Stealing Castro's daughter

a memoir

LEE BROOKS

The true story of how an American man's love for a Cuban woman gave him the courage to cross 900 miles of open ocean alone on a small boat, talk his way out of Castro's prison by convincing his guards that he was a movie star, and outwit a band of ruthless human traffickers… all so he could live happy and free with his soul mate.

iUniverse, Inc.
New York   Bloomington

Stealing Castro's daughter
a memoir

Copyright © 2010 Lee Brooks

iUniverse books may be ordered through booksellers or by contacting:

iUniverse
1663 Liberty Drive
Bloomington, IN 47403
www.iuniverse.com
1-800-Authors (1-800-288-4677)

ISBN: 978-1-4401-7519-0 (pbk)
ISBN: 978-1-4401-7520-6 (ebk)

Printed in the United States of America

iUniverse rev. date: 2/1/2010

For Adianec
Tu eres mi vida

Chapter one

This had to be a dream, a nightmare, but I wasn't waking up. I was having trouble recovering from my interpreter whispering to me that they were sentencing me to nine years in prison for human trafficking. Nine years in a Cuban prison! This could not be happening to me. I tried to keep my composure, but my mind was going numb. I had prepared myself for another all-night interrogation, but now with this, I physically and emotionally had nothing left. For the past four or five days I had had almost no sleep or food, living on Red Bulls and Balance bars while fighting the open ocean for over 400 miles on my twenty-seven foot boat.

I was being held in what amounted to a shed, on a small key off the north east coast of Cuba. The one small window was covered up with a piece of cardboard, so there was no chance of a cross breeze even if they did open the door, which they chose not to do. Not exactly the same sweat box as in *Cool Hand Luke* but not far from it. In the oppressive tropical heat of Cuba, this place had the same effect. There was so much sweat running down my body and onto the floor, I thought it might betray just how nervous they made me. The jeans I had been wearing for the past three days had doubled in weight from my sweat and the heavy humidity. They would fall from my hips as I stood if I didn't remember to put a finger through the belt loop. I was really starting to feel the effects of dehydration; my lips were sticking together, I was feeling weak, and my mouth was completely dry. Hours earlier I asked if I could go to my boat to get some water that I had stowed there. The answer, of

1

course, was no. They were, however, kind enough to bring me a yellow plastic cup filled with foul-smelling water…"Thanks guys, I'll pass."

The shed was about eight-by-ten feet. There was a folding chair that stood behind an old metal desk, and my chair, that had one leg shorter than the others, to add to my comfort. The harsh retina-burning glare of florescent lights set the mood. Two guards stood in the room with me, only one of them armed. They probably couldn't afford the ammo, so I imagined that he had just one bullet that he kept it in his shirt pocket for safety, just like Barney Fife from *The Andy Griffith Show*. Both of them were gaunt and tired looking, no doubt from the austere life of a Cuban military man. As for the other cast of characters, they included my interpreter and a rotating team of interrogators. Oh and the flies…the flies had far less discriminating palates than I did, and kept congregating on the chunks of semi-cooked pork my host had brought to me for a snack.

It had been about thirty minutes since the last group of interrogators left when the door opened. I could hear the wind picking up and rustling through the palm trees outside. The little bit of breeze trickling into the shed was a relief and actually brought up goose bumps on the back of my sweltering neck. The weather outside was getting bad and I could tell a storm was coming; this would make my escaping much tougher. Then He walked in.

I could tell by the nervous reaction of my guards and interpreter that He, this new interrogator, was more important than the others. My interpreter's hands were actually shaking and that really got my attention. I knew immediately by his clothing and demeanor that he was with the Cuban secret police.

There's a lack of due process in this richly beautiful Caribbean island. With a communist dictator at the helm for nearly half a century, an accusation is a conviction. People disappear in Cuba and I was acutely aware of that fact. I'd been successful for the past day or so with my other interrogators by using humor and thoroughly distracting them with highly embellished stories of my life as an actor in Hollywood and growing up in America, that giant magnetic enemy ninety miles to the north. Now the mood in the room was different and I didn't say a word. I barely even breathed.

"Your five friends have already told us the truth." He said, casually.

It didn't occur to me until that moment that she had been arrested too. My tired brain struggled to make sense of this new information. Did she really tell them our plan? If so, what did she tell them? And what have they done to her, to make her confess? I feared that they had beaten or raped her.

My mind raced through all the stupid decisions that I had made over the past couple of years, ones that had put me in this situation where I could lose my life, and most certainly my freedom.

Chapter two

TWO YEARS EARLIER

Cuba had held a fascination for me since childhood. I grew up in Daytona Beach Florida. Though a little more than 400 miles from the island of Cuba, it might as well have been an entire world away. For a guy with even the slightest sense of excitement and adventure, I can't imagine a more amazing place to grow up in than Daytona. Although my family struggled financially, I still managed to enjoy a relatively carefree and exciting existence, spending many years in a trailer up on blocks on reclaimed swampland. With the slightest bit of rain, our home would suddenly be a mile deep into the swamp, teeming with gators, wild pigs and double-headed salamanders. This was a curious child's adventure paradise and it was my 9 to 5 "summer job" literally to wade knee-and chest-deep through swamps, hunting these gators and snakes with a Daisy pellet gun. As I got older, the boy's curiosity moved from the swamp to the more adult pursuits on the beach and I spent several years (until I moved to NYC) as a lifeguard, where I picked up my lifelong habit of superficial relationships. My fellow lifeguards and I exclusively dated young tourists for the week or two that they would be in our city. Life always seemed to be a vacation.

Daytona is famous for car racing and Spring Break, and it is also filled with expatriate Cubans. I used to hang out and surf with several kids whose parents had escaped from Cuba right after the revolution. As a child, I read about, and had been fascinated by, the exploits of Hemingway and his relationship with Cuba and her people. I heard many stories about corrupt officials and secondhand reports of people disappearing. Over the years it seemed as though every adventurous guy I met had a story about Havana. The adventurous spirit inside me knew that one day the allure would win and I'd end up checking it out for myself. Even though the U.S. government did not seem to always enforce the embargo for individuals, I liked to consider myself a lawful guy and never ended up going.

Once Fidel Castro appeared to be in failing health, I knew time was quickly eating away at my opportunity to see the Cuba so many had spoken of. Once Fidel was gone, things would change and it may once again become the Caribbean Disneyland for Americans. I had to see it, this Cuba, and experience it for myself. I knew it was dangerous and forbidden but that made it all the more appealing. Something had been drawing me there for a couple of decades, but I wasn't sure if it was intuition or curiosity. Since I'm neither rich nor politically connected, I knew I wouldn't be granted a special visa. I've known some powerful people that have been able to go legally by getting favors from politicians, but unfortunately I wasn't born in that neighborhood.

One night at a Hollywood Boulevard club where we were celebrating my friend Bobby's last night being single, a few of the guys started talking about going back to Havana one last time before Castro ceded power. Without hesitation I championed my cause and told them I could be ready to leave by morning. I knew I had to get commitments, pin those guys down then and there. If not, the idea would fizzle as soon as the alcohol wore off. Right there under the main stage, saturated with a childish giddiness from $10 beers, five of us decided to make plans to head out in the next few weeks. The next day, two cancelled due to girlfriend issues. Then a week later, another dropped out because of a scheduling conflict. That just left Anthony, a guy I knew although not particularly well, and I. Anthony seemed to have the same adventurous spirit as I and though he had never been there either, at least he spoke Spanish. And he had a great sense of humor. Both of us had just gotten out of bad relationships and I knew it would be a great trip. The trick would be getting there!

The Bush administration had stepped up prosecuting any American who decided to visit Cuba, slapping them with a large fine regardless of the reason they were there. They began to seal up all the usual routes, confiscating the boats that made their daily trips from Key West to Havana, and having officials waiting for planes in México and the Bahamas that had arrived from Cuba.

I spoke with my friends who had already been there, Bobby, Randy and Jim. It didn't sound easy to get there, but it was doable. Anthony and I were set to go but it would be by the seat of our pants. That was until two days before we were to leave. Anthony, also an actor, was called for a last minute audition and said he couldn't go either. Personally, I think he got cold feet and I told him that next time he should audition for a new pair of cojones. I'd go alone if I had to. I thought about the parents of my childhood Cuban friends who risked everything to leave their former homes to get here. Would I be betraying them if I went to their homeland before the Castro government had even been beaten? Something was compelling me to go. It would take months for me to realize that it was probably the most important decision I had ever made.

Bobby tried to talk me out of going alone. He had been there and said it would be difficult having no contacts and not being able to speak the language. I said, "Bobby, what's so difficult? I'm going to follow in the steps of Hemingway, smoke big Cuban cigars, pollute my body with Mojitos and kiss a hundred women."

He waved me off and told me, "You'll probably meet some sweet country girl on the first day, fall in love and spend the next two years and all your money trying to get her off the island."

Chapter three

I flew on the red eye from Los Angeles to Mexico City. Once in Mexico City, exhausted, I had to tackle the difficulties along with my paranoia, of getting a Cuban visa at the airport. Every fear-filled moment I was wondering if I would get turned in or arrested for trying to enter Cuba. Technically, I hadn't broken any embargo yet. I felt a huge sense of accomplishment when the Cuban liaison behind the Plexiglas partition handed the visa to me. After a seven-hour layover, I boarded the plane for Havana, a three-hour flight that would forever alter my life.

Flying into José Marti airport several miles outside of Havana was incredibly surreal. My mind was filled with images of a Cuba from the movie *The Godfather*, bright lights and shiny new cars. However, that was not the scene I viewed from the plane window. The land was very green and tropical, I could see fields below being plowed with what looked like oxen. The island was surprisingly narrow and I could see both sides while approaching the airport.

I wasn't easily intimidated by travel. I had traveled all over the world alone before and had done some crazy things. I moved to New York City when I was 20 years old, with $96 dollars in my pocket, a bicycle, no contacts, and ended up sleeping in Central Park for my first three days. I leaped out of a hot air balloon attached to a bungee cord. I've jumped out of a boat and onto the back of a 5` alligator. This, however, was the most apprehensive I'd ever been.

The initial thing you notice upon leaving the airplane in Cuba is the military presence. These young, very thin men, boys really, in drab green uniforms, all standing around in groups of four to five, looked very serious. As I would discover, all Cubans that work for the government have that identical look. They're very good at wearing these somber expressions, while their green uniforms hang off them, spilling over their oversized scuffed black boots.

The airport has only one pre-board waiting area. Flags from all over the world hang from the ceiling, not surprisingly I didn't see the U.S. flag. The waiting area is surrounded by a glass wall and walkway for departing and arriving passengers. I feared I was going to be arrested, so I kept close to the other passengers, trying to blend in.

The airport has a third-world ambiance. It attempts to be modern, in a bright kind of plastic way, which only serves to make it feel a bit depressing. The ten-foot long escalator was broken, no big surprise there. Enterprising, freedom loving-American that I am, I started to use it as stairs when somebody grabbed me and said, in a very concerned way, "Señor, es broken."

"Ahhh, yes, I know, I was just going to walk down."

"But Señor, it don' move, *chew* must go 'round and take a stair."

"Yes, but you see, these have become stairs, because it's not work-"

I was trying to reason with him. "No, they don' move, last week they move, *pero no mas.*"

This poor guy must be thinking Americans are so stupid they don't even know what an escalator is for. I thought it best not to explain further, so I walked around.

There was a large, crowded room with small tables wrapped around posts where everybody lined up to go through one of a dozen or so doors for immigration. The air was very stale, humid, and smelt like a bad locker room post track meet. I guess there must be a prerequisite about not bathing before coming to Cuba.

A large man in regular clothing walked up to me and very suspiciously asked to see my passport. I handed it to him, a bit confused. Aside from a quick glance at the passport, he never took his eyes off me. I thought, well, there it is, my vacation was over, they're not going to let me into the country. They may even send me straight back to the U.S. He asked me, "What *ees* your business was in Cuba?"

I stammered not knowing what to say, other than that I was on vacation. He challenged me on a few issues, namely, why I was there. He didn't seem to believe I was on vacation. Then, he wanted to know how many times I'd been to Cuba. When I told him, "It's my first time," once again, the large man didn't seem to believe me.

"Where it was that you got your passport from?"

I laughed at that. He didn't. He stared at me and reluctantly said, "OK," and handed back my passport. It was an odd and somewhat frightening exchange. I found out days later that because of my appearance, and that propaganda-fed paranoia in Cuba, a lot of Cubans believed I was with the CIA. Maybe it was the sunglasses. I look pretty much like the stereotype of the all-American clean-cut male, so I guess in Cuba, American = CIA. Basically, I look so American I couldn't even pass for a Canadian.

My vacation, I thought, was not getting off to a very good start. Perhaps I was wearing my apprehension too much. Maybe I should just try to smile, relax and enjoy myself. It's a vacation after all. I asked the immigration officer, with a smile, "Excuse me, senor, if you could please not stamp my passport? I'd appreciate it. Gracias." This little tip I got from Randy, who had done his fair share of traveling in Cuba. The immigration officer looked up, knowing full well why I asked him that. Still, he coyly asked me why he shouldn't stamp it. So I knew why, and he knew why, and he knew that I knew that he knew why, but he wanted to play. I figured, why not just be truthful here. "Because my country doesn't want me here." Immigration guy smiled right back. Right answer, I guess, and he handed me my passport and told me to enjoy my stay.

I breezed through customs and then waited forty-five minutes for my bag. They hand searched every piece of luggage as it came off the plane. Finally, with luggage in hand and a renewed attitude, I walked through the double doors with an open and inquisitive mind to the communist experience.

That said I was not exactly prepared for what I saw. Communism? This was Capitalism on display in a way that would make even Wal-Mart proud. On your way out of the airport, you have to walk through a gauntlet of cigar stands with trinkets, rum, t-shirts and the ever popular books and pictures of Che Guevara.

I stepped out through the glass front doors to enter Cuba and slammed right into a giant wall of heat and humidity. Growing up in Florida, we had our share of humidity, but this was a real tropical blast. Although it took a moment to get accustomed to breathing under water, it oddly had a very calming effect on me. My life and all the stresses of it began to melt away with the sweat that was quickly pouring out of every pore and drenching my wrinkled linen shirt. I was on an adventure!

My Spanish vocabulary was limited to ordering a chalupa at Taco Bell, so I apprehensively handed the cab driver the address of the *Casa particular* I had made reservations with online. My driver began a one-sided conversation with me, in Spanish, not seeming to care that I didn't understand a word. I told my driver *no habla,* he just smiled as he drove us to the *particular.* A *Casa particular* is a private residence that has a special license to rent rooms to tourists. Although Cuba considers capitalism the root of all evil, tourism is one of their top gross national products, and since they don't have enough hotels to handle all the tourists, they have to open up private homes to house them. I guess even communists have to be practical on occasion. Not surprisingly, the people that run the *particulars* have to give the lion's share of the money they earn to the government.

Cuba is a top vacation destination for Canada and Europe. The U.S. is the only country in the world that forbids its citizens to visit Cuba. We can vacation in Beijing or Hanoi if we so desire, but not Havana. Despite this, over 100,000 Americans still manage to fly there every year. The embargo had been one of those laws that were antiquated and the officials knew it, so they just tended to look the other way. But that had changed. The Bush administration was forbidding even *Cuban-Americans* to visit family members who were dying, if it was not on their "once in every three year" timetable. Ironic that the country that claims the most democracy and freedom is the only one that punishes you for visiting the one that has a reputation for having the least.

My cab driver continued his one way dialogue as we drove over the smooth, freshly asphalted road. I just smiled and nodded like an idiot, as the back of my shirt stuck to the Naugehyde seat. Maybe he misunderstood me and thought I said, "Please keep talking and I'll just smile and nod like an idiot." The countryside had dramatic deep green jungles filled with coconut palms and beautiful rolling green hills that seemed unchanged since God made them. I kept my window rolled down, due to the car exhaust that seemed to be pumped into the back seat. The heat was so solid it literally lay on top of me. The air outside had a strong combination of natural smells, grass, weeds and earth that I was unfamiliar with. It was disorienting, but exhilarating, too. I was feeling very excited about the next six days. I could sense that life had an ease here and I realized that I felt happier than I had in a very long time.

I was close to a large city, yet there were no buildings. There were billboards, however, all advertising the revolution. You know, the revolution-the one that ended over four decades ago! Some had pictures of Fidel Castro with messages of hope and survival, while others had comforting statements that together, comrades, we will defend ourselves from the imperialists. Although I was an enemy imperialist, I got a kick out of them.

"Cuban Advertisement"

We were riding in an old Lada, a Russian car. I say old, but I'm sure even a new Lada wouldn't fair any better. I can tell you from experience that all the jokes about Russian cars are true. It was essentially a tin can on wheels. It was painted communist black, like all Russian cars, so that everyone feels equal. From my driver's monologue, the only word I was able to understand was "America." He repeated it often, and every time he would let out a heartfelt laugh. Even this guy knew I was an American.

We pulled up to a stop sign to merge onto a highway. Out of the corner of my eye, I saw something huge coming up beside us. It was a horse. I followed the reins back through the broken out windshield of a '57 Chevy. The Chevy's body was in great condition, with a beautiful red and white paint job. I'm sure the motor, transmission and driveshaft had been removed so the horse could pull it. It used to have 350 horses, I guess it was on its last. I had heard that Havana was like a time machine; old American cars from the 1950's are everywhere. Cubans, I would discover, are probably the most resourceful people in the world. You simply had to be. Inside that Chevy was a resourceful family of seven, including kids. They looked at me as oddly as I must have been looking back at them.

As soon as you cross the railroad tracks, you're in the city of Havana. Nothing subtle or gradual, just all of a sudden there are houses. Even though the houses have not been maintained, you can still see the old Spanish architecture and faded colors. They were built right up to the curb with a small porch, and usually had the front door open. There were people everywhere walking in and out of traffic, not at a brisk, urban pace, but slowly. They took their time to stop in the middle of the street to talk to a friend in a car, they were in no rush, with nowhere to be. Everyone seemed sexy. Even the ugly people were sexy, in an ugly sexy kind of way. It must have been the heat. Cruising around in the cab, I felt like the captain of a high school football team on Friday night because everyone was staring at me. I had the window rolled down, checking everyone out. Women, old and young, were smiling and flirting with me as we drove past, though not in an obtrusive way. They were just having fun.

The condition of all the buildings made me acutely aware of my surroundings. Everything was falling apart. Even according to Cuban authorities, hundreds of buildings crumble every year. In the U.S. and Europe, areas where buildings "crumble" are areas you would do best to avoid at all cost due to the element that inhabits them, but in Cuba, that is Cuba. The government owns everything: cars, buildings, houses, everything. Many of the buildings, even the ones with only a facade left standing, were stunning. Built by the Spanish over 100 years ago, they have a stoic grandness about them. But obviously, the government doesn't have much interest in investing in its infrastructure or even a sense of its own past. So you have crumbling buildings.

"Crumble"

Lee Brooks

We drove through Old Havana. The streets were filthy and filled with people. Although the people are clean, the city in certain places smells like rotting garbage, due to all the, well, rotting garbage. Despite the smell, I immediately felt Havana's energy, with a quality that feels like something is always about to happen. That energy comes from the people, and it feels like they're crouched at a starting block, about to start a race. I found them very intelligent and gently sophisticated. Cuba has a higher literacy rate than most industrialized countries including the U.S. Perhaps it's the one good thing that Fidel has done for the Cuban people.

We came to a stop at a corner, and then my cab driver turned around. He said something to me, which I took to understand that we had arrived. I thought there must be some mistake.

Chapter four

Doctora Rosi

"Excuse me, are you sure this is right? I don't think..."

He signaled to me that this was where I was to get out. I was thinking, this can't be where I'm staying for the week, no way, not in this part of town with dilapidated buildings and all these people with raw emotions. Generally, the condition of a neighborhood defines how safe it is, crime etc. The condition of this neighborhood definitely set me on edge and was one I would assume was crime filled. But Cuba is a country with a very low crime rate, regardless of what the neighborhood may look like.

The cab driver pointed to a building across the street and smiled, I paid and got out. I felt totally naked, everybody looking at me. Concerned that I was about to become someone's lunch I put on my best NYC don't-F-with-me-look and walked across the street.

I took the rickety elevator to the sixth floor, although it would have been faster to pull myself up by rope, and probably safer. I tentatively knocked on the door, and it was opened by Doctora Rosi, a tall beautiful black woman in her late fifties. The doctor must have sensed my apprehension. She gave me a lovely, knowing smile and put her arms around me. It felt like the most natural thing. There is no pretense with most Cuban people. We hugged like old friends for a moment and she invited me to the balcony for a glass of water. My senses were so overloaded I'd forgotten I was thirsty. As I walked through the apartment, I noticed how clean it was, almost sterilized like an operating room. The view from her balcony was priceless. It looked over and above ten blocks of dilapidated grey buildings to the deep blue ocean. Still apprehensive from being in a police state, it occurred to me that just ninety miles across that deep blue Ocean you have freedom: Key West.

After forty-five years of neglect, the buildings have very little color left. Many walls had partially fallen away, exposing stairways or the intimate view of someone's living area. Standing on Rosi's balcony, you could really see the contrast between the richness of the ocean, the big white cumulus clouds floating in the blue sky, and the colorless gray of central Havana.

Rosi had a regal quality about her. Her skin was flawless deep ebony. Her nurturing laugh came so easily, it made me feel like a child around her. Her sincere happiness caught me off guard and opened my eyes, up until that point I had believed that people could only be happy with the freedom of democracy and material wealth. We spoke for a while about Cuban life and how she can be so happy with limited civil rights. "What else do you need for happiness?"

"View from Doctora's balcony"

Rosi explained that, because she was a doctor (and in all likelihood a member of the communist party), she was able to travel on occasion to seminars in Mexico and Europe. She was trusted by the government and had a very comfortable life.

"I have this beautiful view every morning, with some money from the tourists that come to stay here, I have my friends, I have my family."

Without being burdened with the need to excel or to achieve status, she was happy to live her life and let the government take care of her. She had no worries; it seemed her freedom was internal.

I apologized that I would not be able to stay there. I just couldn't imagine having to walk through that neighborhood every time I wanted to go explore the city. I felt guilty and embarrassed in light of our conversation. She smiled knowingly, reached over and touched my hand. Rosi understood it wasn't what I was used to and directed me to a few four-star tourist hotels several blocks away. She asked me to come back in a couple days and let her know how I was doing. She was sure I would see the area with new eyes.

I checked into the "four star" Hotel Telegrafo, across from Park Central. Everything was damp from the humidity. The flooring was shiny ceramic tile, complete with dust balls. There had been a hole in the wall that was patched, but not sanded or painted. I took a shower and climbed into my moist bed to get several hours sleep before dinner. Then the plan was to head out to a few clubs Randy told me had live Cuban music.

I laid there for about thirty minutes, trying to get used to the musty, four-star smells, and wondering what adventures I was missing outside. The pulse of Havana is palatable and was beckoning me. Or maybe it was twenty-five years of fate impatiently calling. I got up and put on my "hey, look at me, I'm a tourist" clothing; cargo shorts, white linen shirt and sandals. The only thing missing was the pair of black socks.

I walked out of the hotel, across the street and into Park Central. Park Central would never be confused with New York's Central Park, either in size or style. This Cuban park is one-by-two blocks of worn out grass with scattered trees and always filled with people. There was a small group of musicians playing and everybody was dancing. Well, not me. I had heard that when there is music playing, anybody who is not moving is not Cuban. Until you've seen a Cuban give their body to the rhythm of music, you have no clue how human movement can affect the mind and body chemistry. Every level of their bodies reacts to a different piece of the music. It's as if the sound is moving from their soul. I guess it would be like watching Shakira on acid.

There was a very pretty blond girl, (yes, there are natural blonds in Cuba) dancing with her eyes closed. The way she was moving, I don't think she was aware that she had no partner. She had moves that would be banned in all Arab states, and in many portions of the Deep South. Her long hair was sticking to her face and bare shoulders, and every time she whipped her body around sweat would fly almost in slow motion. She brought a whole new meaning to sexy. She opened her eyes when the tempo changed and noticed that I was watching her. She smiled kind of shyly, and walked over and sat next to me. Up close, I could see she was probably not even sixteen. I suddenly got very embarrassed about what I had been thinking when I realized that she was about the same age as my friend's daughter. I was old enough to be her father. In the U.S. this moment of indecision and reflection is considered child endangerment. She was a *jinetera* (prostitute) looking for a foreign "boyfriend."

The average wage in Cuba, if you have a college degree, is about $12 a month. Even though the government gives working people a small stipend of food every month, it doesn't come close to allowing for basic survival. It's not uncommon for women with professional degrees, lawyers, engineers, etc. to quit their professions and rely on the "generosity" of tourists to help feed and clothe their families. One day spent with their "boyfriend" and they make ten times their monthly salary. The unspoken agreement with their "boyfriends" is a bit unique for the oldest profession in the world. Generally, it is not a one-hour relationship. It's a companionship, lasting throughout the vacation. They're treated with respect and kindness, or they leave. Sometimes, though, they are young girls, like this girl, and it's very sad to see. This scene I continued to see nightly during my stay. It was infuriating to see men decades older than I with young pretty girls, having dinner at a restaurant. The girls, young teenagers, would be smiling and laughing sweetly. You could tell they would much prefer being anyplace else, but they had families relying on them; mothers, fathers, children and even husbands or boyfriends. I wanted to give them money and tell them to go home. It was the first of many injustices I observed in Cuba.

She said to me, in a rather shy, seductive way, "You like watching me," halfway between a question and a statement.

"Ahh, you got me. Sorry for staring." That seemed to satisfy her in some way.

She sat right next to me, craning her head and her chest back toward the hot sun. "It feels good, warm?"

This was way too tempting and she was way too young. "You're killing me here," I told her, though I don't think she quite got the moral dilemma that I was referring to.

"No," she told me, "I need you lifeing."

"'Living', yes, I get that. Look, you're way too pretty-"

Before I could even qualify that with the rest of the sentence, which was "I'm sorry, but I simply can't." She giggled and gently put her hand on my knee, I felt weak, but I knew I had to stop this before anything happened, before I got myself into some trouble. As she unconsciously ran her tongue along her full upper lip, she asked me my name. I told her, and found out her name was Silvey. "Silvey, you are bone shatteringly sexy, but-if you were older, you know, or even close to legal but…"

I then went into unknown territory for me; giving fatherly advice. This brought a new, softer, safer, energy into the conversation. We actually had a nice conversation after that, friendlier, and I apologized that I had to say goodbye. Silvey feigned disappointment and pouted, until I handed her $10. Big mistake. You never flash money in Cuba. She walked away backward smiling at me, tucked the money into her shirt strap and raised her arms seductively above her head as she went back to dancing. I thought to myself, "Ok God, I passed a big test."

Like I said, you never flash money in Cuba. Out of the cracks of the sidewalk poured five or six young guys who started bargaining for my attention. They were *jinetero*, hustlers. Young con men who work in groups of two or three to entice money out of tourists' pockets any way they can. Their bravado attempts at English made me laugh. One in particular, Alex, a tall skinny dark-skinned kid about twenty-four years old, wanted to shake my hand and talk about his babies. His teeth were brown but his smile would completely set you at ease. I liked him immediately. I knew I was being hustled but it was entertaining. Besides, I was on vacation and had some extra cash. He told me anything I wanted he could get. He told me many times, "Miami will be my home, I know it."

That was his mantra. "Miami. Miami." Almost every Cuban in their early thirties and younger dreams of and makes plans to go to America.

Without much effort Alex, "conned" me into buying milk for his babies. He said that they hadn't had any in a month and he couldn't afford it. The truth is that the government supplies one pint of milk to each child seven and under every day as part of their monthly rations. He said, "You're American. You can help get milk for my babies."

I played along, "I've never milked a cow before but I could try."

He laughed. "My friend, you are very funny. You know my government saves all the milk and good food for you tourists, only you can buy some milk for my babies…" By now, his whole demeanor had changed and the pitch was on. "One is sick. They won't let me buy it. Yes. You'll help my babies?"

Alex looked up with such hope and humor. I applauded his performance, "I couldn't imagine anything else. But, come on, honestly. Do you really have any children?"

He paused for a long uncomfortable moment trying to figure me out, until I smiled. "Ahh, my friend, you are very funny!" And he pulled me across the park.

He was telling the truth about one thing, to a degree anyway. It is sometimes illegal for Cubans to buy milk, or at least very difficult. Alex walked me to a store that only took American dollars, off limits to the average Cuban. We walked with his arm on my shoulder like we were old pals, his way of letting the other jineteros know that I was his mark.

Alex went in first, telling me he had to make sure they had the right milk. He did a quick negotiation with the nonchalant girl behind the counter. I knew I was being taken, but I didn't know how, yet. He motioned me in. The store reminded me of the stories I had heard about communist Russia. The shelves were almost bare. What was there was cheap, low quality, canned food, and this was a step above the stores Cubans were allowed to shop in. The lighting was very dim, maybe one bulb for the whole store. The display freezer had obviously been unplugged for some time and was filled with clothing and miscellaneous junk. Miss Personality-Behind-the-Counter told me, "For one pint (of non-refrigerated milk) it is seven U.S."

Alex was really pushing it. So, that's the con. She, Personality, doubles the price and he, Alex, gets a cut. I said I would take three. I gave her $30 and told Alex to keep the change. He was stunned. Kissed the money and raised it to heaven. I'm sure he thought he'd stumbled onto the most naïve American in Cuba.

I had hoped he would take his winnings and leave, but...no such luck. I told him I wanted to explore Havana alone. He said, "Okay," but as I walked away he remained two steps behind. When I gave him a look, he explained he was just trying to protect me, due to the fact that we were friends and there were unsavory guys around here that would try to hustle me. I assured him that I had experience in that area and I would be vigilant.

The frenetic energy of central Havana was a bit dizzying. I was constantly bumping into people on the sidewalks or in the street. There didn't seem to be any pedestrian rules. There were old American cars from the 1950's everywhere, mixed in with motorcycles and buses. All of them were jockeying for position, because there were no lane markers. There was certainly no such thing as pollution control on cars there, no periodic smog checks. Everything was coughing out black smoke. With the combination of car exhaust and the sweltering heat, I debated another quick shower. The air was very thick and acrid. My nose was burning from the raw exhaust. Despite that, and every reason not to be, I was totally taken. This place was alive, its life burning through the layers of smoke and dust.

I made my way out of the central area, it was much quieter there and I was able to slow my pace a bit. The old narrow cobblestone streets were full of people, it was late afternoon and they were starting to get off work. I was in the local residential area with no tourists and I was definitely getting a few curious looks. I'm guessing not a lot of Americans have walked through that neighborhood. The buildings were amazing, two and three-stories high, with detailed old world architecture, built right on the street. Some had grass, weeds and even an occasional bush growing through the cracks in the façade of the buildings, like there was a battle between man and nature, and man was losing. Every block or so, I would find a building that had partially or completely fallen down. The partial buildings still had tenants in them. I could look right into their bedrooms from below through what was once their outside wall. Most apartments had their front doors open and I was able to casually peer into intimate Cuban life. Even with the poverty and trash that seemed to be everywhere, the thing that kept standing out to me was how clean their homes were. The women were always cleaning, and it showed. The concrete and Spanish hand-painted tiled floors shined. Despite some of the conditions they were forced to live in and under, Cubans seem to take great pride in themselves and their families.

"Old Havana (Notice the tree growing out of the building)"

Chapter five

ADIANEC

Up around the corner I could hear the squealing laughter of children. I was mostly walking in the shadows now, as the sun was starting to fall behind the buildings, but it was still miserably humid. As I came around the corner, standing in the only piece of sunlight, their teacher was seeing the children off for the weekend. She was the reason for their laughter, and she was simply beautiful. The sun was glistening off her tanned bare shoulders. She had her long brown hair pulled back in a messy ponytail. Her smile was bright and full and she hugged every one of them as they gathered around her. I was so focused on the teacher that it took me a moment to realize the children all had special needs. More points for the teacher.

After a few moments she noticed me standing there about fifty feet away. Casually brushing her hair away from her face she looked up. Her smile faded when she realized I was not someone she recognized and immediately went back to her students. But something about her seemed familiar, and I was caught, staring at this woman. "Who is she, is she married, in a relationship… what could she be thinking?

"por favor…alejate de mi!" *("Please…just stay away from me!")*

I continued my walk down the street. Feeling a bit of a sting, I headed back to the hotel. My exploration had lost its flavor, I was getting tired and needed another shower. I was surprised by how disappointed I felt that a stranger had dismissed me so casually. So I reminded myself that I was on vacation and aside from a moment of embarrassment, it wouldn't hurt to go back and try to say hello.

I tentatively made my way back and turned the corner, but the teacher and her kids were no longer there. I was hoping that she had gone back inside to get her things before she left to go home, which would allow me the opportunity to say hello. About ten minutes later (when you're new at stalking it seems an eternity) she walked out of the dilapidated building and closed a big iron gate behind her, yelling something in Spanish to the people still inside. She laughed to herself and then, to my great joy, turned to walk in my direction. She was busy looking through a canvas bag she had slung over her delicate shoulder, until she got about fifteen feet from me. She looked up at my big dumb grin, gave me a look like "you've got to be kidding," then turned and walked the other way.

I am never this persistent when I get shot down so convincingly. If a woman dismisses me, even if she is being coy, I back off. Though having been an actor my entire adult life, most of the women I had encountered and ended up dating were actresses and models. Generally, if you have the confidence to ask, actresses and models rarely say no to a date, but most of these relationships fall by the wayside when they decide you can't help them or their career in some way. However, this was not the usual woman I'd come across, certainly not in L.A. She seemed genuine- a rarity in my world.

I just wanted to see that beautiful smile again, perhaps even directed at me.

"Excuse me," I stammered, but kept my distance in case she knew how to kick. "Do you speak English?" I was trying to be as respectful as possible, so as to not irritate her anymore than I already had.

Another "look" and she turned to walk away, but the "tsk" sound that came out of her full Cuban lips and the dismissive wave of her hand were so sensual, they only acted as aphrodisiacs.

"Que es lo que no entiendes?" ("What does he not understand?")

I thought I'd try a new tactic, relate to her on a familiar level. Not being able to speak Spanish, the only thing I could think of was the Mexican cockroach song, "La Cucaracha!" "La Cucaracha, la cucaracha, dunh da dunh da da-da-da...." That drew a curious but not necessarily enthusiastic crowd. But I've never been a fan of self-censorship, usually to the chagrin of my friends and family.

I'm an actor, not a singer, so I'm sure it was not the smooth sultry sound of my baritone singing that swayed her. Perhaps she just felt sorry for someone so pathetically desperate. Whatever it was, she turned to me, laughing. Finally, a smile for me. My heart warmed. Still, the last thing she wanted to deal with late on a Friday afternoon was some tourist vying for her attention. But she allowed me to walk beside her.

Speaking to her proved another challenge for two reasons. One was because, as I would find out later, she spoke only four words of English: America, hello, Brad and Pitt. The other reason was because she didn't want to. I kept trying to sneak a look at her without pushing my luck. Man, she was beautiful, high cheekbones, full lips and light brown skin. I measured her up. If I put my arm around her, her head would fit nicely in the crevice where my arm meets my shoulder. A perfect fit. The yellow dress she was wearing was clean and freshly ironed but the color had faded a bit from too many washings. I wondered if it was her only one. There was something about her that intrigued me and piqued my curiosity. I asked her name. "Excuse me, what's your, uh, name? *Namo?*"

I pointed like "me Tarzan, you Jane." But my focus was on a drop of sweat that was making its way down the front of her neck and onto her delicate collarbone. I was staggered. She had a refined sexiness to her but I could see she was blind to it. When she noticed my stare she smiled shyly and turned away, putting up her hand to cover her face.

After I collected myself, I asked her name again. Again, like Tarzan. "My name is Lee," thinking that would be a nice ice breaker.

She nodded without much interest, and said her name was "Abla blub bla."

Good name, I thought. Seeing the absolute look of confusion on my face, she laughed and said "Abla blub bla."

Still not getting it, I motioned with my hand to slow down. And she repeated, phonetically, "Ahh-the-ahh-KNEE."

"Adianec," I said in a whisper and then I wondered aloud what that name meant. It was probably something like, "A sultry Latin chick that will leave white boys quivering."

After we walked another four or five blocks she abruptly turned to me and offered her hand to say goodbye. The streets were still filled with people that I assumed were heading home after work, and she seemed a bit embarrassed to be seen with me. She motioned with a slight tilt of her head to the left and said something. "*Yo vivo cerca de aqui, tu no me pueder acompanar asi q es major decir adios.*" (I live close to here, you cannot come with me. So it's best that we say goodbye.) I think I'm glad I didn't understand Spanish.

I guessed that it was "I'm going that way, and you're not." I took her hand in mine, which felt delicate. I just couldn't give her the opportunity to say goodbye, at least not yet. It was bizarre but I felt a kinship with her, this beautiful girl who was in all ways a stranger to me. I instinctively felt that if I let her slip away it would leave a hole in my life. It was soon evident that she felt that way too. She looked up and met my eyes for the first time and her whole demeanor changed at that moment. Her protective stance melted, her eyes softened, and she smiled. Even though I knew she couldn't understand a word I was saying, I just kept talking. "Listen, I know this is strange, but, uh…ah well, you don't even understand me…or do you. Do you? Hhmmm no. I don't know why, but it's not time to say goodbye yet." I just kept going. "Do you believe in fate? What do you believe? I'm really a nice guy, I realize you don't know that. But, please don't leave don't walk away. Not yet, not until I can figure this out."

I kept looking into her eyes, afraid that if I stopped she would leave me. She didn't.

Era un dia muy caluroso, y yo estaba despidiendo ninos… It was very hot that day, and I was saying goodbye to my kids. I was a teacher of eight very special children. At one point I had noticed an American staring at me, and from past experience I was pretty sure I knew what he wanted. A few minutes later I was glad to see that he had gone. But, as I began my walk home I almost ran into him. Why is it that touristas think that all Cuban girls are here for their pleasure? Although this one seemed nice and thought he was funny. (He had sung a stupid song to me). I just wanted to go home, take a shower and eat my rice and beans.

When we came to my corner, I was concerned he would try following me home. I actually enjoyed being around him. He walked and spoke to me with confidence. It was strange, but he made me feel safe. However, he was a tourista and it was time to say goodbye. When I turned to him, he had taken off his sunglasses. I looked into his eyes and they were the bluest eyes I had ever seen in my life. This was the first moment I really saw him. He looked like a movie star. And I don't know why, but I hadn't noticed how tall and muy guapo, he was before. I was afraid he would see how nervous he made me. I know this is unusual, but I think I fell in love with him in that moment.

I asked if she had a dictionary. She understood and shook her head no. There are many English words that are very similar to Spanish, you just have to add an "O" to the end of the word, *dictionario* for one. If you say it a little louder and wave your hands, you're speaking Italian. I managed to communicate, with a lot of laughing between us, that I had one at the hotel. When we got there she waited across the street as I went up to my room.

With an English/Spanish dictionary, our communication became a game. I asked her to go have a Mojito with me. Yet another Spanish word in my growing vocabulary. She awkwardly said yes, and I relaxed a bit when I realized that she had become as curious of me as I was of her. Being with her had that innocent high school crush feel to it, something I hadn't experienced since, well…high school.

We walked a few blocks and came to a very bright store front, which had the aesthetically sterile feel of a laundromat. There were plastic chairs and tables, and the bar was three card-tables pushed together. The music was very loud, coming from a boom box up on a shelf. It was standing room only in there, and we were jostled around, pushing us closer together. I would tell her jokes in English and she would laugh at me, laughing at myself. There were a few awkward moments where I felt the urge to lean over and kiss her. She seemed to sense it and looked down, her face innocently blushed. But I could feel her boundaries begin to melt. A few times as we were pushed together, from the growing crowd, she would put her hand up and touch my arm, letting it linger there longer than necessary. We stayed for about forty-five minutes, neither of us finishing our drink. I could see she was about as much a drinker as I was.

After a moment with my face in the dictionary, I asked, "*'tu tienes hambre'*, are you hungry?"

She applauded my Spanish and indicated she was famished. We walked through the dimly lit, crowded streets toward the Hotel Park Central. I had been told that they had great burgers at the hotel. Why, I don't know, but whenever I travel outside of the U.S. I have to find a good burger joint. Fortunately for me, as far as I'm concerned, the best burger in the world is at a place called, *father's office*, several blocks from where I live in Santa Monica, Ca. They smother them in Roquefort cheese. Truly amazing. They're even better than *Jackson Hole* in NYC. Plus, there's also a place in Paris, a cafe called *Le Terminus* near the d'Orsey museum on rue du Bac. Bernard, the waiter, speaks English and highly recommends the cheeseburger with fries. The restaurant at the Hotel Park Central can hardly be called a joint though, as it's probably the nicest in Havana. Every block we turned down had the feel of a street fair, with people laughing, dancing and flirting.

Chapter six

FORBIDDEN

When she saw where we were going, she pulled my arm and whispered. "No Lee, no, no."

She opened the dictionary and showed me the word "forbidden." I thought she meant only guests of the hotel are allowed to eat there. But if there was an empty table I was sure I could talk the maitre d' into giving it to us. However, the word forbidden has a much more ominous meaning in Cuba. I laughed and insisted she follow me.

As we walked up to the door the doorman abruptly stopped us and said, "I'm sorry, sir, but she," pointing to Adianec, "cannot come inside."

I stood there in shock for a moment, not quite believing what I thought he meant. I looked over at her in disbelief. She just shrugged with embarrassment, having had a lifetime to accept the unacceptable. I had about ten seconds to accept this, and frankly, I'm not very good with change. I'm usually very "proactive" if people are being bullied, and I'm especially protective of women. Adianec's little shrug of subservience just crushed me. I also have just a little bit of a temper. At six feet, one hundred eighty pounds I'm certainly not what you would call a small guy, so when I raised my voice and stepped forward, he fell back through the door. I followed him inside. The manager ran over and I demanded an explanation that would justify insulting Adianec's dignity. They had a quick exchange in Spanish, and then he explained, "Sir, I know this is difficult for you to understand, but in Cuba, we Cubans have certain restrictions we have to live with. I, myself, cannot enter this hotel if I am not working."

I just couldn't comprehend what I had heard. Are you kidding me? She's Cuban and cannot enter a restaurant in her own country. What year was this? I realized I was witnessing what it must have been like for an African-American 45 years ago. In her own country she has to sit at the back of the bus. "She can't eat in a restaurant in her own country?" I asked.

"Oh, I'm sorry sir for the misunderstandings. Yes, of course we have one restaurant in the back of the lobby that she is allowed to eat in, but most definitely she cannot go up to your room, or wander the hotel or lobby." After he spoke we just stood there, staring at each other. I was letting what he had just said sink in, and in his way he was seeming to enjoy my discovery of his country's oppression of her people. After a few moments, I quietly said,

"No, I'm not staying in this hotel. We just wanted dinner."

Dinner was subdued. She seemed a little unsure of me now, and I had second thoughts about my display of anger. But I had to do something. If I were put into a similar situation, I'd defend her in a heartbeat. She seemed to bring that out in me. People don't stand up for themselves in Cuba without risking retribution. They will, occasionally, speak openly in their living rooms on how they feel about Fidel and Communism, but not in public, as they can lose their jobs and maybe even go to jail for showing disrespect to the revolution. Even in private I noticed that most people would not even utter Fidel's name. When referring to him they cupped their hand several inches under their chin, to indicate the infamous beard.

With help from the dictionary, she explained that she tries to avoid those little misunderstandings by staying away from anything that deals with tourists or the outside world. Having a meal in the nicer restaurants is forbidden, but there are restaurants where Cubans are allowed to dine. Unfortunately, they generally cannot afford to eat out. They are forbidden from tourist resorts, hotels and most of the nicer beaches and restaurants, unless employed there. I could tell that she felt ashamed for me to see her this way, and gone was the laughter I had been privileged with earlier. Maybe she thought I no longer saw her as an equal or someone I could be interested in. It actually had the opposite effect; it began to form a bond between us.

After I put Adianec in a cab, I went to the front desk of my hotel and asked if Cubans were forbidden from entering the hotel. They confirmed what I'd been told, and I said I'd be checking out in the morning. I kept the window open throughout most of the night, listening to the sounds of this new world I'd discovered. I laid there feeling very fortunate for my life and the country I live in. But I also felt guilty for all the same reasons. This vacation had very quickly lost its innocence.

I wanted to tell him how embarrassed I felt, almost like a child and he the adult, because he could do anything in my country. I could tell he would try to protect me but I didn't want that, I wanted him to see me as a woman, his equal. He didn't treat me like I was beneath him. In fact, I felt very special being with him. But the government had controlled my entire life. We're trained to always look up to authority to provide for us, and tell us what we can do. Even though it was all that I'd ever been taught, I knew it was wrong.

It was very difficult for Lee to understand our laws. How could I explain it to him when we didn't speak the same language? I wanted to tell him how frustrated I felt seeing foreigners come to my country, and having more rights, more of everything, than we have. If an apartment building falls down, as they often do, the government doesn't rebuild housing for us. They build another hotel on a beach somewhere. But we love having the people come. It would always make me curious to see their freedom, traveling back and forth from Cuba. And we always loved hearing their news from outside of Cuba.

I slept off and on. Mostly off. I couldn't stop thinking about Adianec. The more I thought of her, the more I wondered what her life must be like. I knew nothing about her, yet she already seemed familiar to me. Meeting her was not a mere coincidence, I was certain of that. Too many things guided me to be at her school at that precise moment. I asked God for a little clue into his plan, because this definitely had his fingerprints all over it. No response. Maybe he was pissed off because I hadn't really called much in the past ten years. I begged him for sleep, just to pass the time until I could call her.

With some obvious communication difficulties, we made plans to meet in front of my hotel at 11:00 a.m. I let her keep the dictionary the night before. I had brought two. The other one was electronic and could speak. It sounded like a Spanish Stephen Hawking. I played it for her over the phone. "*Co-mo se lla-ma? Mi lla-mo Lee.*"

She was in shock, and she just kept saying "no, no," and then would laugh her contagious laugh.

When I stepped out the front door of the hotel I discovered that the wall of heat and humidity had moved from the airport directly to the front of the hotel. It was following me. It wasn't the only one. Sitting on the dirty curb was my new shadow, Alex. With a huge smile, and out stretched arms, he announced, with a tone of annoyance, "My friend, what were you doing? I've been waiting," which he would do every morning until I left.

I somehow had forgotten to consult with my, apparently, best friend, Alex. He wanted to know what we were doing today. I asked if he wanted to have breakfast with me and he looked at me like I was crazy for even having to ask. The pace of the city seemed a little more rhythmic, now that I was making my way in it, and of course I had my best friend in the whole world to share it with, Alex.

After breakfast, my shadow and I went to Doctora Rosi's place. Alex stayed a half step ahead of me as we walked, motioning people out of the way to clear our path. I think it was sort of a dominance thing. This was his city and he was going to show it to me. I wouldn't have been surprised if he had tried marking the curb. Once when we passed my turn, I said, "Alex, it's over here."

He quickly pushed ahead of me like a herd dog and barked out, "This way!"

Doctora Rosi was right. I did see her neighborhood with new eyes. *Yo soy Cubano.* I could see it now for what it was, just Cuba. She greeted us both with a huge hug and welcoming gestures. She smelled of baby powder. Now after seeing what was available, or not, at the local stores, it made me curious of the privilege she must have held to have such a luxury item. Her room had been rented, but she called her neighbor, Conchita, who lived one floor below, with a balcony facing the street instead of the ocean. Their building was not as old as the others in the neighborhood, but it also lacked the character. I assumed the Russians had built it in the '60's when they supported Fidel's regime. It was architecturally sterile, but for Cuba, stable. I had confidence it wouldn't crumble during my stay.

Conchita was a very sweet lady. I guess she was in the neighborhood of 137 years old. She was similar in stature to one of the elder hobbits in *Lord of the Rings*, but she became very special to us. She had a penchant for chocolate ice cream, which we brought her almost everyday, and she spent her days watching Brazilian soap operas. She showed me the bedroom with a shared bath. The room had a window air conditioner, which sounded like a hundred screaming squirrels when it started up. There was a night stand with a lamp that had what I believed to be a 6 1/2 watt bulb. And, as is the case in most of Cuba, she did not have glass windows. They were made of wooden slats that shut tight, overlapping to create, surprisingly, a water tight seal. I had been told that this was for safety, due to strong hurricane winds; wood doesn't shatter. The two large windows which covered most of the wall looked out onto an apartment-long balcony with the Hotel Park Central in the background. During the entire tour with Conchita, Alex just followed me around like a puppy dog. Everywhere I'd look, he'd look. I turned on the water in the sink and said "hmm," he turned on the water in the sink and said "hmm." The apartment was very clean and only $25 a night. "Si, I'll take it." Alex nodded his approval.

I told Alex I was spending the day with a friend I'd met. He asked, as a matter of fact, what the three of us were doing. I gave him $10 and promised to take him to lunch at 1:00 p.m. I sat on the large porch of the hotel with my bags and waited for Adianec. The Hotel Telegrafo sits on a busy intersection across from the Northwest corner of Park Central. The large porch wraps around the front and part of the side of the hotel, and aside from providing shade from the scorching sun, it's also a no Cuban zone. If I wandered onto the sidewalk, I discovered I would get inundated with requests. They wouldn't chance coming up on the porch. However, I would hear an occasional "pssst" as the young jinetero passed by, "Señor, you need cigar?" but that was easily ignored.

At one point I went out to look up the street to see if I could spot her. It was 11:20. She was twenty minutes late, or as I would discover in Adianec Time, close enough. The street traffic was absolute chaos. It reminded me of driving in Rome, where there are no apparent rules. Your only hope of survival is just to keep constant pressure on the accelerator and horn. What should have been three lanes was filled with enough cars for five, all driving way too fast. When I stepped out onto the street I was mobbed like a rock star. I had a *People* magazine under my arm that I'd picked up at the Mexico City airport, and when they spotted it, they went into a feeding frenzy.

"*Ay Dios!*" one exclaimed "Tom and Penelope broke up?"

They were devouring the magazine's information. I was beginning to draw a large crowd when one of the lookouts made a clicking sound, signifying *Policia,* and instantly the crowd melted into the pedestrian and street traffic. Slowly, they trickled back and begged me to let them see the magazine. I was no longer a "mark." I had something much more valuable than money; I had information from America.

Around 11:45, Adianec casually made her appearance, right on time, according to her.

She had her arms folded and avoided eye contact. I wondered if I had blown it the night before. She asked me what I would like to see today. I said "Fidel." She almost smiled. Cubans have a love/hate/fear relationship with their dictator of over forty years. I was only beginning to experience the difficulties of Cuban life. I told her I had a surprise and showed her the People magazine. She whispered, "Lee, no!" and tried to hide the magazine.

"*No, es prohibido!*"

She opened the dictionary and pointed to the word that was becoming all too familiar, "forbidden." I seemed to be batting a thousand on the forbidden game. I always tend to find that door. The truth was I was beginning to feel like a clod. Everything I did to impress her put her in threat of arrest. Law #88 states that any Cuban receiving publications from a foreigner can be prosecuted and jailed for up to eight years. I told her we had to drop my bag off at my new room. She insisted that she walk several feet behind me, because of the *Policia*. Again, my look of confusion made her pull out the dictionary. I knew what was coming…"forbidden." That, too, was *prohibido*. Walking together could get her two years in a re-education camp. Cubans are forbidden to have contact with foreigners. My jaw must have dropped because my reaction brought a giggle out of her. It is only allowed in business and then they must have a third-party witness. I could feel my temper begin to boil over, and told her it was bullshit. I'm always very respectful of other cultures when I'm in a foreign country, but there is nothing to respect about injustice. I told her this. Now it was her turn to look confused. Using the dictionary, I explained that in the rest of the world, we have civil rights and freedom of travel…that is, well, except that only in the U.S. we're forbidden to visit Cuba, because Cuba doesn't allow civil rights. There must be a joke in there somewhere, but it's beyond me.

I got off my soapbox. I wasn't sure if I was impressing her, confusing her or scaring her.

Lee was completely different from anybody I had ever met. He had this way of thinking that anything was possible. I would try to explain to him that I couldn't do something and he would always laugh and say "come on, let's go."

Nothing was impossible for him. I asked him if all Americans were like that. He just smiled at me and said nothing. I noticed very quickly that he didn't let anyone tell him what to do. It was a little scary, but exciting. He seemed to get upset at what he said was the inhumanity of the Cuban way of life. Even though it was dangerous in Cuba to speak out, I trusted him.

She really looked sweet that morning. She wore no makeup (which made me wonder if she had ever had any). Her hair was wrapped up in a casual bun, with a few strands left to fall occasionally across her face. I'm not sure if women realize the impact that that has on a guy. She was wearing jeans and a tight fitting t-shirt that read "chocolate," and she smelled great. I noticed that she didn't really perspire. She just glistened, which made me sweat even more. I was aware of how comfortable I was walking through the same streets that just a day earlier left me concerned about my well-being. I got embarrassed a few times as we walked down the street. We would walk through certain "smell zones" that had the fragrance of a sack of dead owls, or at least what I would expect a sack of dead owls to smell like. I would look back at her and she'd smile, seemingly unfazed. I guess you can get used to anything. The "smell zones" came from uncollected trash. Garbage would just gather in a corner somewhere and ripen in the hot Cuban sun. Though Cubans keep themselves and their homes spotless, they put much less or no effort into any communal area. I wondered if it was their unconscious way of rebelling.

I was trying to figure out how old she was. With her mature elegance, I guessed she was older than she looked. When we got to Conchita's building and she caught up to me, I asked her. She said, "*Veinte-cinco*."

She was twenty-five. Twenty Five! My heart sank a little with disappointment. But I hid my feelings. She was too young for me. About a year earlier, I made a conscious decision to stop dating anyone under thirty. I mulled it over for about a second and a half. I'm on vacation, so I decided it really wouldn't matter. In an understated way, she lightly touched my arm, smiled and asked me the same. I mumbled in English and quickly changed the subject, before she had time to translate. She giggled, and although our conversation was strained, her personality was easing through.

Being with her made me unusually happy. I already liked her, a lot. We seemed to have this connection that was organically set, not forced or contrived. I could see that she was getting more relaxed as we sat on the stairs near the elevator and talked. As we spoke, I touched her hand to make a point. She didn't pull back, but her face turned red and I could see the pulse on her throat quicken. I wanted so much to lean over and kiss her neck. The way it softly melted into her shoulder, with that light brown skin, it was more than I could bear at that moment. We just stared at each other for several seconds, until she looked down. I didn't care what we did that day, I was happy just to be with her. Although she seemed to laugh often, it could not betray the seriousness that permeated her eyes. But I could already see that her sense of humor was as dry as mine. She may have been years younger, but she was definitely more graceful and mature than I. We sat and talked for about an hour when I remembered our lunch with Alex.

We took my bags up to the apartment. Adianec and Conchita became immediate friends, talking over each other and laughing. I went into my new room and began to unpack. I unpack like a guy. I toss things onto hangers or in the drawers. Boom, done. After a few minutes, I felt a soft touch on my shoulder.

"*Ay, Lee, por favor,*" she whispered and gently moved me aside.

I laid on the bed and watched her unpack, fold and hang my clothes carefully. Generally, when a woman tries to do those things for me, I feel uncomfortable, maybe even a little manipulated. The women that I come into contact with will usually want something even more in return, or at least I've come to expect they will. But with her, I could tell, it was just her way. I was being taken care of, and surprisingly, I liked it.

When she finished, she motioned me up. I motioned for her to lay beside me. She laughed, rolled her eyes and left the room. After a few seconds just her hand reentered the room curling up her index finger, beckoning me out of the room. I really didn't want to leave my air-conditioner. Once the squirrels calm down and drop the temperature by twenty degrees, it's very pleasant. I actually stopped melting.

About that time, Alex knocked on the door. He said he knew the best *paladar* in Havana. A *paladar* is a private home that has a special license to serve meals. If you can find them they are, most times, cheaper and better than the restaurants. But the food is not a reason to go to Cuba. It's incredibly bland and is pretty much limited to rice, beans and chicken or pork, and on rare occasions, seafood. The land in the countryside is very fertile with deep rich soil. But it is somehow completely under utilized, so vegetables are scarce. You can drive for hours and never see a field that has been plowed since the revolution. Nobody works the land because it doesn't pay and you're forbidden to enjoy any of the fruits of your labor. At one point I had been told the recent account of two young boys who had somehow caught a lobster. They sold it, got caught by the authorities and went to prison. Their crime was putting their own personal desires ahead of the revolution. Everybody, except for the communist elite, must never receive more than anyone else. Which means, not enough.

Chapter seven

Cuban cuisine

The three of us must have looked like the Cuban version of *The Mod Squad* walking down the street. There was the hip black guy, who was walking with extra confidence since he had a pocket full of cash and certainly had more coming. Alongside was the beautiful, sultry woman, Adianec, who was about to have a rare seafood meal. And me, the pasty-assed white guy.

It is a Cuban pastime to sit outside the front door, watch the world go by and laugh. The *chiquitas*, having nothing better to do, would whistle and blow kisses at me as we walked by. I'd give Adianec a nudge to confirm that she had noticed. She just gave me a look like I was imagining things. She already had a way of putting me in my place.

The neighborhood was a mixture of apartment buildings, old abandoned department stores from Havana's heyday, and a government-owned mom-and-pop-type storefront with mainly empty shelves. The area was Stark and colorless, like most of Havana. The intense, bright, midday sun bleached out everything, making it seem even more sterile. Alex pulled on a large red steel plate about seven feet high. It was attached to the building's brick wall on one side with four chains substituting for hinges and it opened into a dark, narrow passageway between two buildings, with barely enough room to walk straight-shouldered. Still, with the sun blocked out and the moisture from leaking pipes, the temperature dropped and made it a nice respite from the heat.

We went through a few doors and nondescript storage rooms until we came to a freshly painted, bright pastel room with the a/c on full blast. It had a very nice set of curtains that covered a piece of plywood that had been a window at some point. The framed pictures on the wall, of Europe and Havana of old, were actually quite charming. There were five round plastic patio tables with four chairs at each table. The room was empty of people, so we had our choice of tables. I suggested the one near the "window," as it was more romantic. The tablecloth was clean and there were real cloth napkins folded upright on the table.

As the waiter/owner/chef/busboy seated us, Alex whispered something to him in Spanish. He nodded and walked away without laying down the menus he had brought. Thirty seconds later, he returned and handed us the menus. I opened mine; no prices. What a surprise. He had switched menus, another Alex scam. Obviously, I'd be paying a premium and Alex would collect the difference. I was going to tell my "best friend" I was on to his scam, but then I thought what good would it do? This was his life. I was a means to an end for him. Besides, we're not talking major scam here. It was never going to be enough money to hurt me, and it would help keep him alive. I had no idea to what extent until the three of us began to make small talk while waiting for the food.

They were both from the countryside, though aside from Havana it seemed the entire island was rural. Adianec came from a province, about eight hours away, called Camaguey and had been in Havana for a little less than a year. Alex was from Las Tunas. And although Adianec had permission to move to Havana, Alex just came on his own. It seems that the Cuban government decides where each person is to live; Cubans cannot move freely. And since Alex came to Havana without permission, he could not get a job or collect his food rations. Therefore, his very existence depended on getting money from tourists.

In Cuba, there is a Presidente of the CDR (Committees for the Defense of the Revolution), similar to a neighborhood watch. The Presidente is responsible for the coming and going of about two hundred people in his/her area. This is the person that reports suspicious behavior to the government, i.e. if you have friends over for dinner, it is suspect as a gathering of dissidents against the revolution. If you want to move to Havana, you ask the president of your CDR for permission. If the police stop you in Havana and see that your official address is in another province, they will call your CDR and ask if you had permission to visit Havana. Cubans don't often talk of these things because to them this is not unusual.

Alex was our translator, and when he realized that all conversation had to sift through him he saw his value grow. He leaned back in his chair spread his arms and rested his hands on the back of his head. By the time our food had arrived, two other groups of tourists came in. Adianec and Alex were excited to find out where they came from. They were enchanted with the idea of what magic laid beyond their shoreline.

When lunch was finished I paid the bill: $75 for three people. Alex excused himself to "smoke a cigarette" (collect his share of the tab). During this meal, I realized I was going to have culinary challenges in Cuba. The food ranges from boring to bad, and the lack of choices are very depressing. One thing I look forward to when I travel is tasting the local dishes. I love to eat. Though Cuba has many things to make up for the lack of palatable food, it's the one downside that could keep tourists away. Well, that and a communist dictator.

At lunch that day I was trying to be so aware of how I was eating and sitting. I felt like I was in a beautiful dream and I didn't want to do anything that might change that. He seemed so interested in my life, but I didn't know why. His life was so much more fascinating. He was an American. I was just a "campesina," country girl. Havana was still new and exciting for me, and now with Lee, there was more to life than I had ever imagined.

I remember being a little uncomfortable at first, that we had a friend of his with us. Alex was very nice, but I wanted to be alone with Lee. Then I thought maybe it was good that there were two of us with him, in case the policia stopped us.

After lunch Alex pulled me aside and informed me, "Adianec, she is not a girl for you. She does not have an understanding of the needs of tourists. I have many appropriate girls for you to choose."

And for a small fee, he would make the introductions. I told him that wouldn't be necessary I was not in need of one of his girls. He patted me on the back in a condescending manner and told me that I was "over confident." He winked and said to not let my pride get in the way when it was time to come see him. He had the best girls in Havana. I knew he was right though, I had a slim chance to embark on a holiday romance with Adianec. But I didn't care. I wanted to spend as much time with her as she would allow. I would be leaving in less than a week and would never see her again. The thought of not having the chance to really get to know her brought a surprisingly deep sadness over me.

For as amazing as Havana is, it's definitely not a return destination. And from what I'd learned so far, Adianec would never be allowed to leave the island. So every moment with her was a gift. There was a mystery about her that intrigued me. Granted that could be attributed to the fact that I didn't understand a word that she said, but that was only a very small part of it.

After getting rid of Alex (he was an easy bribe), Adianec went back to Park Central to get a *Coco*. She went alone, so we wouldn't be seen getting into a Coco together. A Coco is a mode of transportation in Havana. It's a bright yellow fiberglass shell shaped like a coconut, covering a three-wheeled motorcycle frame. Two people sit in the back, with the driver up front. They're fast, noisy and dangerous, due to the non-aerodynamic shape of coconuts. We took most corners on two wheels, and sort of rolled around and in between traffic. That was okay with me, since it slid her onto my lap numerous times. Even with the instability of the ride, she never lost her graceful composure. I became aware, I think for the first time, of the fact that she didn't belong there. Her energy was serene and focused, and Cuba is wild and spontaneous. I watched her and wondered how she had attained her refinement. Anytime she would notice that I was staring at her, she would look away with a smile. Embarrassed, she would reach over to cover my eyes. Just then we took a wild S turn. She was thrown against me and she burst into laughter. I had chalked up a perfect moment.

"Adianec in our Coco"

I told her that I wanted to learn more about the history of Cuba. Subtext; I wanted to learn more about the history of Adianec. She instructed the driver to take us to the Museum of the Revolution. Before Castro's revolution, it was the Presidential Palace where Batista, the dictator before Fidel, held most of his formal state functions. We had to pay to get in, since even propaganda isn't free in Cuba. The palace had surprisingly ornate architecture for Havana; marbled walls and pillars, and a wide staircase that split on the first landing and flowed to either side. But like most of the buildings in Havana, it was in disrepair and needed to be cleaned. There were many bullet holes in the marble due to an assassination attempt on Battista. Like a twelve year-old, I felt an urge to rush over and put my fingers in the bullet holes. I don't know why, but I enjoyed it. Adianec seemed amused. I think my childish moments made her feel more comfortable as she grew to trust me. She came up, put her hand on my arm, and said, *"Ahh Niño."*

We continued forward, and she pointed to a picture of Havana. *"Este lugar nuestra como era La Habana antes de que Batista saliera corriendo de la ciudad."* (This shows Havana just before Batista ran away).

I recognized it as Havana before the revolution, which I told her, "I know a little of your history."

"¿Sabes algo acerca de nosotros?" (Do you know anything about us?)

"I have something on my nose?"

"Te importaria usar el diccionario?" (Should we use the dictionary?)

"Yeah, let's go into the other rooms."

I couldn't get over how beautiful she was and I was hit again with this overwhelming urge to kiss her. I told her, "God, you have a beautiful smile. I really want to kiss you."

"Que, te gustan mis dientes." (What, you don't like my teeth?)

I felt I could understand exactly what she was saying to me. It was as if we spoke the same language.

She then guided me to the large Plexiglas display cases, they contained memorabilia and old pictures of Fidel Castro, Che Guevara, and many other revolutionary guerrillas, who had fought their way through the eastern mountains and jungles to finally overthrow Battista in Havana, New Years Eve, 1958.

We slowly made our way around the first floor for the better part of an hour. The rooms were very sterile and hollow. Since the revolution, not much has been constructed in Cuba for beauty's sake. As we walked, she would whisper her personal opinion of the events, which somehow I seemed to understand.

There was plenty of anti-American propaganda. Some of it was true, but most of it was exaggerations and lies. I found myself defending my country, probably for the first time in my life. Because of all my travels, my eyes are open to the fact that my government is not perfect. But it's my country, and I resented it being smeared by a dictatorship that keeps its people enslaved. To her credit, Adianec was able to see through all the propaganda. With the dictionary, she told me that she loved the idea of America. She said she had always questioned how it could be so bad, if people risk their lives trying to make it to her shores.

Out in the back of the museum is a courtyard and small access building selling chips, ice cream and candy from Mexico. On the shaded patio were a couple of plastic tables and chairs. The food had been so boring up to that point that the sight of tasty junk food seemed exciting. Junk food was now a delicacy. I enlightened her to the ingenious mind of the American male by making ice cream and potato chip sandwiches. One can only assume the overwhelming impression it made.

As she licked the melting ice cream off her fingers, I naturally thought to offer my assistance. Racing through the dictionary she asked me what life was like in Santa Monica, California. I was tempted to tell her that I was the mayor of Los Angeles. She'd never know. I opted for the truth. I told her that I had turned my acting career into more of a hobby about five years before and that I now owned a construction company and bought and sold houses. Her eyes widened in disbelief. She couldn't understand how I could do that, since her only experience was that the government owns everything. I described in as much detail as I could the beaches in Malibu, and how the mountains grew out of the ocean. I explained how I would drive down the wide boulevards in Beverly Hills, with ten foot high stone walls hiding the mansions and secret lives of the rich and famous. And how every so often someone in those mansions would misunderstand my status and invite me to one of their dinner parties.

I told her about the house I had just bought in the Santa Monica Mountains to fix up and sell. She laughed in disbelief when I told her you can run into movie stars in the grocery stores. She said she had heard that the stores in America were always full of food, but that she knew it couldn't be true. She sat there, holding her breath, hoping I'd tell her it was. After a few moments of describing the produce department at *Whole Foods*, telling her about all the colors and varieties from around the world, her enthusiasm began to wane. Her eyes went dark and a deep sadness came over her. I asked her what I had said. She put her hand over her mouth and got up to walk away but not before I saw the tears well up in her eyes. I sat there and let her have some space in the open atrium area.

After a couple of minutes I realized that I had gone too far. I felt like a braggart. My life in the U.S. was one that she would only experience through tourists' anecdotes, smuggled magazines and illegal satellite dishes. She knew this was a life forbidden to her. Her status would never improve while mine can be anything I desired. In her eyes, the truth was that she could never have a relationship with me, an American citizen free to roam the world while she would spend her life as a prisoner on a communist island. In her mind, my life was heaven.

Chapter eight

A KISS

With her arms crossed in front of her and her head bent down slightly, she walked back toward me. I got up to meet her, and we both apologized simultaneously. I put my arms around her and after a few moments she began to relax and then slowly put her arms around me as well. We didn't move for about five minutes, both afraid that this moment would disappear. I pulled away to look at her, brushed her hair away from her face, and looked down into her eyes. All I saw was pure kindness. As I gently kissed her, the sun was beating down hard on us and I could taste the salt from the sweat on her lips. My second perfect moment of the day.

I could feel her begin to get lost in our kiss and then just as suddenly realize where we were and pull away in a panic. She looked around to see that our moment had not betrayed us. She relaxed, laughed at herself and put her arms around me again. I knew she was taking a calculated risk. With the limitations on our ability to communicate, discussing the matter would take a lifetime. So we went back into the museum to check out the upstairs section. Walking up the stairs meant I got to go past the bullet holes again. She held my hand on the way up the stairs and I thought it strange that it felt so natural.

The first thing we came to was a life-size model of Fidel, Che and Camilo, making their way through the dense mountain jungle, on their way to Havana to "liberate" Cuba. From the exhibit, I realized that a prerequisite to being a guerilla fighter was not only revolutionary fervor, passion and will, but also the inability to grow normal facial hair. They all had patchy beards, even into their later years a full beard eluded them.

One thing that surprised me while reading some of the original writings of Fidel, which were on display, was that his intentions in the early years seemed to be the antithesis of what he had become. He constantly wrote of having a free Cuba. His words seemed very sincere and I wondered how could someone turn so drastically? He lambasted Batista for not having free elections during his seven years in power. Fidel was now in his 45th year of dictatorship without a hint of democracy. Did he get frustrated with the sluggish speed of bureaucracy, did he get greedy and self-important or was his initial magnanimous character just a ruse to seize power? He spoke of equality among the classes. He accomplished that by bringing everyone, with the exception of himself and the privileged few, down to the lowest point of survival. Even Che, in a speech made shortly before his execution (of which some say Fidel orchestrated), chastised Fidel for becoming a man who turned his back on being a true revolutionary and now only worked for self-aggrandizement.

Fidel was able to achieve some of his loftier goals: universal health care and a largely literate country. I would love free education and medical services, but not at the price you have to pay in Cuba. You're forced into a lifetime of servitude to pay for the privilege of free services. Fidel had such great promise, intelligence, charm and charisma. I guess it's true. "Power corrupts, and absolute power corrupts absolutely."

I was enjoying getting to know him. He was not at all what we had been told Americans were like. He cared about things and people. He was very funny, or at least I thought he was, I couldn't always tell. As we walked through the museum, I was surprised how much he already knew about Cuban history. He corrected some of the misinformation that I'd been taught in school about the world, especially capitalism and democracy. I knew in my heart that everything he told me was true. In the back of my mind I always knew we were being lied to. Throughout my life, I would sit and talk with my friends and we would discuss how our government was keeping us from knowing the truth. So it was very exciting to finally hear what was propaganda, and what was true.

At one point we were talking and eating ice cream and my head was spinning with all the stories he was telling me. I was living in a whole new world. Looking at him telling me about his home and friends, he had so much enthusiasm, he was like a "Nino." I knew I was in love with him. I could understand almost everything he was saying to me, but as he kept speaking I realized that I couldn't picture myself in America. I was Cuban, I would always be Cuban. I didn't want to get upset, but I knew that he would leave me soon, and I would be alone again. Then I couldn't hear him anymore. I could see his beautiful smile and his mouth move, but no sound, no more words.

I was so angry at myself for ruining a beautiful moment but I didn't want him to see me cry. He had enough respect for me that he let me walk away, very different than a Cuban man, they always try to control women. I guess that's why I never married. When I came back he kissed me, I had wanted him to since we met. It was a very romantic kiss, just like in the movies.

We were feeling a bit carefree and decided to walk the mile or so back to my apartment. It was late in the afternoon and I was a little grumpy knowing that I had to eat very bland pork or chicken and rice and beans for dinner. I had only known Adianec for about twenty-four hours, but we had experienced so much in that time that our relationship already had a comfort and familiarity about it. When we arrived at Conchita's building, Adianec kissed me and asked if she could see me the following day. I stumbled in my reply, a little surprised that she thought the day was over and I asked her to have dinner with me. She sighed, not wanting to disappoint me, but said, (all communication still done by dictionary and mime), her family would worry and she had to feed her dog. I told her, "Now you have two hungry dogs, and this one bites."

She just looked at me and smiled. I guessed that meant that she didn't want the day to end either. She asked me what I wanted for dinner, and jokingly for my own amusement, I said, "Dominos." She cried out like a little girl, almost ripping my shirt pocket. She was so excited she just reeled off in Spanish. *"Oh Lee no te puedo creer, es Dominos! Yo conosco esa pizza por los comerciales de Univision. Dime que es tan deliciosa como luce en la television. Cuanto cuesta? Es verdad que te la llevan a la casa, por favor cuentame como funciona, cuentame todo lo que tu sabes sobre Dominos."* (Oh Lee, I can't believe you, it's Dominos! I know that pizza from the commercials on TV. Tell me if it is as delicious as it looks on TV. How much is it? Is it true that they deliver it to your home? Please tell me everything you know about Dominos!!).

I explained that Dominos was a right of passage for Monday night football. "Pizza in 30 minutes or less." Evidently, at least from what I could decipher from my quick dictionary search, her sister's boyfriend had a contraband satellite dish and she had seen many Dominos commercials while watching Miami TV stations. She wanted details of the taste, if everyone was laughing just like in the commercials and did we always serve it at parties. Her innocence cracked me up. She informed me that they also had pizza in Cuba and if I were a good Niño, she would bring me some in two hours, after she fed the other dog.

In the short, life-risking ride up the elevator, I had already begun to miss her. As I walked into the apartment, Conchita came up and took my hand and asked about Adianec. She wanted every detail of the day, and asked if I was going to see her again. She was as taken by Adianec as I was. We sat for a few moments talking about the challenges of daily life in Cuba. She said it was very difficult and sad for someone like Adianec because she was so young and intelligent and deserved more from life. We talked about the U.S. embargo and how it punished the people of Cuba but not the government. I found myself becoming more involved in these people's lives. She reminded me of the perfect grandmother. She wanted so much for everybody else. For herself, she had everything she needed. As long as it came with chocolate ice cream.

I stepped into the shower, which had an 8``x12`` window view of the ocean, and turned the squeaky knob for water. Nothing happened. After a full day in the Cuban sun, this was not a happy moment. Something growled inside the wall and reluctantly five or six emasculated drops trickled from the showerhead, followed by five or six more every half a second. I thought someone had turned off the water so I wrapped a pink towel around me. The towel was probably about a decade old, and so thin it was like a piece of transparent gauze. I called for Conchita. She came in, looked at the water and said very matter of factly, "Si, Lee, please do not use too much."

"Use too much? It will take three weeks just to get my hair wet!"

Conchita nodded and grabbed my arm, nearly pulling it out of its socket; Hobbits are very strong. She led me into the kitchen and pointed to a blue fifty-gallon container tied to her ceiling. Because the government in Cuba doesn't pay a lot of attention to silly things, like infrastructure, there is no water pressure and usually no water at all. Everybody has the blue containers or tanks that they keep full of water. She said when the time came to fill it, she wouldn't have a big, strong American man to help her fill and lift it back up. I told her to just give me a call and I'd pop on over. They keep the containers or tanks in the highest place in their homes and gravity helps the water flow to the fixtures. She dragged me back to the bathroom and showed me a small electrical box in the shower with a switch. It had a bare wire leading from the box to the neck of the showerhead. The bare wire wrapped around the pipe to heat the water. She said to try to make sure my hands were dry when I turned it on...Really.

During the long process of trying to get my hair wet, with my head down under the shower, I absent-mindedly cradled my hands up over the shower head and touched the raw wire. The sensation is difficult to explain but easy to simulate. Take a bucket of water and a fork, place it within reach of your toaster...

After getting a surge of energy the shower, I wanted to go out and hear music, but there was no telling how long Adianec meant when she said she'd be back in two hours. I still had at least an hour to wait so I took a walk, through the neighborhood. I went back to the patio restaurant at the Telegrafo and had a small plate of chicken and a bowl of rice and beans, while watching Cuban life pass by. Alex walked up and grabbed the seat next to me and ordered his dinner. The only familiar taste for me was the Coca Cola that is served at all tourist locations. This was the time of day when Havana really exploded, people filling the sidewalks and streets as if it were a festival, but this was just another Saturday night. Although still muggy, the temperature drops considerably after the sun sets, and the breeze flowing off the ocean makes its way through the buildings and into central Havana. Cubans are always out at night to cool off in that breeze, and once out they are not quiet. They don't seem to do anything quietly. They talk loudly, laugh loudly, even eat loudly. Cubans laugh often and it is such a passionate laugh it seems almost violent. During dinner, Alex and I talked about what his life would be like in Miami. I could see his mind drift off as if he were already there, so I stopped taking for a while and let him have his fantasy. Pointing to my shirt he told me he wanted to start looking like an American. I took the hint and promised that I would leave him the shirt before I flew home.

Chapter nine

FOOD POISONING

Adianec beat me back to the apartment. I had given her some money before she went home so she could buy the pizza and some chocolate ice cream for Conchita. They were engrossed in watching and commenting on a Brazilian soap opera when I got there. Conchita's place smelled of Pine Sol. She was always cleaning. Enjoying television in Cuba seems to be more interactive than in the U.S. They weren't so much watching as participating. Neither one really acknowledged my arrival. Adianec simply held out her hand for me to come and sit next to her, which I did. There are three official channels in Cuba. Anything else is illegal and can only be received by a contraband satellite dish. One channel is for entertainment usually South American soaps and movies. One is for primarily education, and the last seemed to be the Fidel Channel. Almost every night there is a show called *The Round Table*, where Fidel and his comrades talk about important issues facing Cuba and the world. The U.S. was always a target. The Round Table is on two channels simultaneously, just in case one might decide to change the channel. Even though I didn't understand what he was talking about, I was mesmerized watching Fidel, which I did almost every night.

After sitting on the arm of the couch for a few minutes, I got bored and went into my room to read. Adianec followed a few minutes later with my Cuban pizza. Dominos may not be fine cuisine, but it is, in a broad sense, still pizza. This Cuban "pizza" had very little similarity to pizza at all, certainly any pizza I'd ever seen in my life. The crust was a slice of bread, unleavened, with mashed tomato on top followed with chunks of pasty milky cheese, round slices of some kind of aged, raw meat lay on top. I didn't want her to feel bad, so I took a small bite then offered her some. She turned up her nose. Small wonder. I was desperate for something normal, so I took a few more bites, including some of the mystery meat. I told her if she got some ice cream for us, I'd show her pictures of Los Angeles that were still on my camera.

We lay back on the bed and she put her head on my chest as I gave her a slide show of my city. Every picture excited her. She wanted to know everything, the names of all my friends and how far everything was from my house. She commented on the cleanliness of the streets, something most Americans don't thing about, and asked where all the people were. I explained that no one walks in L.A. We drive to the corner store to get milk. We started to talk about politics and my views on the war in Iraq, which was a major topic of propaganda for Fidel. At that time, I think I was one of the few Americans opposed to the war. She seemed very relieved to find out that I wasn't one of the Yankee imperialists that Cubans are warned about.

She seemed a bit embarrassed to tell me that she had never read the Bible before, though her family considers themselves to be Catholic, due to religion being outlawed up until a few years earlier. She asked me questions about Jesus and the Pope. Our ability to communicate in hand signals had become more efficient. I also briefly explained to her about Judaism since most of my friends are Jewish. She had also never heard of meditation or reincarnation. She was starving for cultural, historical and spiritual information and anything that was not communist propaganda. I could have spent the rest of my life right there and would not have felt cheated. Our conversation went on for hours and hours, until we both fell asleep.

I don't know how long we had been asleep, but I woke up just before dawn, sweating, delirious and vomiting. "You poisoned me." I moaned, crawling back in bed from the bathroom.

She raised her head off the pillow and gave me a look like "Man up, sissy boy." I asked her how people react when they get sick in Cuba. She took my hand, kissed it, then mimed something like, they just don't make a big deal about it. For a while, I was concerned that I'd have to go to a Cuban hospital and feared I'd end up with a lobotomy. Then the electricity went off again, which it does two or three times a day in Cuba, and can stay off for hours. No air conditioning. The heat quickly began pouring into the room. I was so miserable, I asked her to leave. My whole body ached and I needed to stretch out on the bed. I think she was relieved. She said she would go feed Simba, her dog, and come back in a few hours. She wiped the sweat off my face and asked if she could bring me something.

"Yes, I'll take some more poison, enough this time to put me out of my misery." I said, not completely joking. She understood, but was not amused.

It was a lovely day I spent in bed, alternating between sleeping and getting sick. Adianec came in and out. Alex stopped by, wanting me to take him for lunch, and asked if I'd like to give him my shirt now. His concern, I'm sure, was to get it now in case I died. Finally, around eight that night, between the heat and the intestinal wars, I had purged everything out, and began to feel better. I was even a little hungry and had asked Adianec for watermelon juice. "Sans poison."

Surprisingly, she found some.

I did feel bad about bringing him the pizza, although as I told him it did not come from my "cucina." He was able to focus on being sick very well. Conchita and I tried to get him to take medicine but he said he didn't trust Cuban doctors. I liked taking care of him.

We slowly walked to the Park Central Hotel for dinner. I was pretty weak and thought I'd garner some sympathy from her, but she wasn't playing. We had a nice time at dinner, and the doorman remembered us with a friendly smile. I had soup and ordered filet mignon for her. I wondered if she had ever had filet before. As I watched her eat the steak, which actually didn't look too bad, I could see she felt guilty with every bite. At first I thought it was because I was eating soup. Then I remembered from an earlier conversation that it might have been because her family was not there to enjoy it with her. She doesn't like to experience good things if she cannot share it with people she loves. I told her we could order take out for her parents. She laughed and reminded me that they lived eight hours away, but the people she lived with were like family. They had been watching over her since she moved to Havana. Sol, the mother, had been Adianec's mother's best friend for many years. Adianec admitted she felt bad that she was eating like a foreigner while her parents likely only had rice and beans to eat for dinner.

Cuba controls the food consumption of its population, by giving them a food ration card every month. Every person gets a small ball of bread everyday. Then, once a month, they get five pounds of rice, three pounds of beans, a half dozen eggs, a small chunk of processed meat, four ounces of soy meat, five pounds of sugar, cigarettes and matches, a bag of coffee, one half cup of cooking oil and one half bar of soap for body and laundry. Every two months or so they also receive a leg or a thigh of chicken for the whole house, four or five times a year they get some fish, and twice a year some pasta. If you're sick or pregnant you get extra meat, and all children seven years old and younger get a liter of milk often. This monthly ration, with the exception of the bread, lasts the average Cuban about fifteen to twenty days. They must love Februarys. I wondered if it was all about keeping order (give the people just enough to survive and keep them relying on the government). The regime decides what, when and how much they eat, where and how they live. I could not accept that this oppression and suffering was happening a mere ninety miles from the United States.

I came to Havana about a year before I met Lee. I thought that by taking a job in the city I could provide for my family. I guess I was very naïve after I graduated from the university. Everyone in the countryside talks about how much easier it is to make more money in Havana. If you work with the tourists or in the black market that is true, but I was a school teacher. It was, in fact, more difficult to make money, because there is limited housing in Havana and I had to live with my mother's best friend, Sol, her husband and their son.

The monthly food rations given to us by the government do not last more than two and half weeks, and my monthly salary would disappear after two week. I would buy a little bit of food and some basic necessities. There was nothing left to send to my family. The government always promises to do something but their promises are never kept, so we continue to struggle. They control how much money we make, how much food we get and the price of the food we have to buy to subsidize our rations, so they are very aware that it is not enough. The stories that Lee told me about the food stores that never had empty shelves seemed too much like heaven to be true.

I wanted so badly to help her, but there was nothing I could do. When we got back to my room, she read the *People* magazine while I showered. Due to my short-term memory issues, I bumped into the charged showerhead again, and I was exceptionally verbal about it this time. I could hear Conchita laughing in the living room. If it's true that electric shock therapy cures depression, then I was going to leave Cuba a very happy man.

Even though Adianec explained she had to get home early so Sol wouldn't worry, we laid on the bed and I introduced her to the beauty of "Rock and Roll" until dawn (complete with vocals). Music seems to be the one thing where there is no language barrier. The language of music is universal and we found it allowed us to understand how the other felt. She seemed to really get what Rock and Roll was all about, though she had no idea who *"the Stones"* or *"Beatles"* were. Before we fell asleep, I asked her to call in sick at work and spend the week with me. I told her I was going to buy enough food for her and her family to last six months, so missing a week of work wouldn't affect her financially. She self-consciously whispered she already decided to spend the week with me. I happily fell asleep with my arms around her body, and my lips lightly touching the back of her neck.

When Alex woke me up, in the early afternoon, she had already gone. Alex's face for hers is not a fair exchange. Groggily, I told him, "Take the shirt, take all the shirts! Just let me sleep a few more hours. Go, leave."

Chapter ten

PERFECT

Sometime later, I woke up with her running her fingers through my hair. I opened my eyes and she was sitting next to me, smiling. I don't know how long she had been watching me, but I could tell by her face it had been a while. It was very cool and dark in the room. I could see by the slivers of light burning through the wood slats that it was another hot day in Havana. But I had no worries, no place to go and no cell phone ringing with nervous clients. I was exactly where I was supposed to be. The way she was looking at me made me feel loved, and unlike other times in my life, it didn't make me want to run. I actually felt safe. I didn't feel she wanted anything from me, other than just to be with me. I wondered for a moment if my ability to stay present, with so much tenderness and vulnerability was due to the fact that, in a few more days, I'd never see her again. It was safe to love and be loved in this situation because it was so temporal. I wasn't proud of myself for coming to this realization.

Adianec had such pureness about her, everything she did she did with integrity, honesty and joy. As for her physical beauty, it just weakened me at that moment. I honestly cannot recall ever seeing a more beautiful woman. Her hair was down and falling in front of her face, her high cheekbones and her flawless, tanned skin showed not even a hint of a wrinkle. I had no energy for pretense, only honesty. I asked her what she wanted with me. She just shrugged and bent down to kiss me softly.

She was wearing a pale blue sundress, with straps that had big buttons where they attached to the front. I gently picked her up and laid her on the bed beside me. Feeling the skin on her neck with my mouth sent chills up my spine. Her body shivered slightly and I could feel goosebumps rising up on her arms and shoulders. Her breathing began to get heavier and she whispered something to me in Spanish. It really didn't matter what she said, it was in a Spanish whisper. That moment was so personal, it felt like my first time, as if I didn't know what was going to happen next. Her lips were full and soft and I spent the next five minutes exploring them. She was holding my left hand tightly, so with my right, I unbuttoned the straps on her dress. I slowly pulled the front of her dress down, kissing her as the dress lowered. "Perfect, perfect." It had been a while since I'd seen natural breasts. I thought it best not to share my inappropriate thoughts, but...perfect! I slowly brushed my lips across her nipples and she let out a gentle gasp.

We made love and slept, off and on, throughout the rest of the day. We woke up around five that afternoon. She said she had a very special surprise for me. We showered, got dressed and headed out to get a cab. She was playful while we were getting ready. She seemed very happy. I was constantly in awe of how unaffected and modest she was, given her beauty, and couldn't help but wonder how she would bloom if she was ever in an environment that allowed for personal growth. I took her hand and told her, "*Tu es muy bonita...*I feel privileged to be in your presence."

She looked at me silently for a moment, a look all guys dream of being on the receiving end of where you feel like a hero, and she said something in Spanish that sounded so sincere and poetic, I had to turn away.

The day we discovered each other in intimacy, my eyes opened to what love could be about. As I lay in his arms, I felt free again like I did as a child in Camaguey. It was such a personal day. I could not explain to my friends in detail, just that what we had heard about Latin men being better lovers than Anglo men was certainly not true. I never knew so much gentleness and passion.

The sun was still high enough on the horizon to make the cab ride uncomfortably hot. We drove along the Malecon, a sea wall with a very wide sidewalk and four-lane road. The Malecon draws hundreds of people to the water's edge, especially in the evenings. The road is more like a highway used to get quickly from one end of Havana to the other. The wall, about four-feet high, was built out to meet the ocean and takes the full brunt of waves that have built up in the Florida Straits. The waves hit the wall and explode ten to twenty feet into the air, reaching out as far as twenty-five feet before crashing down on top of cars and people. The ocean spray delights everyone, especially the children who test their bravery and strength against nature. Big waves take the feet out from under adults, making for a gut-busting Cuban version of *America's Funniest Home Videos*. The city comes right up to the edge of the road on the other side, and during hurricanes, with the sea level well above the wall, the streets and buildings for many blocks inshore are saturated.

We were coming to the end of land. At the eastern side of Havana is Havana harbor. On the far side of the inlet is a beautiful old lighthouse that proudly looks out over the water. Built around the lighthouse and into the coastal rocks, stretching back along the water for a half-mile is a formidable old Spanish garrison. It sits high above the city on a hill with walls that appear to be over forty-feet thick and stoic cannons daring all who approach. I couldn't see a bridge anywhere, but we were obviously heading in that direction. Then all of a sudden, we went down deep underground beneath the inlet, coming up on the other side. Same sun, same heat, but no city.

The cab dropped us off at the entrance to the fort, "El Morro," and we walked over the stone bridge that crosses the now dry moat. El Morro, built by the Spanish in 1589 to keep the English at bay, is enormous. For several hours, we explored the north side of the fort containing the barracks and offices of Che Guevara. For many years, Che represented to me a hero of the common man, even more so since I read the *Motorcycle Diaries*. His office and the desk and chair he sat in, deep inside the protective walls of the fort with a view high above Havana fascinated me. As I studied his life in detail, months later, I discovered he may also have been a psychopath. He had personally seen to the execution of hundreds of people, many of whom were men that fought beside him. He put them to death for the crime of disagreeing with the revolution's turn toward Communism.

As the sky began to get dark, we sat on the western wall of the fort overlooking the harbor, city, and setting sun. It looked like so many of the romantic European coastal cities I've visited. This time, however, the distance and beauty masked the deplorable conditions that existed there. Adianec had been looking so happy, even hopeful, but at times over our time together, I could see her begin to draw back emotionally. She no longer tried to maintain eye contact or let her touch linger on my hand or arm. I think she knew her emotions were heading into dangerous territory. I took a picture of her sitting on the wall with a large orange sun setting half way under water behind her (when I returned home I printed and framed that picture so I would never forget her).

Something strange and magical occurred to both of us at the fort that day. As we lost ourselves in the exploration of the buildings and surrounding area, we understood everything, every word and detail that the other spoke, this time it was real. It wasn't until we were sitting on the wall that we realized it. I thought she was speaking English, she thought I was speaking

Spanish. It had happened a few days before, but now it was almost a complete understanding.

Now, the surprise for you, she told me.

She said this in Spanish, but I knew what she said. We walked deeper into the now darkened fort where a large crowd had gathered overlooking the harbor. As soon as we arrived the show began. It was a reenactment of some battle for Havana. The actors, actual soldiers that were stationed at the fort, all dressed in authentic seventeenth century uniforms, were marching and setting up the firing of the cannons to protect the city and fort. This occurs every night with the cannon being lit and firing at exactly 9:00 p.m. The sound rumbles throughout the city below.

We came out of the fort with the crowd into pitch darkness. There were no lights to help us on our path. We also became the target of Cuban mosquitoes. We walked through an endless swarm and were stung so many times it was like being in a bad horror film. It was actually painful. They were so thick it was difficult to breathe without sucking in a mouthful and all you could hear was that universally recognized buzz. We walked with some effort through darkness, and into a small village on the outskirts of the fort, toward a dim warm glow ahead. She held onto my arm tightly, with her head resting on my shoulder, trusting that I would catch her if she stumbled.

It was a *paladar* with a beautiful pathway garden. The homemade tiki lamps seemed to keep the mosquitoes at bay. There were bags hanging from trees with the glow of candles emanating from them. Some of the ancient trees seemed alive with their long twisted arms. For a moment I forgot we were in Cuba. They sat us in the back yard next to a pond with a small waterfall. It was perfectly romantic.

An Italian couple sat at the table on the other side of the path and we struck up a conversation. They had just been in New York the past week and expressed how kind and helpful the people were there. In Spanish, they told Adianec, "America is such an amazing place. It was so much more than we had ever expected."

Adianec asked me if all Americans were as kind as I had been. Not something I'm usually accused of. But I told her from my experience, Americans were some of the most generous people in the world. As individuals, I've read, we give more to charities than most countries combined. She was completely shocked by that, her face was almost comical the way her jaw dropped in disbelief. She said they had been taught that all capitalists would sell their own children to get a new car.

"Absolutely untrue!" I told her. "Our neighbors' kids, yes, but not our own."

Communicating with her was getting easier. I was amazed at the pace that she was absorbing English. And my Spanish had almost doubled to four words. Yet the dictionary was still our constant chaperone. And we both had become very proficient in the art of Mime. I asked her if she was a communist. She laughed, seemingly offended, and lightly slapped my hand. Even though she had been fed a continuous diet of propaganda since birth, she was very strong-willed. I have my own mind, she said in Spanish.

Adianec had gotten herself into a tight spot at her school. She defiantly circumvented the rules that teach children the virtues of Communism and the greatness of Papa Fidel. I could see her passion and temper begin to boil as she spoke about the curriculum. This was the sexiest I'd seen her. She had a temper. She said she would continue to do what she thought best for her children, which meant preparing them for a world not suited for disabilities. Teaching them through repetition how to bathe, how to prepare simple meals, how to ride the bus, and how to count money. Learning the communist creed would not get them across town any safer. When she began to wave her finger and animate with her hands, her voice rose with indignation I wished we were alone back in our room.

I won't speak of the ferocity of passion that unfolded after dinner that night…all night. In between, we talked intimately about our hopes and dreams. Mine were generally about me and what I wanted to accomplish, places I wanted to travel to, and at what point financially I'd feel safe. For Adianec, it was all about her family and how she wanted to make their lives easier. All she wanted was the opportunity to get a job that would allow her to earn a fair living so her mother could quit work and "wear her slippers all day." She constantly worried about her little sister and the guy she was dating, because he wanted her sister to quit medical school. She spoke with some sadness about her relatives that had made it to Miami, and how she didn't think they did enough for her grandparents. For her, it was always about others.

I laid there in the dark, slowly combing her hair with my fingers, thinking about how she was so different from the women I meet in Los Angeles. The sense of entitlement that many beautiful women possess had somehow eluded her. About 3:00 a.m., the electricity again surrendered and it didn't take long for the heat of Cuba to seep in. I took her hand and led her out of bed. She was giggling as she dressed in the dark, not knowing what adventure she was heading toward. We walked through the dark and now-quiet streets of central Havana. It was romantic, but a bit eerie. The closer we got to the Malecon, the cooler the breeze. We walked in silence, past the rubble of once-beautiful buildings. The occasional barking of a curious dog, asking us why we were there, was the only disturbance on our peaceful walk.

When we got to the water's edge, we sat on the wall and talked until dawn. The top of the seawall was still a little damp from the waves earlier in the day, but it cooled us. The Ocean was calm, reflecting the moons light. Along the Malecon were many other couples, gay and straight. Although homosexuality is outlawed in Cuba, there is a large gay population there. But in Cuba, it is almost entirely underground for fear of arrest. A section of the Malecon is an unspoken gay meeting area and we were in the midst of it that night as we talked. We briefly spoke with some other couples, but everybody was there for romance.

Chapter eleven

MITZVAH

Shortly after going back to bed we were awakened by Alex, who was growing impatient with me. I had been promising him I would buy cigars from his contact. I told him to come back at one o'clock and we would go have lunch and buy cigars. I dragged myself out of bed a little before one, leaving Adianec in a peaceful sleep, and got in the shower. Yes, I brushed the showerhead again. Yes, it hurt again. Yes, I was vocal about it and Conchita laughed. I was growing happier by the minute.

The truth is I was feeling a little down that morning. I knew I'd be leaving in two days and Adianec would have to go back to her life. The thought of her everyday struggle was weighing heavily on me. It wasn't just her financial situation, there is poverty everywhere. It was the absence of hope that life offered there, the spiritual poverty, something I'd never in my life experienced before, which tore at my heart. I knew meeting her wasn't mere coincidence. It couldn't be.

We had lunch at the Park Central Hotel, as it was the only food I could tolerate. I don't think Alex had ever been in a nice restaurant before, because he watched and mimicked my every move. He put his napkin on his lap, he cut his chicken in small bites, he even said "thank you" when the busboy gave him water. For being such a street-smart hustler, he really had a charming innocence about him. He and Adianec got along very well and spent most of the time speaking in Spanish. It gave me a chance to be let my mind wander.

As I watched her eat again with feelings of guilt, I decided to do all I could to make sure Adianec and her family never went without food or basic necessities again. I would send them my "lunch money." It would be my *mitzvah*, my good deed. She felt a part of me now in some strange way, and I didn't want the burden of worrying about her wellbeing on my mind. One hundred dollars a month to them is the difference between basic survival and having a relatively decent life. And for me it would mean skipping one lunch a week. It was a very fair trade.

Thinking about how I would tell her that her family would not have to struggle so much dramatically improved my mood. I just had to figure out how to get the money to her every month. This must be why I'd met her. Not that I'd ever been a great believer in fate, but God, I believed, had put me in front of that school a few days earlier to help this incredible woman and her family. And who knows, maybe in a few years, if Fidel was no longer in power, I would be able to come back and see her again. Certainly she wouldn't need my help forever, but she would have it as long as she needed it.

After lunch, Adianec went home to feed Simba and check in. Alex's cigar quest took me on a clandestine journey into the deep recesses of the Cuban black market. The room we ended up in, after finding our way through a maze of alleys, hallways and small rooms was creepy. Old soiled sheets taped to the low ceiling partitioned the room into small spaces. Everybody was paranoid and uncertain about the American. Later, Alex told me that one of the sellers thought I was an American spy, CIA. In Cuba they pronounce it "seer." This was not a government-approved cigar store. They were stolen from the cigar factory by enterprising employees, who took a big risk. Stealing from the government would guarantee many years in prison. Even though I'm not a smoker, I was in awe of the variety of cigars. Long, short, thick, thin, dark, light with names like, *Monte Cristos, Esplendidos, Romeos* and *Cohibas*. There were many different ways to make you nauseous. Which is exactly what happened, with the very first inhale of my *Esplendido limited* I turned a nice shade of Irish green. I had purchased three cigars, 2 9/10th of which ended up in the trash.

Adianec came by late in the afternoon and took me to the *El Floridita*, an old hangout of Hemingway's to listen to music. At the end of the bar is a life-size bronze of the *Old Man of the Sea* himself. Standing there smiling, leaning against the bar as he greets patrons. We didn't stay long, since the next day would be our last full day together and we both wanted to spend what time we had left alone.

Walking home in the dark we had a serious and dangerous lapse in judgment. Adianec absent-mindedly grabbed my hand as she was translating something for me. We were unknowingly being watched by a police officer.

He was across the street and whistled for her to come to him. The blood drained from her face. For what she had done (touch my hand), that asshole could immediately send her away for two years. This was something I had already heard about. Her eyes began to well up, as she put her hand to my chest to asked me to wait right there.

She already knew my temper, and was concerned I would do something impulsive trying to protect her. Panicked thoughts raced through my mind. Do I tell her to run as I go over and knock him out? Do we run together and try to escape the island? I didn't know what, but I had to do something. I was not going to stand by as she was dragged off to prison. But I did stand there a moment, impotent in my indecision. She dutifully walked across the street and stood there as that moron humiliated her. I had had all I could take and ran over to stepped in between them. I wanted to insult and humiliate him the way he had insulted Adianec. But all that came out was, "Is there a fucking problem here?"

I was ready to go at it with him. I towered over him with an extra thirty pounds. He wouldn't engage me, or even meet my stare. He nervously ignored me as he quickly wrote down her information. She asked me to calm down. *"Lee. Por favor."*

"Hey asshole, deal with me. You got a problem, deal with me. Leave her out of it."

I could not tolerate seeing him humiliate her. *"Lee, es nada, Por favor, trouble to you."*

"No, Adianec, this is wrong. Let him be a man and deal with me." I turned back to the bully, who still wouldn't look at me. I could feel the blood rushing into my face, tightening my vision, and I knew I was seconds away from losing control "Hey!" I yelled, "I'm talking to you, asshole! You wanna play tough guy, I'll play." He now spoke to her quietly but with concern.

Adianec was getting upset, and scared. *"Lee, solo informacion. He promeza no arrestar me. Okay, Lee? The policia he scared. Goodbye rapido."*

She told me he had said he would not arrest her, but was putting her on notice. I knew what I was doing was stupid, it's a habit of mine. But it was working since he was definitely intimidated. I stopped yelling but kept my face inches from his. He didn't know what to do with this crazy American. Alex had told me that the police are told to protect tourists, especially the rare American, as Cuba needs foreign dollars. And now with one challenging him, he was very apprehensive. Nobody in Cuba challenges authority. But, if he harassed me and I filed a complaint, he might have to explain himself. I was counting on his paranoia. His arrogance challenged, he wrapped things up pretty quickly. I think he just wanted to get rid of the loco Americano.

I didn't say another word, for her sake, but I didn't take my eyes off him.

He never once looked at me, just another bully that turns to chicken shit when confronted.

When the policia saw Lee and I together, I thought my life was over. I was so scared that I was going to go to prison and also embarrassed for Lee to see me have to submit to this man. And of course all the people around us thought I was jinetera, and Lee saw me being treated like one. It was shameful. We had been so careful until that night. Even though I had been denied personal choice my entire life, I still could not understand it. Why do these men in my government think they have the right to suppress my heart, my mind and my life? Where I breathe is my choice.

When Lee came over, I thought he was going to strike the policia. I just wanted him to calm down and not involve himself. It would do no good for both of us to go to jail. Even though the policia protect the touristas, Lee's reaction was more than any policia in Cuba had ever seen. What kind of man does this, he risked his own freedom for me? If this is the kind of man that comes from America, than everything I've ever been taught about that country is a lie.

We were both very shaken by what had just happened. Adianec asked me to not do that again by wagging her finger, and then gave me a kiss for doing it. I understood what she meant. We had one more full day together and then I would have to go back home. I couldn't stop the nagging thought that I was abandoning her. We spent the whole night talking again. We talked about the war, politics, and the ability to vote. I tried to explain with the dictionary what snow felt like and how incredible it feels to be standing on the top of a snow covered mountain surrounded by white peaks and clouds against a blue sky. It was incredible to me, someone who had never seen snow. "It feels cold like an ice cube, but very soft like a feather and when you walk, it crunches under your boots like the potato chips we ate at the museum. At the end of the day you're exhausted, your legs are burning and you can barely walk. The sun is casting long shadows on the course, it's getting very cold and the snow is getting too icy, but you want just one more run from the top, one more chase through the trees. Then you reward yourself with a hot drink by a warm fireplace."

I remember how sad I felt when I thought that I would never be able to sit next to a fireplace with her on a cold winter night. It all seemed so insane that I wanted to share it with her and knew I never could. I told her of my plans to send money for her family. She just nodded, with a slight smile. Cubans, it seems, are familiar with disappointment. They expect to be let down so they're not disappointed. I didn't try to convince her. I knew I would find a way to keep my promise. She hesitantly asked. "When…might you…come back?"

The way she asked, I knew she saw more in this relationship than I was willing to face. She was letting herself be vulnerable, and I was about to give my usual, "it's not you, it's me" speech. Although I couldn't deny the connection, this relationship was out of the question. She was too young, lived too far away and the culture, and communication gap was a warning sign. I told her, "All I can promise right now is to keep in touch. It's just…too dangerous for me to come back to Cuba."

I could see her disappointment and anger directed inward. It seemed at that moment she decided that she couldn't afford to be vulnerable any longer and she put up a wall. She laughed at my jokes and talked, but her emotions became inaccessible to me.

The next morning Alex awakened us, again. She went home to feed Simba as Alex and I grabbed a few eggs for breakfast. She came back several hours later with Simba. He was a beautiful white Canadian Shepherd who assumed that I was his personal chew toy. For the next hour, he constantly had my hand, arm or ankle in his mouth, and his play was not what one would call "gentle." Adianec found this a constant source of amusement. It was good to see her laugh, so I played along, in pain. She told me that they should go, and she would not be able to stay the night with me. She said she would come by in the morning to say goodbye. "Here, let me walk you."

"No."

She left no room for negotiation. In a bizarre way I felt like we were breaking up. I was very lonely at the thought of not seeing her until morning, but I understood that she was protecting herself. I felt torn between doing what would be best for her and wanting my sadness to go away.

Late that night, I walked alone through the crowded streets of central Havana. It felt different without Adianec. For the first time since we met, I felt like a foreigner. With her, I fit in. As I walked by the park, I was approached by a few girls looking to start a relationship, but my heart didn't have any room for company - not the organ they were interested in, I'm sure. The night seemed unbearably humid, breathing was a chore. As I walked back to the school where we had met, I tried to retrace our steps of that first day to see if I could find her apartment. I was so restless and aggravated that night. I just wanted her back in my arms for the time we had left. The streets were dark and confusing, and for a while I wandered in circles, lost. I finally went back to Conchita's and laid down. I wanted out of my skin, out of this misery.

"This is stupid, man. Stop it. You don't even know this girl."

I convinced myself that what I was feeling was empathy and nothing more. Some time after 3 a.m., I'm not sure when, I finally fell asleep.

Chapter twelve

LAST DAY

I woke up at dawn, and took a shower, after which Conchita surprised me with a nice breakfast; eggs, toast and mango. Alex came by around ten. I gave him some money, another shirt and promised to bring him a pair of New Balance shoes, if I ever returned to Cuba. I had promised the rest of my clothes to Adianec's father. I actually came back home with an empty suitcase. Adianec arrived with just an hour left before I was to leave for the airport. By that point, I was so hurt and irritated by her cavalier attitude that I was about to tell her to go back home and forget we had ever met. She could sense my anger and sat on the bed next to me burying her face into my neck. I could see that she was probably in more pain than I. I had a full life to go back to, while she had nothing but the constraints of Cuban life in her future. We sat there for a while as I quietly sang her a Bon Jovi song (*It's my life*). My off-key singing always brought out a brightness in her. Though she didn't know it, I'd forgotten the words and made up my own version, one of the few advantages that come with not speaking the same language.

I put all my clothes, walkman and toiletries into my backpack and handed it to her. I also gave her an envelope, but told her not to open it until I left. It had just over seven hundred dollars inside. That would keep me from having to worry about her for at least six months, in case I had trouble sending money. We sat on the bed again and held each other. Nothing could make this goodbye easy. I told her, "I will never go back on my promise, you have to know that. If you ever need anything, anything, I'll be there for you."

She held my hand and said, "Need you *aqui.*"

I laughed without responding. I couldn't, nor did I want to imagine what lay ahead for her. It seemed so unfair that I could leave at will and she was remanded to her island prison, forbidden to leave or even live with the dignity of basic human rights and necessities.

As my cab drove away, I turned and watched her standing there on the corner in a crowd of people, slowly disappearing into the everyday hustle of life in Havana. The drive back to the airport seemed much different than the one a week earlier, except for the smothering heat. That felt remarkably the same. The forest was still as green, but the billboards did not seem as innocent as they had six days earlier. They were clouded with an ominous darkness, a philosophy that could harm people that I now cared very deeply for. I had learned so much about this culture, but knew I had so much more to absorb. I wanted to make all their lives better, one of them for sure. I looked back at the past week, as an experience that would be life changing.

I watched him drive away from me, I felt frozen on the corner of the street. I couldn't run after him so I went back up to Conchita's. Our room felt very empty. He was gone. I was in two worlds. I still had my heart in his, but I soon had to go back to mine. I had to be strong. I reminded myself that this was my life. I am Cuban, he is American and my dream is over. I need to wake up. I was very sad sitting on our bed, I laid down crying and I could still smell him on his pillow. This past week was a "milagro." I wondered how long this would hurt before I could let him go. Lee was very sweet to me, and said many things about helping us, but I knew as soon as he got back to America, he would forget me. Even though he never talked about it, I was sure he had a girlfriend waiting for him.

I saw Alex on my walk back home. He was wearing Lee's shorts and shirt, and it made me miss him even more. When I got home I played with Simba before my nap. The day before when we were with Lee he had sprayed Simba with his cologne and now even Simba smelled like him. It felt like he was still with me, at least until the cologne wore away.

The sky opened up and cleaned the road ahead of us. It came down so hard we had to pull over. The lightning was a beautiful show, spectacular for me because we don't get lightning in Santa Monica. I rolled down the window and let the cool rain run down my face, and I breathed in deeply the crisp clean air. My mind wandered for some time, wondering if my flight would be cancelled and then I would have to stay another night. If I showed up at Adianec's home, would she be happy to see me? What if I decided to stay and help these people? Undoubtedly, I would end up in prison like hundreds of others that spoke out against the conditions in this place. My plane was delayed for three hours. I tried to call her several times, but the phone lines in Cuba don't seem to be water-resistant.

Ten miles from the Mexico City airport, with my head pressed against the window, I couldn't help but imagine how great it would feel to be with Adianec the first time she saw the outside world. The grandness of Mexico City spread out from horizon to horizon was impressive. I could see fast food signs, Dominos, McDonalds, symbols of a forbidden world that, for a Cuban, only exist while watching illegal TV transmissions from Miami. Once I realized what I was doing, I made myself a promise not to think about her until it was time to send money. This was just another holiday romance. I thought about the life I had. My daily routine was the envy of my married friends. I could pick up and go to Europe on a day's notice. Or take a weekday off at will and head to the mountains for a day of skiing. I had no one waiting for me at home on Friday nights staring at the clock. This was not a time to get distracted by some girl I had met on vacation. I would send money and that would be the end of it.

I arrived back at LAX about 1 a.m. The air was thankfully dry and cool. I like driving in Los Angeles early in the morning, when the freeways seem almost civilized. The 405 - San Diego Freeway - at 2 a.m. was busy, but not bumper to bumper. As I pulled onto the 10 freeway and into Santa Monica, I was seeing all my familiar sights with her new eyes, it was incredible. I felt so blessed to have been born in America, or anywhere outside of Cuba. I felt lucky to have the life I did.

I took my empty bag upstairs, then walked two blocks to the beach. I sat on the water's edge with a slight breeze blowing across my face. The waves were lightly lapping against the sand as they broke. The Pacific was very still. I looked over at the Santa Monica Pier, where the ferris wheel lights were still on. I had always thought they were beautiful, but that night, looking at them, imagining her beside me, they were on fire. My eyes began to fill with tears, which made me laugh out loud. How could I miss her so much? It had to be empathy. I didn't know her and could barely understand a word she said. I walked, through the fog, down the bike path toward Venice Beach, along with a few skateboarders and some homeless drunks.

Chapter thirteen

ALONE

I woke up late the next morning. My guys were already on the job sites when I called them. I headed to the office about 10. My buddy Les, had given me office space in his building in Santa Monica, which conveniently was only a half mile from my home. It's a beautiful old three story red brick building right off the Third Street Promenade.

There were a couple of times in my life as an actor where paying jobs grew thin, and I could barely afford to eat, much less pay rent. Les would give me the guest room in his Malibu home, a stunning house on a cliff high above the ocean. Since he traveled to Europe for business often, I frequently had the house to myself. The last time I stayed for a year, and I would have settled in longer but the house burnt down in the Malibu fires. He was always getting on me about not reaching my potential. "It's time to grow up, be a man, stop playing that childish game of acting." Which was somewhat hypocritical considering all he ever dated were young actresses.

I stepped into Les's office. He had an office phone on one ear, one cell phone on the other and a second cell phone ringing. I took a seat to get my place in line. He's a deal maker, so I have to make things interesting to get his attention when he's at his desk. I started rummaging through papers in his office, and shoved a pile of un-cashed checks into my pocket. That got his attention. When he got down to one phone, he asked me. "So? What's up?"

"I just got back. I want to talk to you about something."

He put a hand over the phone. "You met a girl?"

I nodded. He excused himself from the other call and rolled his eyes. He had done business in Cuba recently and thought he was a "Cubaphile." He took over the conversation, as usual, and asked if I thought I was in love.

"Of course not, I just want to send her money."

"Then send her money!"

And with that he was back on the phone making deals. I sat at the computer for an hour or so to catch up on my invoices. Les came by on his way out to lunch, "Lee, it's great you want to help someone, but you have to know, this is a well known third world con. Beautiful young women get these gullible foreign men to feel sorry for their situation and then they fill up their egos with gratitude and promises of love for coming to their rescue. That's probably what's happening here."

"Les, you know me. I'm not looking for love."

"Okay, good," and he left. He has a way of ending conversations before they're finished.

I drove through Santa Monica to check on my job sites. Santa Monica is a nearly perfect seaside community on the outskirts of L.A. It has a quaint feel to it, but because of the money that lives here it has all the modern accessories. We get tourists from around the world all year long, but it's fairly quiet until the weekends, when everyone in L.A. packs up the kids and heads to the beach here.

I picked up Luis, who has been working as my foreman for several years. We drove to all the job sites together and he updated me about how things went in my absence. Everything was going smoothly, and a lot had been accomplished while I was gone. Admittedly, I can be too detail oriented which tends to slow things down. Luis is the perfect employee for someone like me. He enjoys being the boss. He's tall, thin but muscular, and very quiet. In fact, he never talks...ever. But his quiet demeanor drives all of our clients' housekeepers crazy. His machismo attitude, though sometimes irritating, comes in handy because he wants everything that he does to be perfect. He will do anything to keep me from criticizing his jobs.

I had a late lunch with my friend and client Nicky, who is everyone's Jewish mother, whether you're Jewish or not. We were in the middle of remodeling her home. Even with her kitchen demolished, she would still insist that you sit down while she fed you. Her husband, Doctor Gold, was a Los Angeles gynecologist with the manners of a country doctor. He was about to retire and had delivered babies for generations in the same families. They are a rare couple, married for fifty years, with all their kids grown and very successful. I had to talk to someone who would support me or at least listen to me without judgment. Nicky was always the one to turn to.

We talked about Cuba, Communism, poverty and finally, Adianec. Nicky listened, without responding for thirty minutes and then basically said what Les had said, only in a much more nurturing way. I looked at Nicky and said, "Well, that's my story. What do you think?"

She didn't hold back, but spoke to me out of concern, "Well, dear, I think you should be very careful. Some people can sense a kind-hearted person, which you are. You have a lot to lose." As if to somehow cushion it, she added, "You know, I can introduce you to some very attractive Jewish girls. You don't have to seek so far from home."

"Would I have to convert? I could be a good Jew." I said, teasing her.

"No, you'd be a great Jew." She reached over and patted my hand. "Now, what would you like for lunch, dear?"

Maybe I wasn't describing Adianec accurately. I hadn't considered for a minute that I was being misled, or that she might take advantage of me. But, I was beginning to consider the possibility.

Bobby, my friend who predicted I would meet Adianec, called while I was making my final rounds of the day. I didn't tell him about the "sending the money thing," but he laughed and patted himself on the back for being a perfect intuitive when he had told me I'd meet some sweet country girl on the first day. I had to admit he was pretty uncanny with his prediction.

My triathlon club had an ocean swim late that afternoon, which always seemed to clear my head. But I got out of the water just as confused as when I entered. The suns light was just becoming that end of the day soft orange. It reminded me of Cuba, and I could almost feel Adianec sitting right next to me. Then on the way home I got a phone call from a pretty, petite fitness model, Michelle (not her real name...I don't think), I had met a few weeks before I left for Cuba. This would be the perfect Adianec antidote. Michelle definitely possessed the tools to help me forget the past week. She was the type of girl that didn't bother to complicate her life with things like politics, Communism, poverty or anything that would require thinking.

We agreed to meet at The Kettle, a neighborhood "home cookin" restaurant in Manhattan Beach. We had to meet near her place due to her concern she might get lost driving back from Santa Monica in the dark. "Is the Pacific Ocean supposed to be on the right or the left?" Walking up to meet her, I stood across the street for a moment to watch her look for me, oblivious to guys bumping into signposts as they walked past her. She, innocently, had no idea the effect she had on men. The value of her beauty had escaped her, along with that thinking thing. At dinner, I wanted to talk about Cuba and its difficulties. She had absolutely no clue what I was talking about. "Cuba. It's a country. An island dictatorship, in the Caribbean." I said, trying not to sound too condescending.

"Since it's such a big island, do you think they have both a Club Med and a Sandals resort?"

"I, uh, no, I don't think-"

Michelle wondered out loud if all-inclusive vacations were really the way to go. After dinner we went back to her place. She wanted to watch TV to see if we could catch a commercial she had just shot. No success. About 2 a.m. lying in bed with her, my mind was wandering and I was feeling guilty for being there. Why was I feeling guilty? She was asking me something about something and I just couldn't lay there another minute. I had to leave. She was not Adianec, this was not Cuba, and I had no desire to stay up all night talking with her, like Adianec and I had done every night in Havana. I understood Adianec better when she was speaking Spanish than when this tiny beauty spoke Californian. This was supposed to be living "the dream," but the dream seemed a bit thin now. I couldn't get the Cuban people, especially Adianec, out of my mind. I began to realize that night that my life may seem exciting, but at that moment I realized that it had been a bit too shallow and self-serving.

The following day, I saw on the news that a hurricane was making its way straight for Cuba. Having seen the condition of Havana, there was no doubt that a direct hit would destroy the city. That kept Adianec on my mind throughout the day. I thought about calling her to make sure she had adequate shelter, but I decided against it, I didn't want to upset her. We both needed to put some time between us.

That night I had dinner with my friend Barry, and his girlfriend, Lisa. Barry and his brother, Steve, were the guys responsible for enticing me out of acting several years ago, with a job working as a supervisor for their real estate development company. They are incredibly successful. I thought maybe some of their success would eventually rub off on me. Perhaps I needed to rub harder. After spending a couple of years destroying their company, they set me up in my own business and continue to make sure it remains solvent. Barry is the smartest guy I know, graduating from Boalt Law School while barely cracking a book. Lisa, tall and beautiful, grew up living and playing on the beaches in Malibu. As he is the smartest guy I know, I wanted to get his opinion of how I should handle this situation, especially now that I kept hearing that I was being played.

Barry is the kind of person that will only give his opinion if you pry it out of him, and even then he'll be very diplomatic. If you ask Lisa what she thinks, she will tell you.

With a little embellishment for humors sake, I told them of the week. When I asked about the money and if they had any ideas on how to send it, Lisa said very sincerely. "Lee, congratulations, I think you've found the perfect woman for you. She couldn't possibly be more unavailable. Finally, someone you won't have to leave."

Not exactly the answer I was looking for, but it made me laugh. Barry's said "Honestly, Lee, you just have to make sure you're not doing anything illegal by helping her. That is not something you want to be involved with. You just have to make sure you protect yourself."

So here I was, driven by some unknown power to help this girl, to consciously commit an unselfish act, and everyone thought I was being, at best, naïve. These were all people I trusted and respected. Maybe they were right. It was then that my heart and mind became at odds over this situation. In my heart I felt I knew her, her soul and her pureness. But, what if she was deceiving me? What difference does that make, or should it make? The truth was she needed my help and it wouldn't hurt me to help her. Nobody wants to be made a fool, but I could not walk away and abandon her. I had three more people to consult, my friends Jay and Kevin, and my mother.

Jay and I were actors together for about twelve years until he quit and became a cop in Los Angeles. Jay actually had a solid acting career going, with leads in several low budget action films (he was the *White Phantom*). Several years ago he had an off year and decided to put acting on the shelf and find something steady, something he was equally passionate about. He now has a successful career in law enforcement, having risen to the rank of Lieutenant. He is also the most levelheaded guy I know, and his experience on L.A.'s streets has deprived him of his former rosy out look on life. I called him and after hearing my story, he said it was a very nice thing to do but it was most likely a con. "Just don't get sucked into it any further. You will probably get a call soon asking for more money, for some emergency."

He told me that would be my sign that it's a con.

I've known Kevin the longest of all my friends. We started off acting together doing commercials and theatre in New York over twenty years ago. Kevin had remained in acting and can be seen on TV almost nightly. He is almost childlike in his enthusiasm for helping people, with an embarrassingly big heart. We met for lunch near his home. I was really shocked and disappointed when he shook his head and said, "Lee, you can't save the whole world. I've seen you rescue and then leave women for twenty years now, and this one could really get you into trouble."

I didn't know who in particular he was talking about. My friends were always complaining when I would break up with someone that they loved. I often wondered if they liked the women more than me. After I would break up with a woman, I would continue to watch out for them. I used to direct my exes on who they could or could not date. First rule, no actors. It drove them crazy, "You have no right to have an opinion on my life anymore." This was probably true.

But this situation with Adianec was different. I would have thought that my friends would have recognized that. I actually thought everyone would rally around this. The opposite was true. Universally, they all thought it was a bad idea. But they weren't there. They didn't experience the conditions or see the despair on people's faces. Or, most of all, they hadn't looked into Adianec's eyes. Obviously, I needed to be vigilant. I called my mother in Florida, who is so desperate for me to marry, she would do back flips if I got engaged to an amoeba. But, she is also a mother and very protective of her only son. I told her the story of Cuba and how I was haunted by this woman. Her response was interesting. "I like her, honey."

"Mom, you don't even know her."

"I know, but she sounds sweet."

"Should I just marry the next girl I meet so you can calm down?"

"Okay."

This wasn't helping. "Anyway, I don't know what I should do about her."

"Are you asking for my advice?"

"Could I stop you?" I think we both knew that answer.

"I think what you want to do is a beautiful thing, it's what Jesus would do."

So, now I was on par with the messiah. Well, not quite. "You know I also had sex with her."

"Stop it, Lee."

"Just sayin'." I can only imagine her face when I told her that.

I told her of everyone's responses, and that now I was feeling a bit stupid, having made a commitment to help Adianec and her family. I asked her how I could continue to live surrounded by so much, with unlimited options, and remain insensitive to people who were virtual prisoners. My mother then gave me the one piece of light to date. "I know you try to help too many people, and you can't save the world, but I think maybe God wants you to help this one."

For the next week, I tried to get back to my routine, but something had changed. I felt like I had been partially re-wired. I was seeing everything around me as if it were for the first time. I began to read all I could on Cuba. I found a great book called *This is Cuba*. The author Ben Corbitt, saw the same Cuba I did, but he had spent a great deal more time there and filled the book with facts and anecdotes so vivid, I felt like I was back there. I emailed him and we've been friends ever since. I studied Cuban history on-line and read all the laws and congressional acts on Cuba since the 1959 revolution.

Everyday that went by without word from Lee confirmed to me that I would never see him again. I would lay in bed and think that if he asked me, I would swim across the sea to be with him. I never told him about the love in my heart that belonged to him. I was sure he wouldn't trust it, although now I wish I had. When the phone would ring, I would run to it, in case it was him. I didn't want him to hang up. Nobody had treated me with the kindness that he showed, and I was sure I would never meet another man like him. My whole body came alive just thinking about him. I think he will still be in my dreams when I am an old woman. I will smile when I speak of him to my grandchildren.

It wasn't until the day after he left that I remembered about the envelope he gave me. I knew it had money inside, but when I opened it I thought it must be a mistake. I counted it five times. I had never seen so much money, not even in a bank. I felt like a little child; this was too much. I showed Sol and we just laughed. It was enough money for the rest of my life. Finally, I could give gifts to my family. I was able to buy my mother a refrigerator and washing machine. I gave my grandmothers each $100, and $100 left for me.

I became even more frustrated with the congested rules at my school. Lee had taught me so much about what was happening in the outside world. I wanted those choices of freedom for me and my kids. The heat in our school seemed unbearable after having had an air conditioner for a week. I would bathe the children more often just so they could get a break from the heat. A hurricane came to the west side of Cuba and brought a lot of humidity with it.

I kept seeing the pictures he showed me of his home in my head. I was glad he never saw where I lived. I would have been so embarrassed. Our cocina is half exposed to the outside. My bedroom is in the attic and I can see some of the sky when the sun is out. The bathroom at Conchita's that he found so offensive was one of the most beautiful I'd ever seen. Our shower just had a pipe coming out of the wall and a hole in the floor. Lee had taught me to question and to want a better life.

Chapter fourteen

RE-CONNECT

Even with many people telling me I was being foolish, I couldn't get Adianec out of my mind. I was also baffled by everybody's reaction concerning my need to help her. When did helping someone become a naïve act? I knew my friends were just being protective, but I was sure if they had met her they would have felt differently. Ten days or so after I'd left Cuba, I called her. "Hey cutie, how are you?"

"I see fine, thanks you."

At first I didn't recognize her voice. It was almost childlike in its thinness. She was having trouble catching her breath. I thought that she had been running, but then after a few moments went by, I could tell it was due to excitement and nervousness. That realization calmed any fears I may have had about her true feelings for me. Whatever difficulties in communication we had before were now amplified by our inability to read each other's faces. "Your English is very good. Are you studying?"

"I ahh, umm, *si*…yes much studious."

She had obviously been studying English and was attempting to put together sentences. In spite of that, It was a challenge for us to understand one another. Her accent was very thick.

"I miss him."

I was wondering who "him" was. "Who?"

"*Que*? What?"

"You said, 'I miss him'. Who is 'him'?"

She giggled. "Es you, you es, umm you…" She laughed the whole time she was saying this. "Sorry me inglish, tu know. Umm, you es him."

"Ahh, Okay."

"Song to me."

"Song for you? What—Oh, oh, *sing* for you. You want me to sing?" (I sang to her in Havana, each night as she fell asleep.)

More giggling, followed by "*Si*, yes."

So I sang Springsteen's, *Bobby Jean*. We spent most of the hour long phone call just laughing. I found out three weeks later that laughter cost me $75. I promised to call back in a week, though I wasn't sure if she understood.

I was lying in bed when the phone rang. I yelled at Heidells to not pick it up, I knew it was Lee. My heart was pounding so loud I was afraid he would hear it. He had the same confidence and laughter in his voice. I was trying to show him the English words I had learned but I couldn't catch my breath. He said goodnight too soon, it seemed like five minutes. I didn't even try to sleep that night.

I didn't wait a week to call back. After only five days, I needed to hear Adianec's voice again. We both seemed to be better prepared this time. I had the translation dictionary and Adianec had what seemed to be a prepared statement. It was pretty fundamental, how is your family, work, the weather. And then came the question I was not prepared for: when are you coming to Cuba again?

My pause was too long and put her on the defensive. Very quickly she said, "*es no importa, no importa.*"

Even though Adianec said it was not important, I could tell she was choking up as she said it. I couldn't deny I had real feelings for her, but I was not going to confuse it with love. This was a no-win situation, and I was not going back. I still had some feelings of regret from the last trip for what I perceived to be as disrespectful to the people whose lives had been destroyed by this regime. Though I truly believed the embargo was unproductive at best and ruined the lives of innocent people at worst, perhaps I had no right to challenge it. Though I tried to lighten up the mood, we ended the call without reconciling. I told her the date and time of my next call. I said I'd call in another week.

Before the next call, I was surprised by an email from Adianec. It was in English, sort of. She told me how happy and surprised she had been when she got that first call a couple of weeks ago and she wanted to apologize for pushing me to come back to Cuba. She said she wasn't sure how safe this email address was, since using the internet is illegal for Cubans, and the government monitors all communications. She had a friend who worked in a doctor's office, and she could also translate letters into English. As long as she didn't get caught and we paid, she would continue to allow us to communicate on her email address.

Subconsciously, every time we spoke, I was always looking for Adianec to slip up and reveal herself as the fraud that everyone here was convinced she was. Consciously, I wanted her to be the person I knew in my heart. Even with my protection mode on high, I just wasn't prepared for what would happen with the next phone call.

She was bubbly when she picked up the phone. I think she might have had her sister or a friend in the room because she was being very familiar with me. Her caution had been replaced with a lively enthusiasm. We had been talking, with little headway for about ten minutes when she dropped the bomb on me and took my breath away.

It sounded like she was being coached with her English, because unfortunately, I very clearly heard and understood every word she said.

"We have *problema*."

I was laughing, not realizing the gravity of the situation yet. "Oh yeah, what kinda *problema* do we have?"

Umm, *no mas dinero.*

I couldn't say anything. There was a long silent pause while I tried to absorb what she had just said.

"Hellooo, meester."

"No no, I'm here, I uh I heard you. What do you mean, no *dinero*?"

"You need bring *mas*, ah, more, baby."

That moment gave me the unfortunate personal experience of what it actually feels like to have your blood run cold. I couldn't breathe. She was laughing like it was some kind of fucking party. It literally felt like my blood drained out of my body. Jay's words were echoing in my head. "You'll know it's a con when she calls and asks for more money due to an emergency."

I couldn't believe this. This couldn't be happening. "Give you more. Just give you more money?!"

There was far less laughter now from her. "*Tu* come back now, in Cuba, so I need you."

That's about the last thing I wanted to do at that moment. "Right, right, I, ahh, see. You want me to send you more money?"

"Si, baby, y comes to Cuba."

"Listen, I have to run, I'm not feeling well. I'll call you back." I was lying on my bed looking up and the ceiling began to spin.

My friends were right, all of them. I guess that's why they're my friends. The devastation I felt went beyond disappointment. I was so blown away I couldn't even get angry. She kept calling me her "baby." Yep, that's me, born yesterday. I'm supposed to believe she blew $700 in a month living in Havana.

The fact that I'd been played was bad enough, but with her laughing in my face, it was totally humiliating. That must be her game. I didn't want it to be true but there it was. She didn't even try to disguise it. I was literally on my knees that night asking God, "Why did I have to be such an idiot?! Why? And why the hell did I have to tell everyone?!"

I certainly couldn't face my friends with this. I'd just let the whole thing fade away. Maybe they'd just conveniently forget about it. I decided to not even engage with her again. I was sure she would try one more time to contact me and then realize I was on to her and move to on the next gullible tourist. Even after having had my trust violated, the idea of never speaking to her again, made me feel surprisingly empty.

The next few weeks went by in a fog. Adianec sent several emails and I assumed by the thirteen digit number that kept coming up on my phone that she tried to call many times. I didn't pick up. She finally left a message. Her voice was weak and sad, certainly part of a good scam. She basically followed the same script as in her emails. Lee. I'm sorry. I know I make mistake.

She was sorry. She made a mistake, blah blah blah. The message continued on, "I, I done a thing wrong for you. My friends to say that I need you money, so you come back to Cuba. It selfish, I know it, and I, I feel like stupid girl. I done to need more money, just you."

Then she told me that she loved me.

I didn't quite understand what she was trying to say. She didn't mention the money I had left her. Was it gone or not? I did know, however, that this was a good opportunity for me to walk away. She gave me a way out of the commitment I had made to her in Havana. I would write her an email and explain why it was best that we just say goodbye.

In the email, I tried to explain how much damage her little "con" had done to me. I said, "You can now count yourself as one of the majority of people outside the U.S. who are ignorant enough to believe that all Americans are millionaires. Just so you know, the money I left you was not extra money I happened to have lying around. I am not rich. You picked the wrong American. I work hard for whatever money I have and I consider the money stolen, since you were supposed to use it for food for you and your family for the next six months so I wouldn't have to worry about you."

I also said some other very hurtful things that I will never repeat. I wished her well and said, "If you have any dignity, you will just let this thing fade away and not try to contact me anymore."

She took me at my word.

Weeks went by, but time did nothing to fade my memory of her. My days were spent staying busy at work and training for the upcoming triathlon season, but most of my nights were spent thinking about her and Cuba. If she had just let things be, I would have sent her more money. Because above all, I had just wanted to make sure she was safe.

One night, I got an email from Heidells. He was the son of the family that Adianec lived with. He told me, "Lee, I want to tell you that Adianec is doing not well. We can ever get her out of bed. I have heard the story about the money and you have all the wrong impressions of Adianec. I have known her very well for a long time. She is a very special person, very special. She is so much different than most girls. I want to tell you that I am certain she really loves you and had just wanted to be with you again. I do not know that you know but she is very loyal to family and that money you have left with her went for to them. She buy them basic appliance for her mother and give money for food for her grandparents with almost nothing left for herself."

I could barely read on when he said, "Adianec's birthday has gone by and she had hoped that she would have received a card or just a call from you. When it never came, she stops smiling."

Heidells' letter left my heart heavy and perplexed...actually life left me perplexed, Heidells letter just added to it. It had been almost two months since I had last called her. I spoke with Barry at dinner that night. He said, "Lee, look, you gave her the money, right? Okay, then you don't have the right to tell her how to spend it."

True, but still I felt used, even if she didn't run off with the money. The money was for food so I wouldn't have to worry. Not for luxury items. I was not an ATM.

"Hey." I quietly said to Adianec when I called that night, 2 a.m. Havana time. She was crying when she picked up the phone.

"Si, hello." Each phrase was followed by a long pause.

"I, uh, just thought we should talk and clear this thing up. I'm pretty upset."

"*Si*, yes, I know. Lee, *por favor...*" At this point, Adianec started crying very hard and was having trouble breathing. In between her sobs, she was reprimanding herself for how she was acting. "Stupid girl, *mas tiempo* please we done hang the phone."

"Okay, okay. No, I won't hang up until we're finished. Please don't cry. I'm here, I'm listening. I just want to understand." I meant it. The crying certainly weakened me, but I had to remain distant, to try to find the truth. If she had just made a silly error, which I desperately prayed for, then I wanted to make a strong point so she wouldn't do it again. I told her I felt used by her irresponsible actions. If I was to continue sending money every few months, I wanted it used for food and clothing only.

Adianec just kept saying over and over in broken and sobbing English that she was sorry. This desire to help her was beyond me, it was something much bigger, though I couldn't explain it to myself. It was as if God was whispering in my ear. It would have been easier to command my heart to stop beating then to turn my back on her.

"I never more lie to you, never, never." More intermittent sobbing. "You are good man, very very good, I feel like very *joven*. It, I was stupid. My heart want you here sorry it was bad mistake, I listen wrong to people. No more ever to fool you. *Por favor no mas* money from you, just you."

"Okay, I'm trying to understand, why don't you speak to me in Spanish. We'll sort it out later."

She had so much to tell me and I just wanted her to get it out. So I sat there and listened to a very passionate discourse for ten minutes. Strangely enough, I did understand. Not verbatim, but I grasped the underlying emotions. I couldn't follow the words, but her sincerity came through clearly.

We spoke for over two hours, costing me two hundred dollars. This was roughly the same amount I was to send her every two months. After I hung up, I was content for the first time in over a month. I felt like I had been holding my breath since the last time we spoke. I really needed to know that she had not betrayed my trust.

The next day I made a decision to return one more time to clarify my feelings for her. Making the decision to go back was easy. Preparing for it was not. How would I tell my clients, with their homes in disarray, that I was taking a second vacation in just over three months? I guess I would have to quash my dreams of being "Contractor of the Year." In regards to my friends, Nicky was, not surprisingly, okay with it, but couldn't help worry about me. She apologized for having the "overly concerned, Jewish mother syndrome." The owners of the other house I was working on, John and Fred, like Nicky, had become much more than clients, but still I had every room in their house under construction. They were taken by the romantic aspect of the situation. You can always count on your gay friends to be nurturing. John joked that it would be okay as long as he could be in the wedding. Of course Luis would have the heaviest burden of all, having to do my job as well as his.

That night the phone rang was the first prayer I had ever had answered. It was not something we do often in Cuba. Religion was a dangerous activity until about ten years earlier, when Fidel allowed the Pope to visit. Lee had told me to pray when I needed guidance in my life. Just talk to God in my head. I was talking to him and Lee when I heard the phone. I knew it was Lee. I started crying before I even picked it up. I was so frustrated with our distance. I wanted to slip through the phone cord and be with him in Los Angeles.

He told me to speak to him in Spanish. The first thing I said was how could he give me so much money and just expect me to keep it to myself and not share it with my family. They needed more things than I. And if that was the way he felt, then please he should keep his money. But do not leave me, I would die. I said I knew it was wrong of me to try to trick him to come back to Cuba, but I was sure from the day we met that we were supposed to be together. I had lived my life as a good person and I thought I deserved to be with someone like him. He was everything I would ever need.

It felt like I was dancing under a waterfall as I spoke to him and shared my feelings. It also made it easier knowing that he did not understand what I was saying. I knew that he didn't feel the same as I did, yet. I also knew that my love for him was deep enough for both of us. When he called back the next day and told me he was coming back to Havana I cried, but I wasn't surprised. I made him a promise in Spanish that I would never deceive him again.

I had asked for all her measurements so I could bring some clothes back to Cuba. I was trying to be moderate, with my money and my feelings, but the truth was I went a little nuts. I filled a six-foot duffel bag full of clothes, shoes, and a shoebox full of make-up. Tom, my dentist, donated a box of a thousand tubes of toothpaste and another of brushes, since both are often hard to find in Cuba. I also went to a Target store and got a cart full of razors, shampoo and other toiletries for her family and friends. An old girlfriend of mine suggested that, even though it may be awkward I should also take a box of tampons. I did, and was stunned that Adianec was unfamiliar with them. Just another small example of how Fidel has put them in the Stone Age. It surprised me how fulfilling it was to be able to bring those people so many things they needed. There really is something to the concept "giving is better than receiving". When I was in line at a Target store, a lady behind me asked, "Why all the toiletries?"

"Actually, I'm going to Cuba. Life is pretty bleak there and they barely get enough food to eat, let alone have enough money to buy deodorant and soap. Even if they did most items are hard to find. So I thought I'd, you know, I'd help out a little bit."

She smiled, reached into her purse and asked, "If you wouldn't mind, may I pay for half?"

In hindsight, I should have also mentioned my mortgage.

Chapter fifteen

BACK TO CUBA

Mexico City airport was under construction when I arrived there. It wasn't the best-designed airport anyway, and now it was a completely confusing labyrinth. I tried to sleep a little after I picked up my visa. It was challenging because I had food stuffed in my cargo pants pockets, including sharp cheddar cheese, which was getting sharper by the minute. I wanted Adianec to experience what American food tasted like. It seemed so strange that I was going back to see her. While I was in Mexico, I bought her a stack of fashion magazines in Spanish. Just because I love breaking Cuban law #88. I wondered what law I'd be breaking for bringing her extra sharp cheddar cheese.

I felt a bit more confident landing in Havana this time, now that I knew what to expect. I had forgotten what Adianec looked like and I kept trying to visualize her face, but it was always obscured in my mind. The escalator was working this time. I breezed through immigration and then got stopped by the military as I was waiting for my bags. The young soldier interrogating me, with a uniform two sizes too large, kept asking me the same five questions, "Who do you work for?" "Is this your real name?" "Why have you come to Cuba?" "How many times have you been here?" and "Do you have contacts in Cuba?" I think, "is this your real name?" was my favorite. He seemed nervous and was sweating all over his little pocket sized pad of paper. He would ask a question, wipe sweat off the paper then write down the same answers. He didn't seem to notice that we were stuck in a loop. The questions remained the same, and I kept answering them the same way, over and over again. He was taking his job very seriously, like I was a threat to their national security. This went on for twenty minutes. I finally stopped him and asked, "Excuse me, is there a problem?"

He said, "No. There is no problem."

He then asked the same questions again.

"Listen, do you guys not want me in your country?" I protested.

He looked up at me, stunned. I guess the direct approach was new to him. He hesitantly turned, and walked over to his superior. I followed and asked what was going on. The superior officer said very nonchalantly, "Nothing, you may go."

My teenage interrogator looked as confused as I.

I took my suitcase and the six-foot duffel bag, which was so heavy I had to drag it, and made my second entrance into Cuba. The waiting area was crowded and hot. Yeah, I remembered this. I was having trouble spotting Adianec with all the people milling around. Finally, I saw her enter at the far end of the arrival area and walk toward me. She was being very coy, didn't even look up to see me. When I got to her, I was again taken by her natural beauty. She had let her hair grow, and I wondered if she had done so because I had told her that I liked long hair. She had a blue ribbon in her hair, which made her look like a coed, and wore a new dress with heels. That outfit must have cost her all the money she had left after giving most of it away to her family. I looked around to make sure there were no policia, and then I pulled her toward me and held her tight. She smelled clean, like a bar of perfumed soap. But she made only a half attempt at hugging me back. I pulled away and took her hand in mine to ask her what was wrong, I noticed immediately her hand was a bit damp. She was very nervous, nearly shaking. I haven't had a woman react to me in such an innocent way in years. I remembered how much she softened my rough edges. I knew she was the kind of woman who could make me a better man.

I was very nervous in the taxi going to the airport to see Lee. I wasn't sure if he would recognize me, and I was frustrated with my English, I wanted him to know me, to know my heart. There was so much room for misunderstanding and I was concerned about our fight. I knew it had hurt him and in my fears, I believed we could never survive another moment like that.

I arrived at the airport late and he was waiting at the far end. I tried to act normal when I saw him but I didn't know what normal was in our situation. He walked up to me in his confident way. I guess nothing makes him nervous. I didn't know what to do. He held me tight and kissed me on the forehead like I was a little girl. It made me feel sad for a moment. I thought maybe I misunderstood his intentions, but then he lifted my face and kissed me like I was the only woman in Cuba.

The way he looked at me in the taxi, I felt my face turn red. The look in his eyes was so sensual it was as if we were making love. Then he surprised me, he always surprises me. He started pulling American food out of everywhere. Some I recognized from TV. This man, he came straight out of my dreams. Literally out of my dreams, he had the same blue eyes, I had always seen. He was tall, muscular and treated me with incredible gentleness.

Not much was said in the taxi, though we never took our eyes off each other. Just touching her hand was erotic, but my desire was to get her alone and re-explore her body. However, aside from the presence of the cabby, I was very tired after my eighteen-hour journey, and needed a shower. Then I remembered the food. Like the seemingly never-ending stream of clowns emerging from a Volkswagen in the circus, food kept spilling out of my pants. The first thing I pulled out was trail mix. She laughed with curiosity, having never seen it before. Next were Snickers, Reese's Peanut Butter Cups, a small bag of pancake mix, a jar of Vermont maple syrup, a small jar of PB & J, a bag of Nacho Doritos, and, of course, extra, extra sharp cheddar cheese. All the staples of an American diet in a pair of pants. She looked at me and just shook her head. I was thinking, wait until she sees all the clothes, makeup and electronics I brought!

Adianec thought I'd be more comfortable if we stayed in Miramar, due to my reaction to the poverty and conditions in central Havana. Miramar is the Beverly Hills of Havana, sans the money. It is also embassy row, so there is a great deal of security. I had found a *Casa particular* online, run by a very nice lady named Ada.

Driving into Miramar, I could see the grandeur of Havana's upper class fifty years ago. It had wide boulevards with stately mansions that had been stolen by Fidel's regime. Single-family homes were now embassies, foreign corporate housing, government offices and multiple family tenements. The houses that were taken over for government offices and housing tenements had fallen into disrepair, probably beyond hope. I thought of the families, most likely now living in Miami, which rightfully owned those beautiful structures. I imagined that they would be devastated if they ever returned and saw their childhood memories in such shabby condition.

We pulled up to Ada's home, which was about five blocks from the ocean. Ada came out to greet us as the taxi pulled up. She was drying her hands with a dishtowel and had a big smile as though she had looked forward to our arrival. Her house was a two-story cinder block home, very much like a middle class house in Florida. The difference here is that three families had split the house up. Two large trees shaded the front yard, and the house had been painted a nice two-tone pastel, again similar to a Florida home. We found out later that she had a son in Miami and another in Canada, and they would bring her what she needed when they came to visit, such as paint. I was surprised also to find out that she would on occasion visit them. I was perplexed, "Senora, if you don't mind my asking, how did you get permission and why would you come back?"

I got the same answer that I got from Dr. Rosi. She was older and comfortable, she had her friends and her needs were simple, and the government took care of these basic needs. I asked why Adianec didn't just leave and go to Miami where she had family. Ada explained to me, in English, "I can leave because I am much older than she and I am not expected to give back to the system. But, someone like her," – meaning Adianec – "who is young with advanced education, she owes the revolution and must first fulfill her duties."

"How long would that take?" I asked

Ada smiled and slowly shook her head. "Oh, unfortunately that could last most of her life."

"Sounds like slavery to me."

Ada shrugged her shoulders. "It's a difficult situation for younger people."

After my shower and a quick re-acquaintance with Adianec, I began to unpack. I was too excited to take a nap. I wanted to show Adianec everything I'd brought for her and her family. I had only gotten about twenty percent through the duffle bag when she grabbed me and pleaded, "Lee, please no more." It wasn't that she was ungrateful. She was overwhelmed. She just pulled me on the bed, held me, and told me she loved me.

Lee had brought me more clothes than I had ever seen in any store. I didn't know what to say or do. It was as if I was dreaming. I asked him to stop. I felt bad because he was getting so much pleasure in this moment. But my emotions were unpredictable with him and I didn't want to start crying. The tears would have been from happiness but still they would be tears.

Is this the way American men treat their women? After he slept he said he wanted to play the role of Santa Claus again. He brought me so much make-up and he gave it with so much kindness. Was this just an act? When would he get mean or domineering? My heart would break for sure.

When I woke, it was dark outside and Adianec was reading the magazines I'd gotten for her. I laid there for a moment, just looking at her absorbing the fashions in the magazines. I started to roll over to kiss her and almost fell between the mattresses. We had twin beds pushed together. The frames were made of steel sitting on top of a tile floor. With only a sheet covering me, I was a bit chilled by the AC but didn't dare turn it down. So I pulled her under the sheet to warm up. Since my last trip, I had begun to study Spanish and Adianec, English. Communication was a bit easier, now that we both spoke a little Spanglish.

"*Te gusta*, what I brought." I was so excited to show her what I'd brought.

"*Si*, very much."

"*Sabir*, know of Santa Claus, cause I feel like him." When I said this, I could tell she was very confused.

"Santa Clarita?"

"No, he's not a city in southern California. *Tu sabi, Ho ho ho.*"

She looked at me side ways, and then with a slight smile "Ahh, si si."

I asked if I could show her more of what I had brought. She squeezed my hand and nodded. I pushed through the clothes and brought out several hundred dollars worth of make up, hair ribbons and other things that girls use to tie up their hair. She had never seen half of the things I brought. Neither had I. We had to look through the advertisements in Vogue to figure what everything was. Ultimately my hunger took over and I had to find food. I opened the bedroom door and hit "the wall" of heat and humidity.

Chapter sixteen

The Copacabana

Ada told us that the Copacabana was five blocks up on the beach. I lit up. "The Copacabana? The hottest spot north of Havana?" They both stared at me. I let out a solitary laugh. I live in my own world of humor. I didn't know the place actually existed outside of a Barry Manilow song.

Adianec never stopped talking the entire walk to the Copa. The streets were very dark due to only one streetlight per block, and every one or two blocks we would come upon security officers. The warm, moist, tropical climate relaxed me physically, but being immersed in a police state kept my senses on edge. I had to get used to being watched all the time, as we were, on every block by these security officers hiding in the shadows.

The lobby of the hotel was quiet, with only a couple of employees behind the desk and a few security guys standing by the doors. Whatever conversations had been going on ended the moment we entered the lobby. I felt everybody's eyes on us as we walked to the desk. The uniformed woman behind the desk directed us out through the pool deck to the back of the hotel to the restaurant. I felt like I was beginning to understand the Cuban psyche. Even the government workers, who are constantly indoctrinated with anti-American propaganda, are incredibly interested in us. There were many situations where I could sense their curiosity, but they would never make the initial move to reach out to me. But as soon as I smiled and said hello their stoic demeanor would melt away and that famous Cuban warmth would appear.

"Adianec and I at the Copacabana pool"

We walked out onto the darkened pool deck area into a swimmer's paradise. This immediately became my favorite place in all of Cuba. The Copa has two separate pools. On the lobby level was a very large "regular pool." But down below the seawall was the real beauty, a natural pool over one hundred yards in length. Two sidewalls extended out from the large twenty-foot-tall seawall. Stretching out into the ocean for about fifty yards and connecting to each other on the far end with an enclosing seawall. The top of the pool's seawall was wider than a sidewalk, enabling people to walk out into the water. From the water level to the bottom of the "sidewalk" were two foot tall pillars spread about a foot apart to allow fresh seawater to flush the pool with every wave. It was beautiful, with the moon silhouetted on the water's surface. You could swim in the ocean completely protected. I whispered to Adianec, "I don't know who I have to bribe, but I am definitely swimming in that pool tomorrow."

She smiled, not sure if I was kidding or not.

Those seawalls and pool deck, however, had seen better days. Large chunks of concrete had been broken away, leaving corroded steal rebar and some pretty serious trip hazards. But this was not the U.S. nobody was going to file a personal injury lawsuit. In the subtle moon glow, it was perfect. Adianec literally had to pull me away so we could get to the restaurant before it closed.

Lee was like a little boy when he saw the pool at the Copacabana. It sometimes catches me off guard how he can express freely whatever he is feeling. He doesn't seem to care what people think. In these moments I just wanted to know everything about him. He is back in Cuba. Now my whole world is safer.

The meal was completely inedible. Luckily, Ada gave us kitchen privileges, so from then on I did all the cooking. After dinner, we sat next to the pool and I told her stories of a life that existed across the water ninety miles away.

"You love pool, yes?" Though her face was buried in the dictionary, her English was definitely much improved, slightly better than my Spanish.

"Mucho, tengo amor por la aqua." She laughed hard falling back against the lounge chair. Okay, her English was much better than my Spanish.

"Ay, baby, please we speak *inglish. Porque…*why, do you, *y tambien,* the name, what do you said, in the pool?"

She then mimicked a swimming stroke. "Boxing?"

She knew the word and laughed. "No, mi amore."

"I know, Amore. It's called 'swimming', you swim in a pool."

"Porque you love this, swim?"

I explained to her in a broken Spanglish, with both of us constantly diving into our respective dictionaries, that when I was around twelve, we would ride our bikes to the beach. At first it was mysterious and very exciting. It was like I was on another planet, older guys – teenagers - with long hair walking out of the water with their surfboards and incredibly beautiful girls would run up and shower them with attention. So I grew my hair very long, lifted weights, got a tan and…I think maybe swimming and surfing in the ocean made me feel equal with everyone else. I wasn't that poor kid from the trailer out there. I was hanging out with the rich kids from the beach side schools. We were all the same.

"And the bonita Chicas?"

"Look who I'm sitting with!"

I looked at her. She smiled, shyly and looked down. On the way out we stopped by the disco. Not surprisingly Adianec was forbidden to enter. By now the shock value had worn off.

The next morning, as I cooked breakfast for us, I asked Ada how I could finagle a swim at the Copa. She said I just had to pay five dollars and that because many diplomats brought their Cuban girlfriends there, I could probably take Adianec. She also suggested that we go to *Hemingway's Marina,* where there was another enclosed natural swimming pool.

We got a late start due to Adianec insisting on staging a fashion show with all the clothes I'd brought her. I had also brought a manicure set with a buffer and twenty bottles of nail polish. I decided to give her a pedicure after her fashion show. No doubt this was the most pampering she had ever experienced. The pedicure didn't go well. I never could color within the lines. But I was happy, at least, that I could cross another potential vocation off my list.

He did something funny. He painted my toenails with some of the

polish he had brought. I am sure this is something he had planned to be romantic. A Cuban man would never do this. They guard their manhood as a treasure. There was no doubt it was new to him. He painted them like a man. I smiled and didn't tell him that I had just paid someone to do them. I just let him continue and told him how beautiful they were. I would secretly redo them later!

We walked down 72nd Street toward the beach. One block before we got to Fifth Avenue, I was mesmerized by a large house on the corner, sitting up on a bit of a hill. I found myself staring at it every time we walked by for the next week, and could almost feel its family history. I imagined children running up and down the hill and climbing the large tree in the front yard. But if it was true, it was a very long time ago, before its owners were driven out. The house seemed sad to me, as it was now being used and neglected by some kind of government police or military department. In comparison, most of the houses around it had faired better; they were at least in private hands.

Fifth Avenue is the main street running through Miramar and on into Havana where it becomes Avenue del Malecon and runs next to the sea wall. It has two lanes in each direction with a twenty-foot wide worn-out grass median. Most of the cars driving by were old American Fords and Chevys, looking like an improvised vintage car parade. Acrid exhaust billowed out of the old cars, mixing awkwardly with the syrupy smell of mangos rotting under a tree.

Directly across the avenue was a beautiful Catholic cathedral. Like most churches in Cuba it was being used as something other than a house of worship. In this case, it had become part of the Russian Embassy. The Embassy complex stretches out, covering several large square blocks. It was maybe a quarter-mile wide, with the planet's ugliest concrete edifice rising up several hundred feet in the middle of it all. You can see this Russo-phallic structure from many miles away. A tall, eight-foot concrete wall surrounds the place with shards of colored glass sticking out of the top. "What is the ugly thing, baby?"

She made a distasteful face. "Russo."

"Russians?"

Apparently, it wasn't only the architecture that repelled the Cubans from Russian diplomats. The Russian officials who traveled there didn't quite endear themselves to the Cuban people either. "*Si*, we don't like."

"Why?"

"Hmm. they think maybe we belong to them."

It was hard to believe that they still have any power there, but apparently they still have a hold over the country.

"*Si*, they have no trust with the U.S. so Fidel will embrace them."

Stealing Castro's daughter

In contrast to the Russian phallus structure, which one must travel several light years to find anything approximating its hideousness, was the pool at the Copa. The upper pool deck, the one with the chlorine pool, had salsa music blaring with beautiful Venezuelan women strutting around in Brazilian bikinis. Not wanting to upset or humiliate Adianec, I did my best to focus on the natural pool ahead, though my knees did weaken a few times. I could see out of the corner of my wandering eye that we were drawing attention. Obviously, this pool does not see many Americans.

The deteriorating condition of the concrete pool decks and seawall were much more apparent during the bright daylight. A few of the pillars in the natural pool, holding up the walkway on top of the seawalls were worn down to the steel rebar by the constant wave action. I could also make out an underwater sidewalk running down the middle, lengthwise of the pool about four feet underwater. Colorful Coral reefs had formed on the bottom and walls of the pool over the years. The view made swimming laps, if you had goggles, seem like scuba diving. I immediately jumped in and started playing in the eighty-plus degree water, diving down and discovering starfish, crabs and giant sea urchins eight feet down on the bottom of the pool. I had to coax Adianec into the water. She tentatively walked down the steps, looking elegant in the new black bikini I had brought her, stopped at the bottom then shyly waved for me to come get her and "taxi" her on my back to the underwater sidewalk. She couldn't swim.

The cost of admission came with lunch, chicken or hamburger. We had burgers because I don't care for dark meat and in Cuba, chicken breast simply does not exist. I would ask, in restaurants and grocery stores, "Si, pollo, blanco meat? Blanco, breast?"

I would usually have to simulate the breast as well, in case they didn't understand. I always got the same response, a shrug of the shoulders, "*No, senor. No blanco*, dark."

I've seen chickens walking around in Cuba. They do have breasts'. But something must happen to them after they die in this country...they become breast less. Now, having no breasts on your chicken is not the end of the world, but, it's worth at least some questioning. Not to the Cuban people though, they seem to have no issue about it at all. The Cuban people take everything in stride. They don't seem to question, they just accept and go about their lives. There is an expression there that one picks up quickly in Cuba, "Ay Cuba."

When the electricity goes out, which it does several times a day, "Ay Cuba." Whenever service stations run out of gas, "Ay Cuba." No bus service today, "Ay Cuba." It roughly translates "this is life in Cuba." They expect disappointment, so they won't be disappointed.

Ay, Cuba.

Lee Brooks

Lee was always so sweet. He was the perfect man, a gentleman. But, he complains about the food in Cuba every time he eats. When the hamburgers came he said,

"Ahh Adianec, this is not a burger, it's not even real meat. Somewhere in Havana a family is missing their "perro" (dog)." I guess the food in America is made out of gold.

Adianec had wrapped a colorful scarf around her waist to cover her bikini for the walk back to Ada's. I'm sure her intentions were modest but it only served to accentuate her Spanish figure. Everything about her lit a fire inside me.

About a block up, Adianec saw a motorcycle policeman sitting at the intersection and asked if we could double back and walk over a few blocks to avoid him. Every time something like that happened it bonded me closer to her. I wanted to, needed to do something for her. Living in a police state was not a healthy life, especially for someone like Adianec who had such an innocent and kind soul. I was in a state of confusion within myself. Part of me wanted to be with her completely as she allowed herself to be with me. But, there was that other side, my logical side, which kept her and her situation at a distance. It was true, what my friends said, this was not my fight.

We had gone to the foreigner's grocery store after the beach, and I stocked up on real food. I made spaghetti for everyone that night with garlic bread and salad. It was just plain spaghetti to me, but for them it was a feast of color and flavor. If there had been any doubt of Adianec's love for me before, it was surely settled that night. The way she would look at me throughout dinner was almost overpowering.

As was our habit the last time I was in Cuba, Adianec and I stayed up all night talking and making love. Sometimes we just talked about silly things, and would always end up laughing due to the others faux pau in Spanglish. I think we would just keep talking until we passed out, so we wouldn't have to say goodnight. One night she asked me about Paris, particularly the Eiffel Tower. She had just seen a movie where a couple got engaged on the top of the tower.

"*Es* true for people?" She looked like a curious child listening to a fairy tale. Completely enraptured.

"Get engaged on the Eiffel Tower? Yes, of course."

She had tears in her eyes. "Tell me it is beauty… I, *tu sabes*, I never will go."

That just crushed me! She faded away into her imagination. I knew I would never forget that desire of hers…and I didn't!

I wondered how it was possible that this beautiful, caring woman in my arms never got married. So, I asked. She raised her eyebrows! "I am old and *feo*? I have *tiempo*."

What is "*feo*?"

"Not pretty."

"Oh, ahh, no you're not *feo*. Anything but, you're *muy bonita Chiquita*."

This made her laugh again. I loved watching her laugh, it seemed to temporarily lighten up the deep heaviness that I saw in her eyes. "*Ay, Lee, no mas dictionario*, you talk *inglish Amore*."

She still didn't really answer the question as to why she wasn't married or, at least, close. "Then, why? Why, no *novio*, no *esposo*?"

"*Porque* my Spanish-speak love? I can tengo uno. I am spoiled for you."

That's a good answer. "No, really, why no family of your own?"

"*Mi amore*, I just finish school. I want some air till someone is mi *hefe*."

From years in construction, "*hefe*" is a word I knew. "Your husband will be your boss?"

"*Aqui*, men in Cuba think that, *si*." I nodded. From my observations, that didn't surprise me. "In America, this is too?"

"No, not so much anymore."

I could see she wanted to ask me something more, and broached it cautiously. "You? You have *esposa*?"

From my smile and laugh, it eased her fears before I even told her. "No, never. Not even close. Not seriously anyway."

"*Porque no*?"

"My life works as is. I don't need to complicate things."

That's what I tell women who ask, and it's how I'd lived my life up to that point. As she looked up the words in the dictionary her face changed. Interesting I thought, she sees more with us, more potential, more of a future than I'd imagined.

I had brought a portable DVD player and a case full of movies. We watched the movie *Spanglish*, with Adam Sandler, at 4 a.m. Just as I began to fall asleep with her in my arms, the electricity went out, taking the cold air from the AC with it. It didn't take long for the heat to force its way in. "Ay Cuba."

I found it a challenge to keep from being totally swept up by her. Life with her was effortless. Her philosophy was simple, "do what's right and best for the people you love." Simple, but few people in L.A. truly live by it. I would stare at her as I awoke each morning, she had such a sweet innocence about her and I wondered how she had so far escaped the easier life that so many nice girls we met had succumbed to. It would sicken me whenever I thought about her future and the life she may have to choose in order to exist. How can she survive here and for how much longer? I could see the brightness in her eyes begin to fade as she would question the impossibility of any hope for a future. I figured she had maybe a year before she became hardened. I just had to keep reminding myself, this was not my fight.

Chapter seventeen

Life changing moment

One morning, we called a taxi to take us to the Hemingway Marina. Our cab driver had to haggle (bribe) with the guard at the gate to let him drive through with a Cuban in the cab. He drove us to a private beach area where we had to pay to get in. The beach was was inside the marina with a two hundred yard peninsula separating us from the inlet. The protected swim area was perfectly smooth and we could see the ocean just over the dunes. They had a giant slide and rope swing as alternative ways to enter the water. Venezuelan tourists and Cuba's elite occupied the beach. The Cuban elite are members of the growing class of Cubans with money; usually corrupt government officials or people in the black market. Adianec seemed uncomfortable being around them. She was upset over the elitist officials that spoke of equality and sacrifice for the revolution, then lived a privileged life. I had brought her several spiritual books in Spanish, *Ask and it is Given* and *Many Lives Many Mansions*. She was currently reading one about being in the moment called *The Power of Now*. I told her this was good practice to just be in the moment.

I grew up being taught that everybody in Cuba has an equal life. But, it's a lie, told by the people that live a lifestyle many times better than the average Cuban. They are elitists that preach of the evils of capitalism, while they embrace it. It makes me furious to see it, though we have always heard the rumors. Even doctors in my country cannot afford the taxi fare to take their families to the beach. And even if they could, they would not be allowed to enter where I was with Lee.

We grabbed a couple of lounge chairs under a palmed umbrella for shade, so I wouldn't catch on fire basically. We had silky white sand at our feet and the place smelled of coconut suntan lotion, which immediately took me back to my childhood in Florida. Adianec read her book and worked on living in the moment as I competed with young children to see who could become King of the slide. I teamed up with a couple of 30ish year old boys from Venezuela and we made fools of ourselves going down the slide, rolling and tumbling in a heap, splashing into the sea. No language barrier in the world of immature adult men. After a while of rough play and scaring away small children, Adianec called me over like I was her child. "Lee, baby, sunscreen."

I dutifully but impatiently stood there as she covered my entire body with lotion. From across the park area, my partners-in-crime snickered and yelled some remarks in Spanish. Though I didn't understand what they said, I'm sure it had something to do with my manhood or lack thereof. I didn't care. I was getting accustomed to the way she took care of me, actually much better than I do.

As I went back to my "playmates," I heard a sound that sparked my imagination; it was a whining two-stroke engine. It couldn't be, but there they were. Two jet skis pulled out into the inlet and tore through the water sending sprays thirty feet. I walked down to the end of the dock and saw the sign for Jet Ski rentals. I signed up and ran to get Adianec, so I could introduce her to the "need for speed." If the guilt she felt from our past activities was any indication, I was about to send her screaming to a nunnery.

As we climbed on board the Jet Ski, I looked back at her. She was so terrified she couldn't even breathe. I started out slowly just to build her apprehension. Her arms were fully wrapped around me, her face was buried in the back of my neck and her nails were slicing into my flesh...Life was good. I picked up speed as we came around the peninsula toward the inlet. The waves increased to about a foot and a half, and we began to take some air. Her screams seemed to alternate between absolute delight and total horror. I yelled back, "Hang on tight!"

I opened the throttle up full then dug into a hard right turn. We got lost in an avalanche of warm salty water. I slowed to take a look at her reaction. "Lee, stop, stop!"

Her eyes were huge and her face was a full smile of teeth as she screamed with laughter. I had achieved my goal, she was fully in the moment now. Her cute little straw hat and my sunglasses were nowhere to be seen. Her hair was dripping all over her face as she tried to regain her composure. She was so beautiful my heart was flooded.

That afternoon on the water machine, I had more excitement than I ever had in my life. Lee seemed to have more fun scaring me than being

on the machine itself. Sometimes I felt like I was going to die and then complete delight all in a few seconds. I kept screaming for him to stop but I really wanted to go faster.

I asked if she wanted more. "No, no, no, no mas," she screamed.

I didn't believe her, so I headed straight for the inlet which was under a quarter mile-wide and boiling with waves as the ocean was squeezing through the small opening to get into the marina. We got about 200 yards away from the opening of the inlet shooting off the tops of the waves at twenty miles an hour when I sensed a change in her. I stopped immediately and turned around. The waves were tossing us about making it hard to keep our balance. I asked her, "Hey honey what's wrong? Are you okay? What is it?"

I could see she was really scared. I said, "Baby, I'm sorry I forgot you can't swim."

She shook her head. "Please, Lee, the ocean, to me forbidden, I don't want jail."

I was infused with anger. We were having so much fun that I had forgotten where we were and who she was. Without even thinking I told her, "Amore, a ninety mile ride on this thing and you're free. Let's go right now. We'll be in Miami in three hours." Had she said yes, I would not have hesitated. She had her face buried in my neck and was holding me so tightly the buckle on my water vest was cutting me.

I've never had an epiphany in my life, and I was always envious and skeptical of those who claimed to have had one. Right there soaking wet on a jet ski in Hemingway Marina, insane with anger, I had mine. My mind was so clear, any doubt and confusion had vanished, replaced with an absolute knowing. I was not here to supplement her income and our meeting was not a coincidence. "Adianec, do you trust me?"

She gave the perfect answer, "Lee, *tu estoy* my life."

"I don't know how, but I'm going to get you off this damned island," I promised her.

We barely spoke a word for the next few hours. My anger and determination were like a laser and I felt amazingly inspired and alive. After we got back to Ada's, I finally thought to ask her what her feelings were on the subject of leaving Cuba. She said she had never thought it was a possibility, so with the help of our ever-present dictionary, we discussed it. "Baby, you haven't said anything, I just assumed you'd want to live in Miami."

"*Si, si, mi amore.* I have many emotions for it. My family, maybe it would keep me away."

She put down the dictionary and gave me an unsure and frightened look. "You can stay with your uncle or cousin, couldn't you? I mean, I'll support you financially for a year or two, you know put you through school again."

I didn't even finish the sentence. "*Ay,* Amore, *no mas habla* money. Miami, my dream is not there."

"Well, where is it? It can't be here, can it?"

She was now in deep thought. "No, no not here, *mi amore, es no aqui.*"

"Okay, whatever you want, I'll make it happen." She just laughed and kissed me. "Kiss me again and I'll end the embargo."

"Then Fidel kiss you." I could live without that thought. "How far does your Los Angeles live from Miami?"

"How far does it live? It lives about the same as L.A. to Havana, just easier immigration."

"You would see me there, in Miami? And my family, dog?"

"More than I do now. We have time, think about it. But the offer is for you only."

She said yes she wanted to talk about it but it was all so sudden, she was overwhelmed. What would happen to her family, what about Simba? She had many doubts…I had none.

I was surprised that Lee had mentioned going to America. I always thought it impossible, so many people die during the process. I didn't want to make a big deal about it. Maybe he was just emotional and would change his mind after he calmed down. I didn't want to get my hopes up so I just watched him and waited to see where it would go. Then I started thinking about the idea of being free and many feelings that I had repressed began to show themselves. Mexico and Canada are a dreamer's option, they rarely come true. He didn't mention the option of marrying me I knew he would never do that. It would be too dangerous for him in his country. And I knew he was not the kind of man that marries.

We went out to dinner that night, to a popular restaurant that I had heard about at the Copa. El Aljibe restaurant was located in Miramar about a half mile from Ada's. It was an open structure on three sides. The roof was palm-thatched and had beautiful hand hued plank floors. The elegant waiters dressed in white were very friendly. The customers were mainly older, wealthy men with very young, beautiful Cuban girls and European tourists. The dining room was large, seating about two hundred people, with the space occasionally broken up with two-foot diameter columns holding up the thatched roof. This was immediately my favorite Cuban restaurant.

I ordered their special family chicken dinner, dark meat of course. It had a brown sauce that drowned the chicken with an earthy sweetness, plantains fried crispy and all-you-can-eat beans and rice. By any standards, the dinner was excellent.

We had to revert back to the dictionary because we had no room for error. I was confident that what we were doing was moral and right, and that she would be enjoying her freedom in Miami by the holidays. She didn't share my optimism. She was concerned that what I was suggesting was very difficult, if not impossible, and had many risks. I said, "Baby, that's what Americans are known for. Look, all my life, people have been telling me not to do things because they were too hard, risky and dangerous. People told me that becoming an actor was impossible, but I did it. They said you couldn't swim across San Francisco Bay. Well every year for the past decade, about a thousand people, men and women, myself included, compete in this race called, Escape from Alcatraz Triathlon. It's only impossible until you actually do it."

I'm not sure it was all sinking in, but I was on a roll. I felt passionately that nothing was impossible, especially when what you're doing serves others. I have never felt so sure that I had found a higher purpose than at that moment, when I made the decision to help rescue her.

As we walked back home in the humid darkness, we would come to certain areas that were infused with the perfume of night blooming jasmine. We would stop without a word and breathe deeply, taking both of us back to far away memories. That was a perfect dessert, after my first satisfying Cuban meal. Along the walk we discussed where we should get advice. In Cuba, sharing this kind of plan with the wrong person could get us both arrested, but we knew we couldn't do it alone. Cubans were allowed to leave the island only under a couple of very narrow parameters. With her youth and education the chance of getting official permission to leave the island was razor thin. We had to find the right path, so we decided to go to Havana the following morning to speak with Doctora Rosi. The more we talked about it, the more receptive and excited Adianec became about the idea. We decided that it would be best if she didn't go back to work in order to begin to disappear out of the system. She would also need to see if she qualified for a Cuban passport. It wouldn't give her permission to leave the country, but it would be a start.

Rosi was as beautiful and warm as I remembered. We sat on her balcony, looking out over a gray city with a beautiful blue ocean seven blocks away and a mere ninety miles from Adianec's new life. I told her about the Jet Ski experience and asked if she had any suggestions. I could see that Adianec was a bit apprehensive, but I instinctively trusted Rosi. She smiled, nodded and then thought for a long time before answering. She told me, "It is lovely and I am so pleased that an American has taken an interest in my country. My dear, I understand your concerns for Adianec. I agree that this country is very difficult for such young, intelligent people. But," she took a long pause, "trying to get Adianec out of Cuba will be dangerous and expensive. Do you...plan to marry?"

I said no. "Adianec will move to Miami, not L.A."

She shook her head. "Please, I ask you. You must really think about what you are committing to, before it is too late. You may be giving Adianec false hope, my dear. You may simply grow tired with the difficulties that lay ahead, and there are many. If you marry, Adianec could be in the United States in the next two to five years."

Five years was unacceptable. I knew Adianec would lose what hope she had left within a year. I just couldn't imagine that this idea could be so difficult. It's just ninety miles away and I knew the U.S. had an open door policy for defecting Cubans. "You may find Lee that this relationship has a deeper result than what you're willing to embrace at this time."

We left Doctora Rosi's home a little deflated. I continued telling Adianec that anything was possible with faith. We had to stay positive and focused. I told her how amazing her life would be in Miami. She would be free to travel, read anything, use the internet and most importantly, achieve anything she desired.

Since we were in central Havana I asked if I could meet her family, her second family. We walked through the familiar neighborhood of Park Central. I looked for Alex, I wanted to give him the pair of *New Balance* shoes I'd brought, but he seemed to have disappeared.

I was surprised by how close she lived to Park Central. The tenement buildings in her neighborhood were so dilapidated that I walked in the middle of the street to avoid falling brick. The deteriorating streets were accented with vintage cars, some on blocks. The buildings, of beautiful old Spanish architecture, lined both sides of the street with only a two-foot sidewalk separating the front doors from the busy street. Even though they were falling apart due to neglect and age, the buildings still retained much of their original character; they captured my imagination. There was no grass or trees, only an occasional green bush growing high up out of the side of one of the three story apartment buildings. I thought of the "*Wizard of Oz.*" Adianec lived her whole life in black and white. No color, physically, emotionally or spiritually. One day she would wake up from this nightmare and see life in full color.

Chapter eighteen

FRIENDS

I was embarrassed for Lee to see how poor we were. He knew I didn't live in a palace. Still, when he walked in he looked at everything, all the intimacies on how I live, I was so uncomfortable with him there I just wanted to hide. I was worried he would compare the conditions of my life with the conditions of my heart and think them similar.

We arrived at her home, which was a half block from a train station, just as an old, rickety, rusty-colored train was pulling up to the station. People had their heads out the windows, trying to get some air. Walking into Adianec's home I was struck, as I had been in the past by Cuban homes, by how clean it was. It was such a dichotomy from the outer façade. The living room was about twenty-feet wide and fed into what I thought was the dining room, sans the table. The rest of the apartment flowed back down a very long hallway about eighty feet in length, with all the rooms on the left side. It reminded me of the old railroad flats in Manhattan.

The living room floor was made of beautiful old hand-painted Spanish tile with very intricate patterns of cobalt blue, reds and greens. It was probably hundreds of years old. Right under their impoverished feet were tens of thousands of dollars worth of materials on the American market. On the far wall between the living room and dining room was a stairway, almost a ladder, that led up to the attic and Adianec's room.

The first to come greet us was Nina, a black, skinny Labrador mix. Sol came out from the back of the long hallway trailed by an ever-smiling Heidells.

Sol came and wrapped her arms around me, smothering my face with kisses. She, like most Cubans I had met, had no inhibitions about showing emotions. At no point did she treat me like a stranger. Heidells was a good-looking kid in his early twenties. Tall, thin, with long black hair and some kind of attempt at a Fu Manchu beard. When I would speak, Heidells would translate. A lot of *mucho gusto*-ing. More people arrived from the back, cousins I believe, and perhaps a girlfriend of Heidells. "So, should we order a Dominos?"

That was the funniest thing they ever heard. Heidells turned to me, "they want to know how you like us."

"You mean, you guys in particular or Communism as a whole?" More howling. They were an easy audience. I could stay in Cuba and become a standup comedian. "No, you guys are great. I just keep wondering how you stay so happy, given your living conditions?"

Now everyone was flooding Heidells with questions. "How are they different then Americans?" and "what do Americans think of them?" We talked and laughed for about fifteen minutes before Vladimir, Sol's husband and Heidells father came out. Like Heidells, he was tall and thin. He had a shy smile and a warm, but stoic, presence. He was the kind of man that left the talking to others, although he would not back away if spoken to. Vladimir, like a lot of Cubans, was a non-filtered chain smoker.

The energy in the room could have woken the dead. Every sentence spoken would end in laughter. I really enjoyed these people and I was absorbed in their fullness of expression. They spoke from the heart, with no self-monitoring. However, like other Cubans I'd met, there was a defeatism etched into their soul that I assumed came from decades of despair and disappointment. However their home had so much warmth, I immediately felt part of the family.

Always interested in other people's dramas, I asked what they thought of the Cuban revolution. "I'm curious. What do you think of Fidel, is he a good leader?"

Everyone got very quiet. End of my comedy career. Heidells answered very soberly. "We think it's time for change."

"Time for him to go?"

"Yes. Like thirty years ago." They had more questions. "They want to know what you think of Bush."

"Hmm. Well, I'm outnumbered in my country, for now. But I'm not sure the people near him are giving good advice. And I have noticed dissention begin to rumble amongst my friends"

They broke out in applause. But they were also shocked, that we could express our political views so freely.

They spoke openly, feeling safe in their home. Vladimir was a young boy when the revolution came and Sol had not been born yet, so it was all they had ever known. But they too felt an immediate change was necessary. They thought Fidel's regime had overstayed it's welcome by at least a couple of decades. It was the same I heard from anyone who felt safe enough to share with me. They wanted change, but there was also a fear of the unknown. He was all that most of the population had ever known. Even with all the constant anti-imperialist propaganda Americans mesmerized them. Yet like most Cubans I had spoke with they had a deep fear of the U.S. government. They were afraid Bush would attack Cuba and they thought he hated Cubans. I explained to them that it was just politics and I assured them that it was not in the U.S. interest even to throw a stone at Cuba.

Adianec and I ate at El Aljibe again that night and talked about our options. What about a boat? Too dangerous, half the people who attempt that route don't survive. Marriage was not a good option. It would take too long, and then I would have to turn myself into the State Department for coming to Cuba. I was willing to do that and I didn't mind marrying her to get her out, but I did want her to know that it was a solution for freedom, not a commitment. I would check with a lawyer when I got home. Another way was to obtain a visa to Mexico. She had heard of people who had done it and then simply went to the U.S. border and turned themselves in and got political asylum. It would take connections and bribes, and in the past few years she said it had seemed to dry up as a possibility. I suggested the Jet Ski again. I could rent one of the newer ones from Key West, they were as fast as 85 mph, but the idea scared her.

She was almost panicked, thinking about the possibility that we might get caught. For her it could mean two years in prison. For me, the outcome could be much harsher. She said they randomly listen to phone calls and open mail. We would need to have a special language, a code that would sound like we were saying one thing but meaning something else. I joked with her about speaking in a code when we couldn't even understand each other now.

"Could you imagine the people eavesdropping in on our calls, understanding what was being said better than we could? Then in their frustration they finally break in and say, No, *mija*, he says to meet him at the dock at noon!"

But in that moment it struck me for the first time just how dangerous this could be. We also decided to put really sensitive information in e-mail, since it would be difficult for them to track it to her. Even though the internet is illegal for the average Cuban, she had contacts in offices that for a small fee would let her in after hours or send messages from her themselves.

Nothing was decided. We would both have to work on it after I left. I reiterated to her that this was to get her to freedom, not a commitment, and no strings attached on her end as well. She owed me nothing once she got to Miami. I couldn't explain to myself, much less to her, why I was doing this. I truly felt I had no choice.

My last full day, we stayed in bed later than usual. We were both lost in thought. She rolled over and looked into my eyes for a long time. I think she was trying to figure me out. This was a big life change for her, one that she had barely allowed herself to dream about. I asked what she would tell her family. She laughed and waved her index finger in the air. Something I would learn she was prone to do. It meant no.

Another day at the Copa; that place was like a sedative for me. A midday tropical storm came through violently and chased everyone away but us. We cowered under a concrete overhang and laughed at our reaction to the lightening that was exploding all around us. It was frightening but beautiful. The storm vanished suddenly, leaving the air vibrant and clean. Heavy clouds hung around for the rest of the day, giving a nice respite from the baking powers of the sun. We stayed until dark, both knowing that to leave the Copa meant to prepare for me to leave Cuba once more. On the walk back to Ada's, we held hands and talked about a future time for Cuba.

As we walked by I took one last look at the sad house on the hill. Adianec began to put up her wall of protection once we got to Ada's. Even though I was expecting it, I was still a little hurt. We spoke about it briefly, just so it wouldn't be something that could grow in the future. She asked when I was thinking of coming back, and I must have looked quite surprised because she stifled a laugh. I said. "There's no need. You'll be in Miami in three months and besides, I'm going to Israel and Vietnam in January." I told her I would make a stop in Miami, and then drive her up to meet my family and see Disney World.

I didn't sleep much that night. I was imagining her in Miami, giving us the possibility of growing closer. I think back on my naïve arrogance that night and wonder, if I had known the danger that lay ahead, would I have just quietly left her and Cuba behind.

We spent the rest of our time together that morning just sitting in Ada's garden under the mango tree. We listened to the laughter and playful screams of children in the background, in a language I couldn't understand. There was no use in trying to hide the fact that we were both very sad. As I walked out the door to get into the taxi, she told me again that she loved me. I don't know if it was the depth of her love or because the distance between us allowed me to be open to it, but I knew I had never in my life felt so loved as I did when I was with her.

His leaving, like the first time, tore at my heart. This time it hurt even more intensely. But I was confident that he really cared for me and

that I would see him again. It was hard not building up this wall that he spoke of. The pain I felt when he was leaving was too passionate to feel so I guess I just turned everything off. He wasn't just flying home, he was disappearing behind a wall where I was not allowed. I remember when I was little someone saw a plane high up in the sky and we all ran out screaming and waving. It was a sign that there was a world beyond what we knew.

I took in the country as I drove to the airport and I hoped it would be the last time I saw it. The oppression I saw in the people walking down the streets was in stark contrast to the flowing green natural beauty of the country. The more I experienced Cuba, the more I felt a connection to its people, and the more I resented Fidel Castro and his oppressive regime.

The plane ride home was a sad blur. I started to pretend that she was beside me, flying out of Cuban airspace and into a life full of expression. The visualization of her with me was something that started as I got on the plane in Cuba and became a constant habit of mine from then on. I felt that if I got used to seeing her, feeling her with me in America, then one day she would just materialize.

Chapter nineteen

ON A MISSION

For the entire trip back to the United States, I could smell her perfume on my shirt where she had pressed herself against me. It stayed with me as I woke in my own bed the next morning, and I could almost feel her body next to mine. I was still in a daze from traveling all night, but I called Adianec to let her know I was home safe. It was always difficult connecting a call to Cuba. The infrastructure there is so antiquated that it sometimes takes ten attempts to reach the correct number, if ever. I teased her about being a woman of leisure in a tropical paradise, while I worked my fingers to the bone.

At dinner that night with Barry and Lisa, I told them of our plan to get Adianec out. Lisa put down her glass of wine and stared at me. "You've fallen in love with her?"

"No, I don't really know her, but I cannot sit back and let her suffer under those conditions. You can't imagine how suffocating it is."

"Lee, why would you help someone to the degree of losing everything if you're not in love with her? She could be, and probably is, taking advantage of you!"

"Well, what if she is taking advantage of me. Really who could blame her? I just simply cannot walk away. Even if she is, we still both win. She gets her freedom I get to help someone in need." We were all silent for a moment. "Barry, I need a good immigration attorney to investigate the marriage option." Now it was Barry's turn to stare at me. But since I didn't ask his opinion, he didn't give it.

"Call my brother Bobby and have him contact Peter."

Within hours, Bobby connected me with the top immigration firm in the U.S. That afternoon, I was speaking to their Cuban expert in Miami. He said I might be setting myself up for disappointment if she disappeared after she arrived, which he said was common. He tweaked my ego a bit. I thought, why would she leave me? But instead of touting my limited virtues, I explained that she would stay in Miami. He said that was a very noble thing to do and he understood my need to help as he, too, was Cuban. However, he felt obligated to advise me against that route. It would take two years and the cost with penalties could exceed $100,000 and potentially jail time. That got my attention.

I called an old friend, Newie, who had recently married and moved to Houston. Aside from laughing at all my jokes, she was incredibly sympathetic. I usually give her a call when I'm feeling down. She said a friend of hers was dating a guy whose family was very wealthy and politically connected in Mexico City. Perfect. I told her that could be Adianec's ticket out, I was so excited and falsely impressed with myself that I called Adianec and told her that I had scored our connection in Mexico, and that she should pack her bags.

When Lee continued to talk about his plan to get me out, I was more excited about knowing he cared than the possibility that I would see the world outside of Cuba. I knew that getting permission from the government to leave was almost impossible.

He called me and told me about his plan for Mexico and I just listened. I can remember the clothes I was wearing, the chair I was sitting in. I wanted to live in that moment for the rest of my life. I enjoyed the excitement in his voice, even though I knew that the road through Mexico had closed many years ago.

Over the next couple of weeks word spread among my friends, mostly because I told them of my inspired plan. Time and time again, I heard the same thing. "You know, she will probably disappear within a few days. That's what those women do, they're in a horrible situation and they'll do anything to get out." I would always feel the need to come to her defense and say that she was not like that. This was different. In my gut, in my bones, in my heart, I knew it. But again, I couldn't help thinking, "what if she is?" Who could blame her if she was just using me as a vehicle to freedom? I was sure that I would be okay with it. Basically, I had no choice anyway. My ego was so bashed up I felt like I'd gone through a ten rounder with Tyson. I couldn't be one of those guys that get suckered by a beautiful face. I didn't fit the profile. Those guys are usually old, fat, ugly and rich. I was none of the above…well, at least I wasn't rich.

It's possible that I could be blinded by my empathy and also my recurring need to rescue women. From my earliest recollection, that was my M.O. It was one of the two things I inherited from my wayward father, that, and the need to travel. This fit neatly into both categories. I'm not saying dad was a knight in shining armor. In fact, he was quite the opposite. With his wanderlust and thirst for Milwaukee's Finest, he would disappear for days or weeks or sometimes months at a time, without word or notice. He would head out for work in the morning and return on the wind a lifetime later with stories of exotic places called Atlanta or Phoenix. As a young boy (at this time we still lived in Detroit), such destinations seemed galaxies away. Though his spontaneity left me with subtle abandonment issues, (I would listen for the sound of his truck pulling into the drive every night as I fell asleep), I was transfixed with his inspiring stories of all the people he met along the way. Although his unannounced itinerary was confusing and painful, it gave the family a reprieve from his violent late-night returns from the local bars.

I can clearly remember, lying in bed, tensing up as I heard him stumble through the front door, calling my mother's name. Then the argument of that particular evening would start and, soon after, the sharp sound of his open hand across her face. I would fly out of bed shoot down the stairs, barely touching even one, run into the kitchen with my 5 year-old chest puffed out and with the deepest authoritative voice I could squeak out, screaming, "leave my Mommy alone!"

Successful in my mission, father and son would spend the next hour "bonding" as he would bounce me off the walls. So these are the two things I inherited from my father; an obsessive need to travel/leave and a duty to rescue women, or at least an unsettling, knee-jerk reaction to any injustice or bullying. Not surprisingly, I have spent my life jumping from relationship to relationship, leaving soon after arriving, or as soon as the damsel was out of distress. Lucky for me, I've found the perfect location and occupation for my dysfunction...Hollywood. Since practically all young actresses and models are in some form broken, in need of attention, or possess a deep aura of sadness, I can repeatedly relive my childhood - insert Freudian joke here.

Even with that awareness, my priority had to be getting Adianec safely out of Cuba to her family in Miami. I decided for the sake of her freedom to suppress any romantic fantasies that might develop. If I were bringing her to the U.S. for personal or selfish reasons, there was the lingering possibility that I could or would grow bored or disillusioned, then she would be lost in that nightmare forever. I had to keep her safe by remaining detached.

One day I was at Jay's house, the former actor turned L.A.P.D. officer, for a Saturday BBQ. I called up Adianec and put Jay on the phone. Jay speaks fluent Spanish. I wanted her to feel another connection with freedom and for at least one of my friends to "meet her." After that call, even Jay, whose cool-headed, rational nature, which borders on the cynical, seemed to have a different opinion. I knew she would charm him.

I felt more comfortable with my relationship with Lee when he started to call me and have his friends speak with me. I knew he was making me a part of his life. Barry and Jay sounded a lot like Lee, except they spoke Spanish. They all had the same humor.

Newie called back a week later with bad news. Her friend said she was not comfortable asking her boyfriend for help. This was the first of what would be dozens of dead ends. I was deflated and embarrassed to call Adianec. I had convinced her that it was a sure thing. She was very quiet and then said, "I know, Lee, that I am like prisoner of here. You a good man, *gracious mi Amore.*"

"No, baby, that was just one of many options. Let's start giving them all some energy so the right one will come along."

I tried to sound optimistic, but I was very disappointed.

I felt so bad for him when he called to tell me his plan did not materialize. I wasn't surprised, just disappointed for him. I had told two of my friends what he was trying to do. They had the same expectations as I. We talked about how lucky I was to have him in my life. I knew how much he wanted to take care of me. I wanted him to know that sending money was enough. Escape was too dangerous for both of us.

We began to entertain all offers. A few showed their true con colors immediately. They told me they needed two thousand dollars up front and they guaranteed me they had the connections in the Mexican government to have Adianec in Mexico in two to four months. "We just have to start greasing palms…" Uh huh, grease this.

A month or so later I found a lawyer in Mexico City who said that he could do it legally in six months, I checked him out. He had an office and was a certified lawyer. I sent him five hundred dollars for the paperwork and then spent the next couple of months being played. One more parasite and the list continued to grow. Everybody knew somebody and that somebody was guaranteed to be able to help. Every somebody turned out to be nobody.

Christmas day came and I felt disappointed and embarrassed that I had guaranteed she would be in Miami by now. As the months passed, I realized that I'd been staying home a lot, with the exception of dinners at Barry and Lisa's house. I would always think of Adianec, lost in Cuba, whenever I did anything special. I had stopped dating for fear that I might get emotionally involved with someone and then not have the option to do what was necessary to get Adianec out. She was beginning to worry about me and so were my friends. I was just trying to keep my eye on the ball.

Lee Brooks

I could hear a change in Lee's voice. His energy was very low, and he didn't laugh as much as he used to. In my imagination I saw many holiday parties in Los Angeles, so I was surprised when Lee was staying home so much.

In Cuba, Christmas was not permitted. But, I loved the idea of it. There were so many things I had to learn. I was afraid of being free one day. I thought with all I didn't know, I would be like a baby.

I began to read everything I could find on the internet about the laws in Cuba, our laws regarding Cuba and on Cubans who flee the country. The Cuban Adjustment Act of 1967 says that Cuban citizens wanting to come to the U.S. would be granted permanent residency after being in the U.S. for one year and one day. The law was changed after the Mariel boatlift incident in 1980, when Fidel Castro emptied his prisons and asylums and had the inmates mix with regular citizens, letting the entire bunch float to the U.S. Now Cubans caught at sea are sent back to Cuba, but the ones who could touch *one foot* on dry U.S. soil could stay. It is called the "Cuban Wet-foot, Dry-Foot Policy."

The more I learned about the embargo, the more I knew it was immoral and illegal. It has been stated in federal court that it squelches the constitutional rights of Americans. Not to mention that the Cubans who remain on the island are paying a heavy price for this game of tug of war. There is no doubt in my mind that, regardless of the embargo, Fidel Castro carries the entire blame for the existing conditions. He has taken a paradise and created a prison. I've spoken with many people who have also visited the island and they share my passionate anger.

I bought a map of Cuba that included Florida and the Bahamas and hung it on my bedroom wall. The close proximity between Cuba and Florida frustrated me. One quick boat ride and she would be free. My mind was constantly trying to solve this problem. Once I decided to be proactive, I don't think an hour went by without some deep contemplation of the subject.

One afternoon at the office, Les asked if I was sure I was going through with the plan. He knew a Mexican national who lived in Havana part time. "I'm telling you, he says he absolutely can bring this girl to Mexico on a temporary work visa."

Les gave me the man's number. I was relieved after I spoke to the guy, who claimed to have done this successfully many times before. We found the solution, the key to Adianec's departure door. I immediately called Adianec and gave her the good news. This guy did business with the Cuban government and said he knew the right people. He was heading to Havana in a few days and would meet with Adianec to get all her information. I told her, "If all goes well Amore, you should be in Mexico in three months."

"You come to Cuba y see me?"

It had been several months since my last visit. I made arrangements to fly to Havana via Canada. I needed to stop in Vancouver and visit my friend Tom, who was producing a movie to be shot sometime in the following year. Tom had offered me the role of comic relief, always the bridesmaid. I'd stay for a couple of days so I could meet some of the people involved in the film. It would also give Tommy and me time to wreak havoc in Canada. A year earlier I had shot a small role in the movie *Sideways*, which had become that year's sleeper hit. Ironically, it seemed to have awakened my dormant acting career, even reminding friends that I had some talent.

I called Adianec to see how her meeting with the Mexican national went. They had the meeting at a club where Cuba's elite go to "separate themselves from us," as she puts it. I know being at this place made her uncomfortable. But the guy took her Cuban ID number, and said he would call her in a few weeks. She said, "He was a little strange."

"Did he say anything? Did he do anything? He didn't try to touch you, did he?"

"No, touch ahh no. Um, with his eyes, Si he touch."

I wasn't sure what she meant. She said there was something inappropriate in his actions toward her, and that he spoke to her a bit too familiarly so she excused herself and left.

I didn't care how bizarre this guy was, he was going to get her out of Cuba. He was freeing her, and in a sense, freeing me too. I didn't feel I could get my life back until she was out of harm's way. I had finally found her route to the U.S., allowing me to breath for the first time in over six months. Even though she didn't quite feel she could trust this guy, based on Les' recommendation, I believed he would come through.

Chapter twenty

SIDEWAYS TO CUBA

After a few fun days in Vancouver, I caught a late night Vancouver-Toronto-Havana flight. The in-flight movie was *Sideways*. It was moments like that I wished I could have shared with Adianec. I fell asleep before the movie started and woke up around 2 a.m., about ten minutes before my appearance in the film. Everybody onboard was asleep, threatening my ego and wishing for a quick jolt of turbulence to wake everyone up. Here I had a captive audience and everybody was asleep. I don't know of any actor who does what we do to be inconspicuous.

Flying into Havana was less stressful now. I had my original immigration officer to check me in and he seemed to remember me. I didn't have to ask him not to stamp my passport. I walked into the arrival area dragging my overstuffed, six-foot duffel bag. Adianec was waiting right outside the door. I was always so happy to see her. She was constantly on my mind now. I felt my time in L.A. was just a waiting game until I could see her again. "Hey, welcome to L.A."

She didn't quite get the joke. "*Que?* We are in Havana."

"I, ahh…oh, Havana? You sure?"

"*Si, mi amore.*"

"Just practicin' for when you come to visit."

"*Seguro?*"

"*Si, mi amore.*"

We did a quick money exchange at the *Cadeca*, which always left me feeling aggravated. Fidel puts the Cuban peso equal to the U.S. dollar with a 20% service charge. So, anytime I would send Adianec money or exchange it at the airport, the Cuban government would steal $200 for every $1000 I brought in.

I was so nervous again to see Lee. Every time he came back to me, my life opened up. I didn't understand everything he said because he talked about so many different things that were new to me. But I always learned so much from him, even with the complication of our different languages.

He had told me that being in Cuba was like watching television on a black and white set. He would talk about the rest of the world, New York City, Los Angeles and the big cities in Europe and Asia, and how there was so much color and order. It gave me different eyes to see my country with all the buildings falling apart and nothing painted in over 45 years. I realized for the first time that he was right. My country had no color, spiritually or physically.

Even in the middle of winter, the Cuban heat is oppressive. I pulled food out of my pants pockets again during the ride to Ada's. I mixed it up a little this time, with the exception of the extra sharp cheddar, Adianec's favorite. Ada told us as we pulled up that her current renters were staying another day, so she found us an apartment a few blocks away. We had a two-bedroom with a kitchen all to ourselves.

I made us a cheese and olive omelet as Adianec unpacked my suitcase, and looked through her new wardrobe, this time with unabated enthusiasm. She tried on a very tight, slinky black cocktail dress that I had just brought her, which quite literally made my knees buckle. We sat on the balcony and shared the omelet. I liked watching her face when she ate, discovering new tastes. Everything that was in my daily life was new to her.

Adianec confided in me how nervous she was to go to America, thinking the women there were so sophisticated and glamorous, and she was just an insecure country girl. She asked about my two days in Vancouver and the flight. I had to confess with some embarrassment about my disappointment that everyone slept through my movie.

Being involved in her life really put things into perspective for me. I admired her lack of pretense and materialism. I had no doubt that some guy would grab her up immediately upon her arrival in Miami. I certainly wasn't relishing that idea. I realized then how close we had become.

Lee was very excited this time. He was in a movie on the airplane. He laughed because he was the only one awake to see it. But I also saw real disappointment. I knew he wouldn't say something to me that wasn't true. To look like he does, of course he was an actor. And I think even more beautiful than my Brad Pitt. But everyone says he can't be in the movies, why would he keep coming to Cuba? A year later when his movie came to Cuba, everyone went crazy, saying that he really is a movie star. We were all very excited that he was in a famous movie. He laughed when I told him that and assured me he was not a movie star.

We spent the next three days swimming at the Copacabana, dining at the El Aljibe, sharing all night conversations and my favorite pastime, unleashing her Cuban passion. She asked if I wanted to see the beautiful beaches of Cuba, and I replied, "Of course." On the fourth morning, Heidells picked us up in the family 1953 Chevy De Luxe. Although it is illegal for Cubans to own a car, they are allowed to continue driving the same car they had when the revolution started. They just no longer own it. Now it belongs to the revolution.

The handle to the back door was missing and had to be opened with a pair of pliers. The heat in the car was like a blast furnace. Adianec got nauseous immediately and had to slide back out until it cooled off. It had that old car smell, like decomposing vinyl. I guess it's what the fifties smelled like. It had so much room inside you had to raise your voice to have a conversation with the people in the front seat. In the front passenger seat was Heidells girlfriend of the week.

As Heidells turned the key, the car made no attempt to start. It sounded like it was out of gas. Everybody piled out of the boat before we all instantaneously combusted from the heat. As the woman sat under a tree, the boys tinkered. From experience, I've learned that if you don't know how to fix it, give it a good whack, and pour a little gas in the carburetor. Heidells did something similar to that and the car started.

As we were driving through Havana on the Malecon, the car sputtered a few times. I asked Heidells if that was common. He said no. I told him, "It sounds like your fuel pump is going."

He turned around and gave me a condescending laugh, subtext: "Yankee, don't tell me about my car." I explained to him, "I do know a little bit about cars, you know. I was born in Detroit. This car and I practically share DNA."

Every time he hit the gas, the car would sputter. I saw that we were heading toward the tunnel that goes under the Havana port. "Heidells, I don't think this car can make the hill coming out of the tunnel." He ignored me.

Sitting at the bottom of the tunnel in a stalled car is not the safest place to be. The phrase "I told you so" did enter my mind, but I was too busy waving oncoming traffic into the other lane. The tunnel was dark and, chokingly, lacked ventilation. We told the women to walk up and out, to avoid getting hit by a car and also so that they could breathe. Heidells said, "They will send a tow truck soon."

"How do you know that?" I asked him. He told me that people break down here all the time, so they have trucks waiting at both ends. Sure enough, within five minutes, a late fifties tow truck, looking like a goofy cartoon, came clunking down the tunnel.

Senor Tow Truck Guy just dropped us off at the top of the tunnel and left without a word. We were on flat land, so Heidells tried the key and it started. We got about a mile down the road until she gave out again and we coasted past a forest of palm trees into a turnoff of what looked like a hospital. Again, I suggested a fuel pump problem. Now I was just irritating him, so I backed off and let him work on it.

Usually a situation like this would have me stressed, but I was in Cuba, so I decided to just go with the flow. Ay, Cuba. Heidells thought we might have dirty gas in the tank, so he said he was going to check the tank. I was a little confused on how he was going to drop a gas tank here. He popped the trunk and there was a plastic red gas can sitting in his trunk with a hose sticking out, feeding through the floor, supposedly to the fuel pump up front. I started laughing. Heidells was laughing at me laughing and said that the gas tank had rusted out years ago, and they had substituted it with the can. It was another brilliant example of Cuban ingenuity. What else are you going to do if you can't get spare parts from the U.S.?

We were stuck on a side road; the land around us was saturated with palm trees that were budding with coconuts. Our car was up the road about 500 feet from the highway which lined the blue Atlantic Ocean. There are worse places to break down. We just so happened to be at the end of a driveway where some guy was working on two cars. The guy had tools, and hopefully, some knowledge. He asked a few questions, looked at the engine, tried to turn it over and then had the audacity to suggest it was the fuel pump.

The nerve of that bastardo!

Heidells started taking apart the fuel line and filters to clean them, certain it was a dirt problem. He was in complete denial about the fuel pump, although I'm sure since he was Cuban, he could probably build one out of a vacuum cleaner. A few guys showed up to help out our new neighbor with the two cars. They turned their attention to us and immediately began trying to solve a "fuel pump problem." I stood there, amazed at their speed and ability to communicate without speaking. They were crawling all over the car.

One guy was working with an auger bit to get the right sized hole in the car's hood. Another was taking a plastic bag I brought from L.A. and was making different sized gaskets out of it. The third person had a variety of tubes and hoses and was using the "gaskets" to slide them together to make a long leak-proof fuel line. The last guy took a plastic liter soda bottle and created a hand held gas tank. It was like watching three *MacGyvers* fix a car.

When they had all finished they told me to get into the front seat. They handed me the "gas tank" full of gas that now had a fuel line leading from the top of it, out the window, over the windshield, down through the new hole in the hood, then delicately perched an inch above the barrels of the carburetor so the gas could drip into it. The flow, gravity fed, would depend on whether I was holding the bottle up high or low. They primed the carburetor, turned the key and she started. We had drawn a crowd which erupted into applause.

"Thanks, guys" and I held out three, five Peso bills.

I tried to give each guy five bucks, not only for their trouble but for their ingenuity. Adianec said they probably wouldn't take it, and they didn't. They politely declined the money. Here I was offering them half a month's pay and they shyly refused. This time I understood without having to have it explained. Getting paid would have meant they did it for money and not just for the sake of helping another in need. Helping in Cuba is when you do it from the heart without reward.

We laughed the entire ride home. If someone saw the *policia* they would yell and I would bring the bottle down out of sight. This would negatively affect our performance and the engine would start to stall, then I would sneak it up quickly to get a burst of horsepower. We laughed at our nervousness, knowing we had a bomb in the car with us.

Gas mileage using this form of fuel delivery system is pretty poor. I knew I was in control of fuel efficiency, so I was dancing with the bottle to find the right gravity level. One block from Heidells' house the bottle ran dry. We coasted forward, rolling to a stop five feet from his front door. Luck o' the Irish. We went inside to say hello to Sol and Vladimir, and I was invited down the long hallway. "Vladimir, can I have one of your cigarettes?"

He handed me one, smiled mischievously and said something. Heidells translated. "He said, be careful, American, these cigarettes are for real men. Very strong."

"Real men have cancer?"

One drag and my lungs exploded in fiery pain. As I coughed for ten minutes, Vladimir came over to pat me on the back and laugh. "Very good, very good."

Their kitchen was half outside, exposed to the elements. I could tell they were a bit self-conscious about my seeing their living conditions. The building, walls and ceiling were literally deteriorating around them. I had grown extremely fond of these people and found myself angry that they had to live like this. Their stove was no more than a Bunsen burner. The showerhead was a rusted out jagged piece of pipe sticking out of the wall. The bathroom tile had long ago seen its best day and the shower drain was just a hole in the floor. I thought about Adianec having to shower there, and again, I was reminded of the dichotomy of her refinement versus her surroundings. I told myself that it was almost over for her.

As I cooked dinner that night, Adianec came up behind me and wrapped her arms around my waist. Concerned about my quietness, she asked me what was wrong. What could I tell her? This place exhausted me and yet being there I felt so relaxed. Maybe it was being with her? I told her, "Nothing. I'm just relieved, that's all. Just so relieved this thing's almost over."

I knew there was nothing I could do to change the situation in Cuba. Aside from gathering an army of actors, writers, musicians and a handful of Jewish accountants to invade the island, I was kinda out of ideas.

I could see that being in my home had put a burden on Lee. I know that he is such a caring man. I think he works out his muscles to hide his sensitivity more than anything else. I admire the way he always wants to help. He feels he has to protect everyone. But I explained to him that this is life in Cuba. You cannot acknowledge anything that is beyond your ability to change. And in Cuba nothing changes.

When he speaks of me going to Miami, I get a little scared. I don't tell him, but it's not my dream to go to Miami. The only reason I would leave my family is to be with him. But I know that would scare him. Most things don't, but I can see he is afraid of love. And this love I have for him is so crazy. I tell my friends and we just laugh. My friend, Yanela, tells me I am the luckiest girl in Cuba, and that my situation with Lee is like a fairy tale. I know it's true, I am lucky, but I'm also concerned that he will soon get bored and go away.

The next morning, we spent a few hours swimming at the Copa, and then I convinced her to take me to the local beach for Cubans. She said, "No, Amore, you don't want. It will feel sad."

I insisted. The "beach" was a twenty-minute walk from the Copa. There was no sand, just jagged concrete blocks and sharp rebar sticking out of the water. As far as you could see, there were kids diving and doing back flips off dilapidated concrete piers, eroded sea walls and the remnants of decades old buildings that sat crumbled right on the waters' edge. The breaking waves of the clear blue sea were in stark contrast to the grey remains of civilization that lay there. It had a surreal beauty, brought to life by the frenetic movements of hundreds of children climbing up and over the broken walls and slabs of concrete. Every step I took was precarious and contrary to the acrobatic grace of the children who spread out over at least a mile down the shore.

As we sat and watched the action, I videotaped some of it. She kissed me in a sympathetic way and rubbed my head. I was not depressed, almost the opposite. These kids, though risking life and limb, were ecstatic and completely lost in the moment. Every now and then, one would notice the CIA agent and stop and stare. But overall, this was as good as life got for them.

I went through my usual guilt trip as she helped me pack. This time, however, I took her home in a taxi and left for the airport. Saying goodbye was growing increasingly more difficult. "This goodbye shit is becoming a bad habit."

She nodded and mumbled "*Si*."

"Well, what are ya gonna do about it?"

Sadly, she said, "*No se, amore.*"

"Honey, I know having to say goodbye is difficult, but this is our life for now, and we have a plan. One day soon you'll be flying in to see me from Miami, and in return you'll also be the one leaving me behind, and sad."

"Mmm, I feel so better."

Even with limited English, the sarcasm was universal. "Yeah, it's a gift."

Chapter twenty-one

I NEED MY LIFE BACK

I called the Mexican national guy a few times to check the status of her visa, and with each successive call, I felt more and more that I was being played. I stayed in denial for several weeks, not willing to accept that we had been conned again. I told Barry and Lisa one night over dinner, neither of whom trusted Adianec, that I had hit another snag. Barry asked how long I was going to keep digging in. "Look, Lee. Everything I've read, everything I've heard on the subject…it's nearly impossible."

He was right, even though I didn't want to admit it. "Promise me you'll set a time limit. Okay? That's all I'm asking. Just set a time limit."

"I promise," I responded, with my fingers crossed.

At barbeques and dinners, I started becoming the fodder for jokes. As a result, I slowly began to retreat from everyone, except Barry, Jay and Kevin. Even though they were doubtful, they stayed emotionally supportive. I was really getting fed up with all the unsolicited comments and hurtful jokes from friends and acquaintances.

Over the next two months, we wasted time, money and energy dealing with several more leads which proved to be nothing but dead ends. My resilience had taken too many hits. The worse I felt, the more I called her to keep her spirits positive. If she lost hope, our plan was doomed.

One evening I drove to Redondo Beach to have dinner with an old friend, Kirk, whom I had met in acting class many years earlier. I told him of all the failed attempts, of the physical, emotional, and financial toil they had taken.

He listened quietly as I told him the entire story. He then repeated something I had told him a few years earlier when I was debating leaving acting: I had asked him, "Kirk, how long do I bang my head against this wall before it takes my life?"

I clearly remember that at that time, it was what acting had become, a series of repetitive slams to the head and ego. He explained, "You've done more than anyone would or could expect to help this girl, right? Especially considering that you have no intention of having it flow into a relationship. I know this is hard to accept, but I'm afraid it's time to reconsider and just support her financially in Cuba." Before I could interject, he continued, "You need to get on with your life man. And what a life it is."

He told me how envious he was of my life and asked me to consider that this was just another adventure being fueled by empathy. He said one final thing on the subject, "Lee, you're a great guy and I'm sure she is everything you say, but you don't owe her your life, man. Look at all the amazing women in this town that would love to have you rescue them. This just may be another wall you're banging your head against." He, like everyone around me, thought I was either stupid or naïve.

Driving home, I put the top down to feel the cool ocean mist. I think I was just trying to feel something beyond depression, even if it was uncomfortable. I didn't have the support of a single person, except perhaps a desperate mother hoping for a matrimonial miracle. Maybe I was misled by my sense of responsibility. Perhaps it was a misguided adventure. Why am I doing this? It was just too damn hard. I really didn't know her or her family, and I was exhausted.

I needed food at home, so I stopped by *Trader Joes*. As I walked behind the cart, I was almost in a trance, going over the conversation I would have with her in the morning. I had no doubt she would understand. I had to accept that I had to let her go.

I would tell her it was just too hard, that I no longer had a life. What else could I say? "Maybe we just should settle for what we had?" Certainly her life was better now with me supporting her. I would do her no good if I fell into a paralyzing depression. I needed my life back. That's the refrain that just kept running through my head. I needed my life. This fantasy would only destroy me as I dreamed of what could never be. The more I focused on it, the more I was convinced the whole rescue idea was insane and impractical. My old life was tugging at me, all the years of doing what I wanted, when I wanted, going wherever I wanted to go, not answering to anyone. I missed that. I missed my life and I needed to be happy again.

On top of that, I was losing money by the boatload. All my traveling now was only to Cuba every few months and it wasn't cheap. I had much less coming in, due to my lack of enthusiasm about going out to get new remodel work for the guys, or researching homes fresh on the market to flip.

I can't explain the feeling of utter despair I felt that night. My fear was talking to me and I knew I'd never hear from him again. I don't call him very often. It's a month's salary to call America for ten minutes. But I had to hear his voice at that moment, even though he would probably call me later that night. After twenty minutes when he didn't call me back, I panicked. He always carries his phone with him because of his clients.

I laid in bed and could hear a conversation in his head. he was going to end it. I knew I was imagining it, but it just kept coming. My heart was pounding with the thought of never seeing him again. I kept calling and with every unanswered ring I knew it was true. I knew I had taken too much of him, and if I really loved him I had to let him go back to his life so he could be happy again.

There were many times I would hear Lee's voice calling me, and then a few minutes later he would call. I had gotten so used to this bizarre occurrence that a few times I would be at my sister's and say I have to go home, Lee's calling. She would always say "How can you know that?" I didn't know how to answer her, I just knew.

When I got to the car, my cell phone displayed seven missed calls with the familiar eleven digits, Cuba. I called her back with some concern. She never tried more than twice. I knew something was wrong. She picked up on the first ring. She had been crying and I asked what was wrong.

"Lee, I never want you hurt. I don't want a burden to you."

She said she had had a bad dream, and then she repeated almost verbatim the conversation I had just had with Kirk, and even the debate in my head. She said, "I want you…walk away. I understand. You need your life."

My head was spinning. Did I accidentally dial her number at dinner and let her in on the conversation? That had to be it. How else could she--? I mean, she couldn't be that tuned into me. I knew she loved me, but…this was spooky. As we spoke, I checked my phone for recent calls, and it did not show that I had dialed her number that day. I briefly told her about the conversation at dinner and asked her how she knew. She said she had been able to know when I would be calling, and could feel whenever I was upset. Then she said, almost with fear in her voice, *"Lee, my love for you is crazy."*

We spoke for hours that night. We talked about our options and decided to continue advancing the cause but to try to not get too emotionally wrapped up in it. We agreed we should date other people because we didn't know if or when she could escape. Although we never spoke of exclusivity in the past, it had just happened. Her ability to have an emotional connection with me some

2,500 miles away confirmed that this relationship was not an illusion. "Lee, amore, I need you happy. Is too much, I don't wanted this of you."

That's what I wanted to hear. That's what I had decided, but the more we talked, the more we spoke, the more I saw I didn't. "I can't seem to just let you go, baby."

"You have girls?"

"What? Are you serious? I'm just a bit too preoccupied."

"Maybe, si, better for us, maybe just not have sex to them."

"Wolves at the door, mi amore." She didn't understand what I meant. "No, *mi amore*, I can't. Not yet. Let's just keep trying, but we'll put more thought and less energy and money into it. We have a few more options on the table, so we'll just let it run its course." This was becoming an evermore painful and confusing time in my life.

I decided to tell anyone who asked that we had stopped pushing for an escape. Though none of my friends understood or agreed with what I was doing, I knew in my gut that had they met her, they would be on board. Barry had been speaking to Adianec whenever I called and he was around. As she became more real to him, his involvement increased. I realized throughout this ordeal just what a real friend is, and who my true friends were. Despite their objections, Barry, Jay and Kevin always stood beside me.

I was at a barbeque at Lisa's parents' house on Broad Beach in Malibu. Danny, Lisa's dad, has the kind of presence that gets your immediate attention, similar to that of General Patton. He's about the size of a front door, so when he slapped his tree trunk-like arm around my shoulder, I said, "Yes sir."

He commanded, "So, fill me in on the *Cuba situation*."

When I finished giving him the *Reader's Digest* condensed version, he informed me that he had contacts in Mexico. I was not surprised. Danny has contacts all the way to Washington DC. "Call me on Monday and I'll push it through."

My spirits lifted. People don't say no to someone like Danny but now experience had taught me to wait before I told Adianec. By the time I called Danny Monday morning, he had already spoken with a lawyer in Mexico. On his orders, I immediately called the lawyer and told her our needs. She was very upbeat and said she had a colleague in Mexico City that had done exactly the same thing several times, and that she would call me back in a few days. Just when I thought all hope was lost, we got a jolt from the heavens courtesy of Danny. I called Adianec and gave her the news. Two days later, the Mexican lawyer called me and enthusiastically said, "Yes, no problem, we can start working on a visa next week. We will need $10,000 dollars up front and another $4000 to $8,000 upon completion."

"I see. And when, exactly, do you figure that will be?"

"In four to five years."

Every time we got slammed, I would tap into my reserve tank. There was nothing left in the main. I really needed to see her now. Looking into her eyes always melted any doubts away. Things at work were cool so I decided to leave again. It had been a few months since I had last visited Cuba.

Chapter Twenty-two

Meeting the family

Adianec greeted me at the airport as though I were a conquering hero. Any feelings of reservation I had felt had long since vanished. In that moment where I felt like I had let her down, she turned it around and made me feel like I hung the moon. The pockets of my pants were weighed down by the copious amounts of food in them. I had gotten a little more daring with the food on this trip. This time I filled my carry-on bag as well. Even bringing some sourdough bread so I could make French toast. Even though I was disappointed at having to return, I loved seeing her and being with her. I resolved to make the best of it and treat it as a romantic vacation.

Again, upon arrival, Ada informed us that she had overbooked her house, but this time we got an incredible place, by Cuban standards. It was two blocks from the beach, closer to the Copa and we had the entire upper section of a house. It had a large kitchen with a stove, an oven and a dining room. The bath had been recently tiled, though they had some how neglected to install a toilet seat. There was no raw wire wrapped around the showerhead this time. So, no shocking surprises.

A large tropical storm followed me the day I arrived. The house had windows (wooden slats) on three sides. We left them open as we fell asleep to the rhythmic, pounding rain and the percussion of a wild thunder storm. A warm ocean breeze flowed through the house. It was the best nap I had had in years. This was the kind of nap you read about in books, where you wake up refreshed and energized. Adianec told me, with some apprehension, that her mother was in town to meet me. Both her mother and sister would be coming over the following night.

We walked around the neighborhood that night. The post-rain temperature was actually pleasant and the air had a clean aliveness that only a thunderstorm can create. There were heavy clouds illuminated by the moon, and the stars were huge and bright. She asked what the night sky was like in L.A. "We don't have a night sky," I joked.

It's not much of a joke. We really don't have much of a sky that isn't obscured by the lights of the city. Even though I thought these stars were some of the brightest I'd ever seen, she said in her hometown, you can touch them. I told her, "Yes, but you'd get arrested because in Cuba the stars belong to the revolution."

She laughed. "*Si, si*, it's true."

I had only just arrived, yet I was already feeling that deep loneliness I felt whenever I fly out and leave her. Just looking at how happy she was and knowing that she would not be leaving with me in six days, if ever, was a crushing thought.

The Copa was great as always. My life would be perfect if I always felt the way I did whenever I swam there. When we came up from the natural pool to get lunch, we sat next to a guy from Canada. His company had transferred him down to run their factory in Havana and he explained to us the con that the Cuban government pulls on investors in Cuba. He said that the Cuban citizens are the government's chattel. The government tells the citizenry where to work, and everybody makes just $12.00 a month. Then Cuba charges the foreign companies $800 to $1200 a month per person. They do the same with the doctors they so gallantly send overseas. Castro, in his genius, had created a land of educated slaves for use at his financial pleasure.

I hinted at our situation, hoping to get some help or advice. He told me to be very careful, I asked him what he meant. "You're being watched and followed 24 hours a day."

I was baffled, but also very intrigued. It was sounding a bit James Bond-ish. He shook his head. "Look at you. You are the enemy, and you even look the part. You may find it amusing, but they take it very seriously. Do you really think they would just let you roam about their country freely? You are being followed buddy, and everything you do and every person you meet is in your file."

"My file, they have a file on me?" I said incredulously. He nodded. The thought of this felt a little adventurous and cool, but I didn't like the implications for Adianec. I wasn't sure if this guy was playing the drama card.

Meeting the parents of someone I'm dating is something I've been pretty good at avoiding through my life. It signifies intent to commit, which I had managed to dodge so far. But I was genuinely looking forward to meeting Adianec's mother and sister. I laid out a smorgasbord of junk food that I had smuggled in. We had Nacho Doritos, chocolate-covered almonds, spicy Chinese snack mix, chocolate chip cookies, Spanish olives and a half dozen other foods. I watched Adianec get more and more nervous as the time of their arrival approached.

The taxi pulled up out front and Adianec ran down the back staircase and around to the front of the house. I could hear her giggling all the way. Her whole life had been such a struggle and I loved these brief respites of ease.

Her sister's boyfriend, Oscar, came up first, followed by her sister. Her sister, Laura, was a petite blonde and about as pretty as a girl can be. They were both uncertain about how to react to me, so I offered them some snacks. They both froze for a moment, trying to take it all in. I didn't realize until later that it was too much for them at once. Adianec brought her mother in and introduced her. I tried to speak my rudimentary Spanish with her but all it did was confuse her, or at least that's what her face conveyed.

As soon as all the introductions were made, there was a knock at the door. It was the lady who had rented the apartment to us. She wanted to write down everyone's identification number. As everyone obediently pulled out their papers, I became protective, taking all the papers and then just stared at her. She stared back. "I need to have those papers, it's the law. Nobody can have a gathering without recording for the government all who attend."

"You mean like Nazi Germany?" I said angrily.

"It's the law." She repeated. I looked at Adianec for a clue as to what to do.

"Lee, we have to." She was embarrassed.

We all sat down and her sister sat on her boyfriend's lap and they were very amorous all evening. That is very common in Cuba, where social boundaries are much more relaxed than in the U.S. Watching them try the snacks was very interesting. Someone would take a small bite of something, and if they liked it, they would excitedly pass that same piece on to another person. There was more than enough of everything, but they were so used to scarcity and having to share that they couldn't conceptualize that there was an abundance.

Adianec suggested that I show the videos I shot of Los Angeles. I had taken the camera into my local supermarket and taped the produce section. It did look beautiful, but they didn't believe that it was real. They truly thought it was staged and that all the fruits and vegetables were fake. I could sense their tension and discomfort, so I changed tapes to the Third Street Promenade in Santa Monica at night. There are blue LED sparkle lights hanging in all the trees that line the walk. Laura, who spoke better English than the other three, told me, "Everyone is curious why the trees are so beautiful?"

"Because of the lights," I responded.

"Yes, but why do you have the lights?"

"Well...it makes the trees beautiful."

That answer made them very anxious. Why would anyone do something just to make it beautiful? The night was not going well. I don't know if they thought I was a liar or just arrogant. I was actually just trying to be a good host.

I turned off the tape. Now I was embarrassed and uncomfortable, and made an excuse not to continue. The night ended abruptly and Adianec trailed them out. I felt bad for her. She had had such high hopes, and now her family had serious reservations about this stranger that wanted to smuggle her out of their country. After about ten minutes, she came back up, looking a bit haggard and immediately occupied herself with cleaning up. I waited a while before I spoke. I told her it was natural for her family to be skeptical, but it didn't change a thing. I said she should just reiterate to her mother that she was not coming to be with me, and that L.A. is 2,500 miles from Miami.

My mother has always lived in the country. She has had a simple life. Not only has she never seen a foreigner before, she has also never even heard English in person. Lee intimidated her with his appearance and confidence. My mother was so nervous to meet him. Sol told me that when my mother got back to her house that night, she told Sol that Lee was the prettiest man she had ever seen. But she could not understand anything he said, which made her not trust him, and that she was very concerned. Afterward, Sol convinced my mother that she knew Lee well and that he was a very good man.

The next morning, we called for a taxi and met Heidells, Adrianna, and Marika at the bus station that would take us to Varadero beach. Adrianna talked to Marika the entire ride while Adianec read a fashion magazine. Heidells and I talked politics and I asked him if he would like to escape to America. He said, "Oh yeah, that would be amazing, man, but, no, no, I can not leave my mom and dad alone."

I never had that worry with my own parents, but I admired it in Heidells. We made a stop in Matanzas, a fishing village with a large serene bay. Matanzas is not small, but it somehow conveys the feel of a small village. On one of the inlets sat many old forgotten fishing boats, the fading paint hinting of the bright colors they once were. All brass or anything of value had been absconded with long ago. Just the worn-out shells remained.

When we finally pulled into the lot in Varadero, we had to walk a couple of miles to the part of the beach where Cubans were allowed. We walked through a small grove of palm trees burdened with coconuts and onto a silky white sand beach. We rented some plastic chairs and set them up under two palapas. (I was about as white as the sand, though not as silky.) Adianec and I went into the water so I could teach her to swim. The sandy bottom almost glowed through the water. I swam out about a quarter mile where the water was so clear I could make out the current swirls in the sand, eighty feet down. I swam back to Adianec who was floating on her back. The sea was very calm.

Cuba and all our difficulties faded away for a while as I held her, letting the warm current carry us down the beach. The water was warm, maybe too warm. It didn't cool us from the heat of the day, but it was wet. Down the beach in the tourist area we could see sailboats, paddle boats and catamarans, with people zipping back and forth to shore.

"On the beach near Havana (Cuban section)"

The ridiculousness of our situation was apparent at moments like this. We were so close to my country and her freedom, less than 100 miles of water.

Just to test the demarcation line of which beach belongs to whom, I asked her to walk with me to the tourist area. She was hesitant, but followed me. Sure enough, when we came close to all the "fun," a Cuban security guard walked toward us and waved his finger at Adianec. I told her to go back to the others, while I rented a four-person paddle boat and brought it back down the beach for all of us. Even with all my years growing up in and as a lifeguard on Daytona Beach, I have never had so much fun in the water as I did that day. "You know, beyond all that water out there is a shore line." She nodded. "No, I'm just sayin', one bold move and we commandeer one of those vessels, and then bing bang boom, we're eating Domino's by sunset."

"Okay, I trust you."

That was easy.

We put some serious mileage on that boat, used it for a diving platform so far out that the water was a deep, dark blue. Adianec, not being able to swim, asked to go closer to shore. She was more comfortable if she could see the bottom.

We went up to the shack for lunch, it only had three items on the menu: burgers, chicken or pork. I ordered chicken, and then grilled the cook on what a breast-less chicken looks like. "Seriously, I'm curious. Why are there no breasts on any chicken in this country?"

Everyone thought it was funny, especially the cook, but nobody could come up with an answer. I still don't know. We spent the rest of the day at the beach whispering about a Cuba without Castro, which everyone agreed was long overdue.

Everybody slept on the bus on the way home, happily exhausted. We spent some time at Sol and Vladimir's house that night with Adianec's mother. She was much more relaxed with me, perhaps due to the familiar surroundings. I teased her, with the help of Heidells' interpreting. "You should have come to the beach with us. We almost took a boat to Miami."

After Heidells' translated what I'd said, she put her hand to her mouth in astonishment. It is the "forbidden dream," especially for someone her age. She grew up in this dictatorship and was a good follower who, though she knew it wasn't right, never made waves. Heidells told me, "She thinks you are very bold."

"Tell her I'll pack her in my suitcase and take her to her brother."

Again, she had the same reaction, but this time with more laughter. "She said, maybe one day she can go for a visit."

I also let her know that I would do all I could to get Adianec safely to her uncle in Miami. "Heidells, tell her I won't do anything that could harm Adianec."

"She said she knows that Adianec trusts you very much."

I talked my way up to Adianec's bedroom. It was in the attic. The ceiling was raw rafters with sporadic small holes in the roof. The walls were painted pink with watered down paint, not quite covering up some graffiti. She had an electric fan nailed on the wall above her bed with pink lace hanging down around it, her attempt to make it pretty. The mattress was absolutely the lumpiest anyone could imagine. It looked like a movie prop. I told her to buy a new one in the interim. It was like sleeping on a mountain peak with a bag of gravel for a pillow. Her attempts to make the place a home made me sad. On the windowsill were three pictures of me. My acting headshot was framed, another one from the week we met was held by her teddy bear, and the third was one of us kissing, surrounded by dry flowers. She was nervous the entire time we were up there. For me it was nice to have a visual of her surroundings whenever I called her.

We took her sister out to lunch the next day. I think I had finally been accepted. I was curious why she hadn't joined us at Varadero the day before. I could see Adianec didn't like the question. Laura kind of laughed and said, "It is my boyfriend. He is very jealous of me and forbids me to go to the beach without him."

This upset Adianec and they got into a brief argument in Spanish. She was very independent and wanted the same for her little sister, who had, to Adianec's dismay, dropped out of medical school because of him. Oscar worked in the black market, selling cigarettes and jewelry to tourists, and would sometimes be gone for days. Whenever he returned, he expected her to be there, at his beck and call, with the house spotless.

Adianec and I had dinner alone at El Aljibe. She was wearing the black cocktail dress I'd brought her months earlier. Apart from that dress, all of the nicer clothes and jewelry I brought her went back with me on the return flight. They were too much for Cuba and could get her in trouble with the authorities. The dress was all black and strapless, with a gold ring that connected to the dress on the front and wrapped around the back of her neck. It fit her snugly, perfectly wrapping around her breasts, flowing onto her small waist, then stretching over her hips and halfway down her tanned thighs. There was no wasted material here. It looked like it was designed for her. She looked so beautiful, so elegant, and she knew I was totally smitten with her that night. As we walked through the restaurant, every man and woman watched her glide to the table. I held back several feet just to watch the show. A lot of cigars dropped during that walk. As I spoke to her that night, I wondered to myself if I would ever let my guard down, and if I did, could this become love. It was the situation I didn't trust, not her. I knew from experience that the feeling of love is easy to cultivate on vacation, but that it rarely withstood the reality of everyday life.

We spent the next couple days at the Copa, and then all too quickly, it was time to go home again. This time, she was less of a mystery. I had met her family, and Laura and I had become friends. That morning we took a taxi to Adianec's home and I spent a few nice moments with her mother before it was time to go. With Heidells' help, I told her that it was very nice to see her again. She responded, yes, maybe I'll be in Havana when you return.

"Ask her if she needs anything from America."

"She will say she needs nothing. I don't need to ask."

Adianec was a little cold toward me but I had come to expect it. I knew it was the only way she could avoid breaking down in front of me. Instead, it was me who broke down, not in front of everyone, but privately while en route to the airport. All of a sudden, my heart broke.

I was always sad when he left Cuba. I would go up to my room and cry for a few hours until Sol came up and told me to come back to reality. This time it was my mother who came up wanting to spend time with me. I had not spent any time with her this trip because Lee was there, and I think she felt a little lonely.

I love my mother, but she was really bothering me, I wanted to be alone. She kept saying, "Please nina, don't cry."

We talked about him for a while. I told her about my sadness. She asked me how I could love him so much when we have trouble communicating. I told her we communicate with our hearts. She said "nina, I hope he understands how much you love him."

Chapter twenty-three

DANGEROUS DECISION

I had two lives now, the one in L.A. and the one in Cuba, with Adianec. The one in Los Angeles seemed only to be a way station between my trips to go see her. I was getting fairly good at changing the subject whenever anyone would bring up Adianec. I felt it was just none of anybody's business. I had gotten so protective of her I took every slight about her and our relationship as a personal affront.

I was completely out of inspiration on how to get her out. Every morning getting out of bed, having to face another day of disappointments was a continual struggle. Even breathing at times seemed a chore. Due to my frustration with the absolute unfairness of the whole situation, and having to walk this path alone, I would often doubt Adianec. I had to be okay with the possibility that she, even unconsciously, was using me to help her escape to America. I would have to allow her to walk freely out of my life and disappear once she was in Miami. All my friends believed I was being conned, so be it, I would probably do the same in her situation. The outcome, her freedom, had to be more important than the sum of my needs.

I had called her uncle in Miami one day to talk to him about which family member would take Adianec when she escaped from Cuba. His wife got on the phone and suggested we just put Adianec on a speed boat. They had connections with someone they trusted. It would be quick-one week. I was hesitant. There was danger of getting caught, or worse. She said, "You are thinking like an American. The journey to freedom is not on a first-class ticket. This was a way of life for us, you understand this? Chances have to be taken."

Maybe she was right. Maybe I was thinking like an American. I called Adianec and put us on a three way call. After an hour, we decided to go for it. There was a spot on a boat leaving in a week. It would be $12,000, paid in installments. Her aunt hung up and Adianec and I started laughing in disbelief. She could be free in one week if I paid $8,000 in three days. After that, she had to stay home all day and night, packed and ready to go. She would get a knock at the door and then "disappear" for a few days, reappearing in Miami as a dry-foot Cuban.

Adianec sat on the cold, dark beach with a group of strangers, including several small children. They were all explorers about to set out on an uncertain journey into a dark angry ocean. Nobody spoke a word, except for the occasional "Sshhh" from a reprimanding parent to one of the agitated children. After several hours there was a flash of light out in the darkness of the ocean. A man told everyone to move quickly into the water and swim toward the light. When people complained he responded harshly, "Then leave here, go back to your stupid lives. There will be no refunds. You lose your money and your chance of freedom." Adianec had never learned to swim and was afraid of water, but she was desperate to come to America to be with me. The entire group was getting battered from the waves, trying to get to the boat, sacrificing whatever possessions they had to the water. Finally on the boat, it was obvious there was only enough room for half of them. The two smugglers pushed and shoved to get all paying customers aboard, making the boat so heavy the twin motors strained to pick up speed. Adianec had a large man sitting on her legs and with every crash into the waves she felt the sharp pain of all his weight. After two hours at sea the boat suddenly and violently broke in half from the excessive weight and heavy seas. Adianec was thrown into the frigid, murky water without a life preserver, and was immediately separated from the group. She was alone. All she could hear was the water crashing around her, and her own voice crying out to me to come save her. In my mind I could see her go under the water in a panic, still calling out my name as the cold water filled her lungs. Her trip to freedom would end as that of so many Cubans before her. I screamed out loud, a deep primal scream, and bolted straight up in bed. I couldn't catch my breath, and had tears rolling down my face from the nightmare. It seemed so real I wanted to call her right then to make sure she had not gotten on that boat.

I knew I was struggling with the fact that she couldn't swim and was afraid of deep water. Every time I started to fall asleep, I would have another vision. I called first thing in the morning to see that she was okay. She couldn't be happier but she told me in our code language, which we had invented when we first decided to smuggle her out, not to mention it again. She was concerned her phone could be tapped. In fact, when she hung up her phone, I hesitated and I heard two male voices whispering in Spanish a split second before the line went dead. She was being monitored, or someone in her house was. I was concerned she would be immediately arrested. I called back, again using our code, and told her she was right. "Castro was in our lives."

Adianec had told me it was my decision whether or not she took the boat. She trusted me. But I couldn't shake the visions I had in my sleep. They were worse than nightmares. I tried to convince myself that her aunt was right I was just being a candy-assed American. This would be quick and easy, a four to five-hour boat ride and our problems would be history. I was tapped out financially, so I went to Barry to sponsor the trip. "Lee, bro. You know I'll always lend you money, but not specifically for her escape. You can do with it as you see fit."

"Thanks Bear, I really appreciate it."

He asked if he could give his opinion. I nodded. "If it was me, I wouldn't do it. It's far too risky. More can go wrong than right, and let me ask you this how guilty would you feel if she died in the water, just like a lot of these escaping Cubans have?"

His questions fed right into my fears. I couldn't handle the thought of her drowning and losing her like that. I told him, "Good call, bear. I won't be needing the loan."

I called her that night. "I'm sorry amore, but it doesn't feel right. Something else will come up, but this isn't our way."

I also called her aunt, who thought I was being stupid. "You've put me in a bad position with these smugglers, do you know that? I already told them Adianec was on board. They will never trust me again. This is our last chance."

"Well, I don't know what to tell you, I am sorry to put you in that position but I have a bad feeling and my decision is final, Adianec is not going on that boat." Vladimir's niece took her place on the boat. Five days later that boat broke apart in heavy seas on its way to Miami. I couldn't take any solace in the validation of my visions. Fifteen people died that night. Only two survived.

I was never comfortable about the boat ride. Too many people have died and disappeared on that short journey. I also have a fear of water I think because I never learned to swim. I would have taken the risk to be with Lee, but I was relieved when he cancelled the trip.

When I heard that the boat sank, I was in shock, but I was thankful that Vladimir's niece was one of the two survivors. I knew I would not have been. Her survival story was amazing. The man that helped her survive, a doctor, drowned before they were rescued.

Stealing Castro's daughter

The survival rate of Cubans trying to escape from Castro's grip is not favorable. Sometimes they disappear in a hungry ocean and sometimes at the hands of the military. Government personnel have killed more Cubans trying to escape by way of the ocean than fleeing East Germans trying to escape over the Berlin wall.

This is just one example:

On July 13, 1994 Seventy five men, women and children tried to escape from Havana harbor on an old wooden tugboat. Three Cuban patrol boats with steel hulls chased down the old tug and caught up to it about five miles out to sea. They repeatedly rammed the old tugboat, until the tug started to breakup, and victims began tumbling off the deck and into the five foot rough seas. Some in the machine room were trapped and drowned while pleading for help. The Cuban boats then turned their high-pressured water cannons on the remaining people, blasting them off the deck and into the water. The three government boats then began to circle the survivors creating a vortex of waves in an attempt to drown the remaining people. This took place as a Cuban coast guard boat looked on. A Greek freighter on its way to Havana saw the massacre and intervened. On that day forty one people were murdered, the youngest was six months old.

A captain of the Cuban Coast Guard boat years later admitted that they knew in advance of the escape plan. They laid in wait until the old tugboat was under way before they attempted to sink it. He also admitted that directive for the ambush came from above. An Amnesty International investigation concluded that it was an official operation and that those killed had been "victims of an extrajudicial execution."

About two months after the boat disaster, she called me. It was very unusual, not to mention expensive, for her to call. She was almost singing, she was so happy. I told her to cheer up. "I did it, I found a way out."

She laughed and explained that Sol had won the lottery, and the prize was a Visa to the U.S. I had no idea what she was talking about. She explained it to me briefly, but it was too complicated a subject for our Spanglish. We could finally breathe again, and she said it would take three months (all the escape plans seem to take three months). Vladimir's brother had a friend in the U.S. Interest Building, not an embassy, since we do not have diplomatic ties, and they could have Adianec attached as a family member. I knew he wasn't doing it out of the kindness of his heart, so I asked, "how much?"

Considering that the average wage is twelve dollars a month, I was thinking maybe a thousand. She hesitated, "It's *mucho*. He wants $8,000."

We were sitting in the living room talking when the postal man knocked on the door and handed Sol a yellow envelope. It was from the U.S. Interest Building in Havana. Without even opening it, we knew

what it was: Her invitation to apply for a family visa to the United States. She had applied for the lottery in 1998 and now eight years later, they had picked her name.

We were all screaming, all of us so happy for them. Sol said to me, "you are a part of our family. You're coming with us to America."

Vladimir's brother knew an official in the U.S. Interest Building that would take a bribe to connect me to the family. I was so happy to have found a legal way to be with Lee. I had also been thinking a lot about what life in America would be like. I could do more for my family, I could learn about all the things Lee has been trying to teach me. I would soon be free.

Having gone through all my savings, I knew I had to go back to the "Bank of Barry" and say I changed my mind about the loan. Barry, always the businessman, told me to offer him a deal. We'll give him $10,000, but he doesn't see a dime until she has her exit visa. "And it's not a loan. It's a gift, *if* you agree to make this the last attempt."

And I thought to myself, "Okay. This will be my last attempt…if it works."

I went on the Internet to research this lottery. I discovered that the U.S. gives out tens of thousands of residential visas every year, with Cuba receiving the most of any country, 20,000 a year. In Cuba alone, the U.S. Interest Building gets over 100,000 applications a year. For the past several years, Cuba had put an end to the application process, so the U.S. has gone into its archive of applications to fill the quota. Sol had actually applied six years earlier. A very small percentage of winners actually make it to the United States. Cuba has had international pressure put on them to allow the winners to leave, so they allow it as long as the applicants pay a hefty sum for "processing," way beyond what a Cuban makes in an entire lifetime. The high fee essentially locks Cubans out of the process. Still though it just didn't make sense to me how this man could attach Adianec to Sol's visa.

I called her to clarify and let her know what I had learned. When I called, I could hear the laughter in the room as everybody there seemed to be celebrating. I explained everything to her and she said, "Si, I know. Please, do not worry, this man, he has a way." She explained that she would be called to go in for her interview at the U.S. Interest Building. The man was going to call her within two weeks.

Weeks later she could be on a flight to Miami. The laughter in her voice was amazing. I didn't want to get my hopes up again because every letdown took more out of me, and I didn't think I had much left. But this did look promising. Vladimir's brother was involved, and since it was family, how could it be another scam?

After about ten days, the man called Adianec and said he'd be by the house to speak to her and give her the details. He told her to have the money ready soon because he had to pay his American contact at the Interest Building. She told me she was assured that this was it. He had done this in the past and it had worked. She asked about the money and it gave me a chill. Barry just that day told me he thought that this was their payoff. He believed Adianec and the money would disappear within a few weeks. Barry had always given me good advice. If he had doubts I had to at least listen. I joked with him, "Well, either way this will end my obsession with helping her."

I was able to be more productive at work, I had to, I was sure that I would have to pay the costs for Sol's entire family. But it would be cheaper and less stressful than having to send them money for the rest of my life, or Castro's life. A few weeks went by and everyday I would call, hoping that she would have an update for me. She had called the man several times and he told her to be patient. His American friend had flown to the U.S. and would be back in two weeks. We were really stressed now because Sol and Vladimir's interview was less than a month away and Adianec had to be attached to their application. I told her I would come with the money soon, but we needed assurances. I told her to make Barry's deal with the man. This "carrot" had been hanging over our heads for almost six weeks. "You have to get aggressive with him. We're running out of time."

I asked her to speak with Vladimir's brother, to see if he could light a fire under the guy since they were friends. She said she had also found a backup plan, another man, another embassy. This time it was the Mexican embassy and this new man, her friend knew for a fact had done this at least five times before. He could get her to Mexico City on a work visa, due to her university degree.

Finally, she got the call. The man said she would have her interview in one week and she should have some money ready. I gave her a long list of questions to ask so I could make some sense of this plan. "Baby, this whole thing makes no sense to me. I need you to ask him some specific questions. If he can't answer them, then tell him no deal. It's just too fishy."

"Mi amore, he is Vladimir's friend to his brother. I sure our trust is safe."

"Okay, you trust him, I don't have that luxury. Now, these are important questions. I want to know if the visa is real or counterfeit. Tell him, I would be willing to come to Cuba and give him the cash when you are safely in Miami. Are you getting all of this?"

"*Si*, yes, I do."

"Okay, good. Now, also, how can he put you as a family member when you're not? There are just too many holes that need to be filled before he gets any money. Do you understand? I know you're excited, but that is when you can be prey to a scam."

She just laughed me off. "Okay, I ask Amore, es difficult explain you when my inglish es so bad."

"That's another thing. Don't you think it's probably a good idea to learn the language of the country you're going to be living in?" I was getting irritated that I wasn't being taken seriously. She couldn't tell that I was annoyed. Our conversation, as usual, was fragmented and difficult, as we both still relied heavily on a dictionary. We said goodbye, and I felt even more frustrated.

One week later, no call. The frustration now boiled over and we started to argue and snap at each other. I accused her of being lazy and not aggressive enough on her end. Sol and Vladimir had their interview and it went well. I told her, "You have to speak with him tomorrow and you have to be the one calling the shots, okay? We have the money. We're paying the piper. You have to give him an ultimatum. Let him know we have another plan and he has one week or we go with the other."

I felt we had no recourse but to call his bluff. After a few days, he called her back and said he would stop by in a week. She told him that would not be necessary. He had played his game to the end and she called him a liar and thief. Vladimir's brother also called him and backed him into a corner telling him, "Adianec is family. You can't do this."

He came clean. Although he did have the connection, he was more focused on his own escape and was using Adianec as backup money, in case his escape plan failed. I am still left in deep awe that human beings can be so vile and reprehensible when it comes to their fellow man.

When I found out that we had been lied to again I was very angry. I was afraid of Lee's reaction because we had been here too many times. I thought he would say okay that was the last time. He was under so much stress. I knew he couldn't go on much longer. And now we would have to start again. Lee was quiet at first and then frustrated, but I was relieved when after just a few moments he came back and said, "Baby, it's okay, we will find another way. I don't believe God wants you to suffer on that island any longer. Please just keep believing." That was my boy, always seeing another option in the future.

I felt like I had been sucker punched. I just sat there, not knowing what to do, or say. Though my anger was directed at Adianec, I didn't express it. I just listened and gave her a pep talk…but this blow definitely hurt.

In an attempt to remove myself from the pain and disappointment that consumed me, I began to distance myself from Adianec over the next month. One night she reminded me that it had been over four months since we had seen each other, and she asked me to please come back to Cuba again. I was aware that seeing her, being with her, always cleared things up for me. She recharged my batteries, and in the past being with her had refocused me. This time I wasn't too sure it would help. My social life had completely disappeared and the few times I did leave home to grab dinner or see a movie, I went alone. If for no other reason, I had to go and give her the money for our final attempt. A man, Alain, swore he could get her to Mexico.

Chapter twenty-four

ANOTHER CON

Surprisingly, Ada was not overbooked at her house this time, and Adianec and I had our old room back. I'm used to Cuba being hot, but this was surface of the sun hot. The heat in the room just seemed to laugh at our air conditioner. I took a cold shower and apologized to Adianec that I would need a short nap before "reconnecting." She rubbed my head and back as she read the magazines I had brought her. I had also brought language tapes, CD's and books for her to improve her English. We were still using dictionaries for most of our communication, with both of us having a couple-dozen word vocabulary in the other's respective language. We had also developed our own shorthand Spanglish. I wanted us to get back to being optimistic and visualizing her life in America, I wanted to get back to that hopeful place. She thanked me for the books and tapes and said, "I know how important assimilating into the culture is if I am to be successful." I laughed.

"Wow, dem is big words for a sassy country gal. I think someone has been practicing that line."

"Is that funny?" she said with her index finger in motion. Meaning "warning" do not be a smartass.

"Uh, well…No? No I guess not." She had given me an opportunity to compliment and show her I was proud of her and I blew it.

I really wanted Adianec to have all that the U.S. had to offer her in her new life. I think, though, she knew I was feeling confused. I told her, "I don't know, I just—I just feel kind of beaten. It's like my life has just been replaced with this dreamlike, depressed existence."

I don't know if she understood. I wasn't saying it to make her feel bad.

I assured her that I was still dedicated to her escape and that there were no strings attached. She owed me nothing after she was in Miami. She had an unusual reaction to that. She double-checked with the dictionary. Then in her sexy broken English, she said, "Lee, I want you aware, I love you. In the world this is the thing you should possess no smallest doubts."

She confided that she wanted to be honest with me about her real intentions. She didn't want to go to Miami. She wanted to come to Los Angeles, so we could get to know each other. It came as a surprise, yet it didn't make me want to run away either. I told her, "That sounds like a beautiful idea. Of all the woman I've met in the past ten years, you're the one that I am the most comfortable with."

Of course, that came with a caveat. "But, we'll have to take things as they come."

Everything in my life seemed to change when he was in Cuba. I laughed more, ate a lot more and I just felt happier. Lee, to my knowledge had always been honest with me, and I had this secret I had to confide in him. It was a beautiful secret for me, but I just didn't know how he would feel about it.

I never had a desire to go to Miami. I never seriously thought of leaving Cuba until he mentioned it. But more than any dream I had ever had, I wanted to spend my life with Lee. I didn't care if he moved to Cuba or if I escaped to L.A., although now my curiosity about America was constant.

I knew I shouldn't have been so aggressive, but he had to know that I was not going to move to Miami. I am actually much more independent than I showed Lee. When he is around he just takes care of everything so quickly and I find myself following him. I loved the way he tilted his head when I told him I wanted to come to L.A., like he was trying to hear more than I was saying. He said something about waiting, but I knew by the way he smiled that he wanted me with him.

We had always been acutely aware of one another, due to having to really focus and concentrate when the other spoke. Even though Adianec's English had improved, it was still rudimentary and she had a strong Cuban accent. Comprehending what she was saying was especially challenging when she got excited. Her speech would become a blur of foreign vowels, and her hands would start a whole conversation of their own. It felt like I was dating Ricky Ricardo.

One afternoon, we went to Adianec's home to find a hiding spot for the money. I had brought the $8,000 for the Mexican tourist visa and Cuban exit visa. I had no idea how Alain was going to pull it off since Mexico rarely allows Cuban tourists anymore. If a Cuban was allowed to leave for vacation, they would undoubtedly not return. We knew some government ministers would have to be bribed, but that was Alain's job. If we somehow got double-crossed or if someone got nervous, that'd be it, Adianec would go to prison.

With bribery involved, this whole plan was getting very dangerous. The only card we had was the cash and Adianec knew not to give out one dime until she had both visas. To keep the upper hand, she told Alain that I would come back and pay him when he had the paperwork finished. The fact was she would fly out the day she received the visas, leaving no time for me to travel to Cuba.

I was so worried about the money, especially with the problems we had when we first met. I hid the money in the belly of my stuffed monkey. I slept with it and took it with me if I went to my sister's house. I never wanted to take money from him again, but this time was necessary so we could be together.

I didn't feel I had any other option but to trust Alain when he said he could get me to Mexico. I had a constant pain in my heart in these situations. I had to rely on people that I knew might be putting me in a position to steal my money because they knew how desperate we were.

We had to be very careful. One tiny slip-up and Adianec could be discovered. She decided to wait to tell her family about this plan. She didn't want to jeopardize their safety. We spoke in whispers that night. We were both feeling paranoid, and yet she was very excited and optimistic. "*Ahh, mi amore,* I feel this one es good. I believe it!"

"I wish I shared your enthusiasm, babe."

"No, really, I think it true."

"Amore, I need you to listen to me. I'm really tired. I want this so badly for you that every scam we fall for takes a piece of my life away. We have to make sure to be careful. I want this to work, so let's be smart. I don't think I have another attempt in me if this fails. Do you understand what I'm saying?"

She did. "It is that for me. I'm tired, too." And she hadn't even told her sister or family yet. "If they know, they many problems in my government. I cannot say our truth till I say goodbye."

"Well, this one seems to be the closest yet, so let's be very careful. Maybe we shouldn't speak openly about it over the phone."

She had met Alain and his family. She knew where he lived and she said, "I trust him, Lee. I do."

She asked me again about the power of prayer and visualization. We decided to act as if it had already happened and she was free. I asked her what it felt like to shop in a grocery store, watch a movie, buy a foreign magazine, or just move freely about. She played along and I just laid there and watched her come alive. I would prompt her every so often or laugh at her misconceptions of life on the outside.

That trip had a desperate feel to it, for we both knew we were at the end of our rope. We were battered and bruised and I think running out of faith. We spent most daylight hours at the Copa, but the majority of the trip was intimate. We made love constantly, day and night as if our lives depended on it. I'm certain it was a part of the absolute desperation we were feeling then. I just couldn't get enough of her, her smell, or the taste of her sweat. It was as though I was trying to take a piece of her with me. If this was going to be the last time we saw each other, I wanted to create the ultimate memory.

The last morning, we followed the same last day routine that we had become accustomed to. I dropped Adianec off, said goodbye to the family, and headed to the airport with a feeling of heaviness and emptiness weighing me down.

Chapter twenty-five

A FINAL EPIPHANY

Back in my other life in L.A. the next night, Barry said, somewhat apologetically that, "now that Adianec has the cash, she, and the money, might disappear. You know that's a possibility, right?"

It made me wonder, again, if I had kept my self emotionally distant enough to handle such an outcome. The old self-protective part of me actually wanted her to disappear. My relationship with her left me feeling vulnerable and anxious. At the same time, I had grown so close to her that I felt slighted by his lack of faith in her integrity.

"I know it's possible. So what? As I said before, who could blame her?"

For the next several weeks, Alain had us jump through a series of emotional hoops and manipulations as he tried every way imaginable to get Adianec to hand over the money. His story finally grew thin and he revealed himself to be the con man that he was.

It was raining when I went to Alain's house. I could see on his wife's face that it was over. How could I let my heart sink again, how could I tell Lee I had been fooled again? His wife admitted that he was not going to help me. It was a scam to make money so he could get off the island. She told me to go and forget about it. I went to my friend's house and cried. That was my last hope, and it washed away with the rain.

It had been almost a year and a half since we had first met. Nothing had been achieved, and every attempt at rescuing Adianec had failed. I didn't call her for a few days. I didn't call anyone...I was spent. I wasn't even angry this time, just dazed. When I did call her, she was the first to throw in the towel and say we couldn't do this anymore, that it was impossible. We decided to keep our options open but to get on with our individual lives. She said, "I need you happy again. You sacrificed too much."

It was what I would expect her to say. She was always thinking of others.

My friend Michael was going to Cuba, and said he would pick up the cash from her. Barry said, "Lee, if that cash actually makes it back, I'd be shocked. Prepare yourself." I had to agree. Why would she give it up if our relationship had all but come to an end?

She did give it back. Barry was shocked and I won the "Ass of the Year" award for not trusting her. From that point on, Barry was a fan of Adianec. He said that it showed a tremendous amount of integrity, and if he were in her position, "I don't think I could have given the money back. No way."

Now Barry and my other friends were coming up with ideas to help her, but I was too far gone to pay any real attention. They finally saw in her what I did, as someone who was truly special. I guess I had always known she was just another example of my need to rescue women. The difference this time was that I had failed.

Adianec and I spoke less frequently and my depression was compromising my ability to function. Several years prior I had gotten involved with a group called the *Art of Living*. They teach meditation, stress management and have worldwide charities. It is an incredible group of people including some very beautiful women. I went to meditate one night and through a series of events began to date one of those beautiful women, the yoga teacher. Barry was beyond happy that I was regaining my senses and nicknamed her, "Yoga Girl."

About three weeks after I started dating Yoga Girl, I was startled out of my sleep at 3 a.m. by another "epiphany." I stumbled out of bed, turned on the light and grabbed the map of Cuba I had hanging on the wall. The Coast Guard watches for boats in the Florida Straits, the ninety miles between Key West and Havana. Cuba knows this and patrols that area of their coast as well. What if I were to take a boat, (learn to drive it first, of course) 200 miles due east of Miami to the Bahamas, and then another 250 miles straight south and pick Adianec up on a deserted beach on the eastern side of Cuba. I knew those waters were dangerous for boats due to reefs, currents, storms and pirates. But certainly neither the U.S. nor Cuban Coast Guard would expect anyone to be that stupid...well they hadn't met me.

I was so excited by the prospect of rescuing her that I couldn't sleep at all that night. Immediately at dawn I called an old buddy who used to be a Navy

Seal. He loved the idea, until I asked him to come along. He said, "Buddy, even I'm not that crazy. Best I can do is help you with logistics."

I brought the map over to Barry's and he got caught up in my enthusiasm, or at least until his logical brain woke up. Yet he was on board, at least figuratively. But I had to promise to do it right, be prepared, and turn back at a moment's notice if things got too dangerous or didn't work out.

Barry brought in our friends, Bill and Phil. Bill was a writer and producer of a long running sit-com, and Phil was an insurance lawyer. They both grew up around boats on the East Coast and were both insane enough to get involved in this adventure. Their best piece of advice was to not to even *think* about making this trip unless I could find a Boston Whaler. Phil's brother said, "You won't have to worry about the Cuban Coast Guard. You'll quit or be dead before you even make it past the Bahamas." Great, thanks. He continued, "Do you know what you're looking at here? It's too difficult for a knowledgeable, experienced sailor and impossible for a novice, impossible."

Hmm, impossible…

I called Adianec immediately after and told her about my plan. She said she would have to think about it. She didn't want me to do anything dangerous. I said, "Look, every time we rely on someone else, we fail, right? We fail and keep failing, because we rely on others, but not this time. This time I'll be in control and it'll be up to me."

I really didn't like the idea of being on a boat alone in the middle of the ocean with no experience, but I didn't tell her that. I asked Bill, who is an adventurer at heart, if he would like to go along for the ride. Though he loved the idea, he and his wife were expecting their second child, so her response to him when he broached the idea came as no surprise.

I thought Lee was crazy to take a boat all around the Bahamas. He said it would be an innocent adventure, but I knew people died often in those waters. I trusted that he was smart and would be better prepared, but I didn't want him to be a part of this. I couldn't even think about the possibility of losing him.

I was up on my game again, but at this point, all my friends thought I'd lost what little bit of my mind I had left, so all they could do was wrap me in rubber and stand beside me. I told Yoga Girl that I had another plan to get Adianec out. "I'm not sure if it'll work or if I'm even going to go through with it, but I have to try."

She didn't seem too phased and didn't ask any questions. We were no closer than that first night we went out. Several weeks later, just before Christmas, she acted as though she had never even heard of my plan to get Adianec out. She politely asked me to leave.

One night over dinner, Lisa asked me, "Lee, do you realize you're planning on, literally, risking your life for a woman that you *still* won't admit to loving? That's unbelievable. That means you are either, insane, or not confronting the truth."

The real truth is, and I think most guys would agree, sometimes it's easier to commit to a physical act for another human being (that may take your life) than it is to commit to an emotional involvement that will leave you vulnerable. Cops and firemen risk and lose their lives everyday for strangers. I knew her, valued her and she was worth the risk.

For me the potential pain that comes with being vulnerable is worse than the prospect of death. I'd committed to helping her escape from tyranny and a life of repression. Why is that less noble or romantic than saying I love you? This plan and all past attempts to get her out represented my commitment to her.

I kept studying the sailing charts and found the perfect beach for her rescue. It was on an attached island, not far from where Adianec grew up, called *Cayo Coco*. It was almost due south of Andros Island in the Bahamas. We decided on one month from that day. The first week of January was just before the winter cold fronts blow in with northeastern storms. After that, we would have hurricane season, so it had to be our window.

The last year of my university training I had visited Cayo Coco, so I was familiar with it. I had my doubts it would work, but I trusted Lee. I called my friend Yanela and told her of the plan and said we need to make a reservation at Campismo. I was so tired I had lost my ability to judge what was possible, so I just let him continue with his plans and waited to see what would happen.

I didn't have a moment to waste, as I didn't know anything about boats. I've skied behind them, dove off of them, but they have always been within sight of shore, and I was never alone. I had to learn to read charts, plot a course, program a GPS and captain a boat…all in one month. Also, I also had to deal with that nausea thing. I tend to get seasick in a Jacuzzi.

I went to the coast guard station in Marina Del Rey, near Santa Monica, and lucked upon a cadet who gave me some tips on getting in and out of the country by water. Unfortunately, their boating course didn't start until February.

I began to spend all my free time on the internet. I learned that the vast majority of Cubans escaping to freedom do so by boat, and many drown in the process because they are trying to outrun coast guard boats or they are in un-seaworthy vessels. They attempt a midnight dash in high seas, or simply get in the water on an inner tube, raft or oil drum and hope the currents deliver them to Florida's shores. I was going to do none of those things. The guys and I had agreed I would obey all laws and stop on our way in if the U.S. Coast

Guard flagged us down. According to my cadet, getting flagged down was highly unlikely since we would be leisurely motoring in from the Bahamas.

I shared my new plan with all my friends except Jay, since he was a cop and I didn't want to get him into any situation that might jeopardize his career. I just told him I had a new plan. He knew not to ask any questions about it. Everyone I told was concerned about the legal ramifications, but in every case I read there was a precedent that it was not breaking the law to bring in a loved one. Cubans have the legal right to emigrate here freely. It was illegal if the person got paid. Not only was I not getting paid, I had already blown through my savings and was now sinking deep into credit card debt.

I studied ocean conditions every night before bed. Some days, my route had two-foot sea conditions, and other days it could be ten to twelve feet. I bought some charts and researched where I could stop and refuel on the way down. One thing that both Bill and Phil, experienced seamen, were concerned about was my running out of fuel. The biggest island in the Bahamas was Andros Island. It was a little over 100 miles long and ended ninety-five miles from Cayo Coco. The problem was it was mostly uninhabitable, which meant I had a longer run without fuel or help if I needed it. At some points I would be on my own, over a hundred miles away from any form of civilization. My midway point for fuel looked to be "Fresh Creek," a small marina on the upper third of Andros.

I wasn't too concerned about actually driving the boat. I was going to be in the open ocean, what could I hit? I cringe at the thought of my naiveté back then. Barry's sister-in-law, Joann, was an avid sailor who knew everybody in the Marina. She gave me the number of Sam, who I hoped could teach me everything about long distance boating, sea conditions, safety, chart reading, and navigation…all in four weeks!

Sam and I exchanged text messages and decided to meet that night at Marie Callender's in the Marina. Sam immediately became my all-time favorite teacher. She, all 5`8`` of her, slender and blonde, looked like she stepped off the cover of a southern California beach magazine. Beautiful Samantha was a captain of one of the pleasure cruise boats in the marina, and she was going to teach me to drive a boat so I could rescue Adianec. Proof that God has a sense of irony.

Over cherry pie a la mode, I told Sam my plan and the time constraints I was under. We went over the charts I'd brought and she found several areas of concern. One was the entrance into Fresh Creek. She read it out loud, "Due to barrier reef, only expert visual navigators should attempt and only in perfect daylight conditions." She looked up at me as if I should have an opinion.

I said, "It probably won't matter anyway, I've been told I don't stand much of a chance of surviving the Gulf Stream crossing." She took that into consideration, nodded, and never mentioned it again that night. Not exactly a confidence builder.

We had another problem. At the southern tip of Andros Island, there is a narrow government cut (man-made) through a very long barrier reef. The cut was on an ocean shelf that went from 6000 feet to 25 feet in depth. She said the wave action could be explosive. Trying to maneuver through that narrow cut would be tricky, but the only available route was to head back west forty miles, and then due south ninety miles to Cuba. I asked. "What do all the little asterisks dotting the chart on the forty mile backtrack and then continuing about half way to Cuba mean?"

She said, "Well, that's the other troubling thing. Those are warnings of rocks, just below the surface."

"What does that mean?"

"It means that there are rocks...just below the surface." We both laughed. "The water is very clear and shallow there, so you can see, but if you want to avoid them, you're going to just have to go slow. Very slow. I'll talk to my Dad about it."

Her father had sailed the Caribbean for decades and would hopefully be familiar with it, but in truth the area I was planning to venture into was pretty desolate. Sam told me that aside from pirates and smugglers, not many boats ventured through there. I had visions of dirty, long- bearded men with hooked hands, pegged legs and old English accents saying things to me like "Aarrrrgghhh."

She, like everyone else, was concerned about fuel. From my research on the twenty-seven-foot Boston Whaler, I learned that it had twin 225 horsepower engines and a 200-gallon tank. With its posted fuel consumption, I told her I should get to Fresh Creek with twenty gallons to spare, fill up the tanks and then land in Cayo Coco as she hits fumes.

Sam said. "You're not taking into consideration wind and currents." She explained about the added component to fuel consumption, wind and currents. A 200-mile leg would grow by as much as fifty miles, leaving me at least twenty miles short on fuel. "I thought I was paying you to deliver only good news." She smiled and looked down.

"So, is it possible for me to be prepared in four weeks?"

"If you're willing to study every book I give you and do practical work with me every other day? Then yes, you should be able to make the trip as long as there are no major problems."

There would have to be precautions. GPS with two backups, emergency transponders and a satellite phone, just in case I get washed off the boat. To make sure I had enough fuel, I'd strap an optional gas tank on the deck, thirty to fifty gallons should be enough.

That night I found a place in Miami that rented Boston Whalers. They had one in stock of the type I wanted. The reason why it had to be a Boston Whaler is because they say it is unsinkable - but they said that about a boat called the Titanic as well. I reserved it for a week starting January 4th. Now it all seemed real, there was no turning back. Although I was scared, I was also very excited. This was by far the biggest adventure I had ever been on. Actually it was the biggest I'd ever heard of. I figured two days to get there, two days on Cayo Coco and two days back with her on board, and if there were any problems we had an extra day.

As far as the Cuban authorities were concerned, I would simply dock at the marina in Cayo Guillermo, which was a much smaller key connected to Cayo Coco by a 200-yard long bridge, stay at one of four resorts there and go scuba diving. The second day of diving, I would leave early in the morning, pick Adianec up on the beach several miles away on Cayo Coco and head for home.

The boat I was renting would do up to forty five miles an hour, a bit faster than the old Soviet-era boats used by the Cuban Coast Guard. Samantha checked with her father about boats entering Cuban marinas. Sam's dad had docked near Cayo Coco many years ago and said it was a very beautiful area. He said, "the Cuban Coast Guard is notorious for confiscating boats. It's a well-known fact that they are modern day pirates." I had to make sure all paper work was in order. As an American arriving there by boat, I would undoubtedly arouse suspicion. Picking up Adianec on a beach could be tricky if they followed me, so I would have to establish, for a day, or maybe two, that I was heading out to dive.

There are only two access points to Cayo Coco. One is the ocean and the other is a several mile-long bridge, running through swamp land, connecting the Key to the mainland. Cubans, unless working at one of the tourist resorts on Coco or Guillermo, are forbidden to cross the bridge. The only exception is to get a special invitation to stay at Campismo, which is a beach campground on Cayo Coco. It is only for Cubans, and is by no means resort quality but it sits on a beautiful beach. The lucky invitees stay in one of the single-story cinder block dormitories. Somehow, a friend of Adianec's had gotten an invitation, and could bring Adianec. On the morning of the rescue, she would take a walk on the beach, and disappear. Her friends would report her missing and she would be presumed drowned.

My lessons with Sam were intense but also a blast. I learned how to program a nautical GPS, a compass and read charts to figure out manually the same thing. When the time came to actually drive a boat, we rented a twenty-one foot mid-console and headed out for a late afternoon cruise. The water leaving the inlet was choppy, making the boat feel very unstable and the air reeked of ammonia from the bird droppings on the breakers. Unable to hear because of the loud engine whining and the wind blowing, we were forced to communicate with hand signals. It was rough that day and every wave soaked and beat us up. I was getting seasick and the ginger pills with the acupressure wristbands only seem to work when the boat was tied up at the dock. I slowed up a bit to ask her if I should expect this rough a ride for my 800-plus mile journey. She said, "Well, you'll have a better boat. It'll be much more stable, but you should expect very high seas."

We continued out about fifteen miles and surprisingly the seas calmed to gentle rollers. With the constant California sea haze we were out of sight of land. We shut off the engine and sat there for a while as the sun began its fall into the western horizon. We talked about the loneliness and fears I would have to deal with alone at sea. "Feels pretty desolate out here, Sam."

"Yep, it does. Get used to it. I'm going to put in extra waypoints to keep your mind occupied but still you'll have to decide how to deal with the stillness."

"Good, I want the ocean still."

"Oh yeah, well, the ocean probably won't be. It's the solitude that will literally drive you crazy."

"It is a strange beauty out here, though, isn't it? I feel free."

"Yeah, I love that feeling."

I felt quite defenseless out there. The ocean was dark and murky with the haze seeming to close in on us. Being an adult, I know there is no such thing as sea monsters, but when you're out there, it does seem possible. Anyway, how do we really know? Surely any witnesses get eaten.

She gave me a quick nomenclature lesson to keep from running into things. "Port" is left, "Starboard" is right. You pass oncoming boats on your left. Very important in boating that you stay clear of things, as boats don't have brakes. "I wonder if my cell works out here."

"Not if I toss it in the water."

I couldn't get it out of my head that she said the ocean wouldn't be still. What was I going to do then? "I'm really concerned about fighting the waves. How bad do you think it will be?"

She looked at me, no joking at all. "Lee, it could be very bad. You need to prepare for that. My dad and I sailed those waters that are on your first leg. I trust my dad, but I was really scared one night, the squalls in that area come out of nowhere. And the waves can hit fifteen to twenty feet. He sailed the waters around Cuba and he said they were very treacherous."

My throat tightened. "Sam, I can't do that. Seriously I wouldn't be able to handle that" I was waiting for her to contradict me. "Would I?"

"No, not up until a few years ago, not a chance, not at your level." Oh shit. "But technology has really gotten better since then and you have people virtually with you the whole time. I'd call in every hour if I were you. But regardless, you will hit big seas."

"I think I just wet myself."

"You will."

I called Adianec and told her about my adventure. My excitement was contagious, affecting our conversation, even in our code. We called the boat a "car" and Miami now became "San Francisco." Hopefully, our conversations about driving to San Francisco would fall on apathetic ears.

My nights were spent researching the internet, pouring over every last detail of the plan in my head and studying for my "finals," because Sam was going to test me. I learned how the earth was divided into quadrants, and I finally understood the importance of latitude and longitude lines. Even though I was learning a great deal quickly, I never deceived myself into thinking that I could drop my guard for even a second. What I was doing was very dangerous at any skill level. And extremely stupid according to my friends.

After a few boat rides with Sam, she said it was time to fly solo. In boating, leaving and re-entering the dock are the dangerous and difficult tasks. This was definitely a challenge for me, and I threw splinters, hitting the wooden dock more than once. I had fears of docking at Fresh Creek where they had a narrow dock slip with an eight-knot cross-current racing out to sea. The first time I soloed, I never even left the dock area, I just kept circling around and re-entering the dock. Some salty old seaman came up and jumped on my boat and within twenty minutes had me making perfect landings. Afterward I bought the old man a beer and told him my plans. He gave me a half-toothless grin, shook his head and said, "Yes, yes, yes," like he knew exactly what I was talking about. He told me, "With twin motors, boy, you can turn that boat on a dime, just by using the throttles."

He explained the technique to me and said to practice out at sea before I came into Fresh Creek. It would help with the current. I asked him if he thought I'd make it, and he said, "Buy me another beer, and you'll make it."

Barry wanted me to do a trial run, fly to Cuba and stay at a resort in Cayo Guillermo to check the place out. That, of course, would be the intelligent thing to do, but I had problems. I didn't want to tell Barry that I was broke, and this upcoming venture was going to put me over $15,000 in credit card debt. Also if someone recognized me on my return with the boat, I would have some explaining to do. Lastly, and most importantly, I just didn't have the time. Besides, when have I ever done the intelligent thing?

Not only was Adianec getting more excited, she was growing more confident as well. She said she looked forward to taking the "car" to "San

Francisco." I was beginning to feel a bond between us, and I wondered if it had always been there or if it was forged out of our struggles. I was feeling energized that finally our future was in our hands.

With Christmas just a few days away, I wondered if it would be the last one that Adianec would be forbidden to celebrate. I had become very circumspect of my fortunate life since I met Adianec. Just being allowed to celebrate the birth of Jesus, Hanukkah or Kwanzaa, or anything else you might choose, is something I have always taken as a birthright. The diversity of expression that we as Americans take for granted is something Cubans are forbidden to even dream of without fear of persecution. The more I began to realize and appreciate these things, the more I knew I would expect a deeper sense of humanity in myself in the future. She had changed me.

I went out and Christmas shopped for her. I bought her some clothes, I was doing all I could to draw her to the U.S. I spent Christmas Eve with Jay, his large extended family and friends, including Jay's father and mother who had come up from San Diego. It was, and is, a warm place to be over the holidays. The way that Tammy Sue, his wife, decorates their home, it feels like you're in the northeast with snow surrounding the house. There were fat Santas and elves everywhere. The Christmas tree had brightly colored gifts double-stacked out four feet from the base, Tons of presents and family that was my idea of the Christmas spirit.

I called Adianec and everyone took turns on the phone to wish her a Merry Christmas and safe journey. Because of Jay's job as a cop, I still hid the details from him, so all he knew was that something was happening in about a week. Jay's mom, in her intuitive grace, gave me several gifts that she thought I might need. One of those items would end up saving my ass in the next two weeks.

When Lee called me from Jay's house I could feel the love and warmth that I had read about in Christmas stories. They were all very nice on the phone, and I felt as though I was there. I thought I could even taste some of the food Lee and Jay were trying to describe to me, except for the thing called "egg nog." The laughter in the background sounded so beautiful. I have come to realize that Jay had the same sense of humor that Lee had, and they both would laugh at their own jokes. It was the best Christmas I ever had. I could feel with confidence that one day I would be with that family for Christmas.

The next two weeks flew by. I was constantly preoccupied with every single detail of my trip. I had my team; Barry would be the contact who I would call from the satellite phone, Phil would give final instructions and Bill would be the weatherman. If Bill said to stop or go back, that was the deal, he was to keep me out of trouble ahead. He had found a website that had accurate real-time weather and sea conditions. Bill also had a copy of my waypoints and would get updates from Barry on my progress. Barry had a page of phone numbers to call and keep my mom and friends updated.

Weeks earlier Sam and I had gone over every detail of the chart. She had set up a series of waypoints. These points are coordinates on a map that pinpoint an exact spot. From these waypoints, I would have to make a directional change and on long straight runs, she would set a waypoint in the middle just to give me a sense of accomplishment.

Adianec and I spoke on the phone the night before my departure. This would be the last time we'd speak until I picked her up on the beach. If something went wrong with either one of us, we would have no way to pass on the information. There was no excitement in either of our voices, just anxiety. "I can't talk long baby. I'm tired and need to sleep tonight."

"Okay, my love, you have all you need?"

"I do, yes, for sure, it's all good. I'm really looking forward to being alone for a few days, the wind, the sea spray, the vomit…hmm, can't wait."

We both tried to laugh. "I need you to be careful. I need you in my life."

I tried to dismiss the danger, and play it off as the ultimate guy fantasy. "Honey, this is a guy's dream. I am the envy of Los Angeles, trust me. I wouldn't do it if it were dangerous."

She wasn't quite buying it. "I'm sorry, I just don't want you to go. We can stop now." Her voice became more desperate. "Let's stop now, Amore. Fly out to see me tomorrow instead."

"And miss my chance at an adventure. Stop being such a chick."

"Promise to turn back if the water gets big."

"I promise. Now, we're all set, right? You know where and when to meet."

"Yes, yes, it's all written in my *mente*, my mind."

"Well, alrighty then, matey, I should cast off."

"What?" I think it was the Popeye voice that confused her.

"Sailor talk, baby."

"Wait, one more thing. I really, really love you crazy deep. Please don't do this. I'm really scared."

"I'm scared I may have to turn in my balls if I back out now. I'll see you in a few days and then for as long as I don't bore you."

"Never."

"*Te quierdo mi amore.*" I could never say "I love you" to her in English… too real.

"I love you, too. *Mucho… Amore*, please go back if the water get big" Her voice began to quiver and fade.

We wished the other good luck. Within a few days, she would be free, or we would be in jail, or worse. She was terrified that I would disappear at sea. I didn't want to concern her, "Don't worry. It's an easy ride. It's a pleasure cruise. I'm going to get to see things I'd never see otherwise."

I didn't sleep that night and had a very busy day at work. Always the same things when you're trying to leave town. Life doesn't simply stop because you're going on an adventure to rescue a woman from a communist dictator. There's still work, bills, your responsibilities. After work I grabbed my three large bags, full of scuba gear, boating gear, and everything else I would need, then headed to Barry and Lisa's house for dinner.

Even though it felt a bit melodramatic, I made a verbal will with Barry prior to leaving. I gave him the combination to my safe where had a bag full of gold coins. He was to periodically send money to Cuba. I said to tell my mother that all my future residuals should go to Adianec as well. My mother was my beneficiary with the Screen Actors' Guild. I knew everything would turn out okay, I was just trying to dot all the i's.

I'm usually a pretty upbeat guy, but that night I felt like I was trying to punch my way out of a rubber bag. I was in a foul mood. My flight was to leave just before midnight, but at 9:00 p.m. I told them to take me to LAX. I had had enough of waiting around.

The plan was intricately laid out. I would arrive in Miami just after 6 a.m., grab a rental car, and pick up enough supplies, food and water to last a week on the boat. Then I'd stop by the hotel we would stay at when we returned and drop off Adianec's tickets, clothes and personal papers she would need. Next I'd drop gear and food off at the dock, check out the boat and get the key, take the rental car back to the airport and then a taxi to the boat. I would head out by 9 a.m. with enough time to cross the Gulf Stream and dock in Fresh Creek hours before sunset…easy. What is that joke about telling God your plans?

"The rescue attempt"

Chapter twenty-six

JANUARY 5, 2006

I checked in at the terminal and headed to the gate where I was told the flight was delayed two hours. That would cut into the sunset time buffer I had given myself and perhaps put me into rougher seas. The marine forecast for my first leg said seas in the morning would be two to four feet, increasing to eight feet by afternoon. The thought of the large waves made my stomach turn. I had attempted to memorize all my coordinates in case I lost my charts and the pre-loaded GPS unit. As I went through my bag, I could not find my handheld ship to shore radio. Without that, I had no way of calling for help in case of emergency, or calling the dock masters to advise them of my arrival, which is mandatory. I would have take time to pick one up in Miami.

Out of sheer exhaustion, I fell asleep and woke up to the pre-boarding announcement. I looked at my watch and saw that we were thirty minutes beyond the delay time. The plan was in motion. I couldn't change anything now and there was no way to contact Adianec. I would just have to have faith that I could reach Fresh Creek before sunset, which was just over 200 miles from Miami. The manufacturer's stated top speed for the twenty-seven-foot Boston Whaler is forty-five mph; I would need every bit of that.

When I finally got my bags and rental car in Miami, it was just past 10 a.m. I should have been on the water an hour earlier. I had to do so much running around in a city that I was unfamiliar with, something was going to have to give. I decided to forgo dropping off Adianec's things at the hotel. I'd just find a good place to hide them on the boat. The e-mail that she sent me pick-up instructions and a phone number, with I would memorize on the ride to Cuba and toss it at sea.

I pulled up to the dock in a controlled panic. It was a beautiful day with a few heavy white clouds hanging in the sky. The marina was very big, filled with an array of ships, a few so large and high tech they looked like floating UFO's. There were ships' masts reaching into and filling the sky as far as I could see to my left and right. My excitement was building. I carried all my bags to the dock and walked over to take a look at the "rescue vessel." It was magnificent, much roomier than it looked on the internet. It appeared to be about twelve feet wide and could fit ten people. It would be very comfortable for two.

I was at Yanela's house with my family when Lee was supposed to leave on the boat. It was even more difficult because we had not been able to speak for a couple days, due to Yanela not having a phone. I knew if something happened to Lee I would never forgive myself. But Lee is not a person that you can tell what to do or not to do, that is the man he is. I wished, though, that he would be careful and not take any unnecessary risks. Even though he said the trip was going to be easy, I knew that was not the case.

Still frazzled and short on time, I checked in with the manager inside the store, who told me, "It'll be ready in about forty minutes."

"Oh, uh, actually I have to pick up my brother in the Keys in two hours and I really need it in fifteen minutes if that's alright."

He said he'd get someone on it right away. I made it back to the boat in twenty-five minutes. I was now four hours behind schedule.

I jumped on my freshly washed boat and popped a seventies rock CD, a little Springsteen, some Bon Jovi (and AC/DC for increased heart rate) into the boat's sound system, something to lift me up as I prepared and unpacked my bags. Batteries for the GPS and drinking water were both kept very close, Balance bars and Red Bull in a dry, handy compartment. There was a seafood restaurant with outdoor dining on the other side of the dock eight feet away. The diners were watching me with envy thinking I was going out for a day of relaxation. As an actor I've played a range of different roles, so this was just one more. I was acting like I had been doing this my whole life.

The manager came on board and went over the different systems; toilet, lights, engines and so on. He told me I could go all the way down to Key West, but to stay within twenty miles of shore, "Seas are very rough today." As a side joke, that I'm sure he has overplayed for years, he poked me and said, "No quick trips to Cuba for you boys!" For a moment I thought that my cover had been blown, and then we both burst out in laughter. I asked him, "Could you do me a favor and turn the engines over while I stow the scuba gear?" Another ruse. I watched him intently out of the corner of my eye as he went through the procedure. Hopefully, I'd remember it the next morning. When the first motor turned over, it rumbled like a Harley Davidson. This was pure guy stuff and my adrenaline was pumpin'.

I had brought a packet of earthquake wax, so I fastened down the GPS and my video camera onto the dash. I needed the GPS so I could easily glance down as I was driving and the camera was to keep a video diary of Adianec's rescue (my friend Kevin wanted to make a documentary). I slowly backed out of the slip without bumping the dock; a small victory. I turned her around and headed into the causeway, which was so filled with other boaters I had to wait my turn as if I were on an on-ramp to a freeway. As I passed under the causeway bridge, I looked up and watched the cars pass over the grates above. Even though I had felt almost paralyzed with anxiety when I first boarded, being the captain of that boat made me feel powerful and my senses were very acute. As I passed yachts heading in the other direction, the passengers would wave and smile, like we were all part of some wealthy, secret club. I would confidently tip my cap and hoped that they hadn't painted "RENTAL" on the side of my boat.

I made a quick call to Barry and my sister as I passed within 100 or so yards of a docked cruise liner towering above me, amazed that something so heavy could float. I picked the speed up a bit. The inlet seemed so far away, and I had to make up a great deal of time. Moments later, I heard a siren. I was being pulled over for speeding. The sheriff's boat pulled up along side me, and the sheriff asked, "Where you from?"

"L.A., sir," I said sheepishly.

"Around here we relax when we take our boats out...slow down."

He smiled. "Yes sir" I said laughing.

He spun his boat back around, leaving me shaking.

I studied the waterfront mansions on either side of me as I slowly passed by, knowing the next time I saw them Adianec would be beside me. She had never before seen such architecture or landscaping. I loved the idea of what her reaction might be. The closer I got to the inlet, the more chaotic the water became. My throat tightened as I headed out to sea.

As I passed through the inlet, I felt immediately alone. I had no idea what lay ahead. All I saw was water and a few boats. This ocean was more turbulent than the Santa Monica Bay. The color of the Atlantic started to turn dark very quickly. I pushed the throttles down and opened up the full force of 225 hp. I was skimming across the tops of the waves at thirty-eight miles per hour, heading straight out to sea. My whole body was shaking from nervous adrenaline. It didn't take long before I was the furthest boat out in the ocean.

I looked back at the diminishing skyline. The boat was getting more difficult to stabilize as the sea seemed to get bigger.

Suddenly, there was a wall of water building up both in front of and to the right of me. I quickly pulled the throttles back but it was too late. I slammed into what seemed to be a five or six-foot wave and got drenched and banged up as it broke all around me. The water was warm and salty. It was simultaneously frightening and exhilarating. The boat seemed to handle the large wave well but it had pushed me off course a few degrees. As I looked back again at a barely visible Miami, I got hit by another big wave, this time knocking me clear off my feet. I jumped up quickly and grabbed the wheel as a third wave, much bigger than the previous two, came and spun the boat sideways. I was fast losing the ability to stay on course.

Things continued to deteriorate the deeper I plunged into the Gulf Stream. The waves started to come from every direction and I was fighting as hard as I could just to get back on course. As soon as I would realign, I would get hit from another direction. I was getting worried that I had made a terrible mistake and was just not strong enough or experienced enough to handle this on my own. I started to panic and pray for a way out "God, don't do this to me! Not now. I need help, need you, I can't do this on my own."

I was almost turned over by a heavy eight-foot wave. There was no let up now. The waves were spinning the boat around so violently and constantly I could only focus on the GPS. I had no idea what was coming next.

Water, foam, sky and a spinning horizon were all jumbled together. I was repeatedly getting slammed to the wet, slippery deck. When a really big wave would hit, I could hear the boat's fiberglass hull cracking. The steering wheel had a knob on it, making it easier to spin the wheel for docking with one hand. If I wasn't being slammed to the deck, I was being pummeled onto that steering knob, which kept stabbing me in my solar plexus. The same spot every time. Soaking wet, I kept yelling, I had no idea who it was directed at but it did seem to keep me focused. "Come on, bring it to me! Is that all you got? Load this baby up! Let's do this!"

There was no respite and I knew I was in serious trouble. Now I was really yelling at the heavens trying to conquer my fears. "More, more, come on, bring me more." Apparently, there was more. "AAAAHHHHH, FFFFAAAAKKKK!!! OKAY, OKAY, no more, God please."

How could this be? I was in disbelief, but I didn't see how I was going to make it across the Gulf Stream. All my stupidity was rushing out to greet me now. I hadn't put on a life vest, nor did I put the spare GPS or phone on my person in case I was thrown overboard, which meant no one could find me. At one point, I could no longer read the shaky GPS screen. Things were racing by so fast, my vision was blurred, I just tried to keep the sun over my right shoulder, but even the sun was spinning around. I was being tossed around in a huge ocean, but my world felt very small just then. The only thing that existed for me was the cockpit of my boat. I was only twenty-five minutes in, and I remembered her words "Baby, please go back if the water gets big." I had failed her. I was going to disappear in this vast ocean, and she would never know what had happened to me. I thought to turn around but…

With every big wave, I was taking in a mouthful of salt water and choking. When I would vomit, which was quite often, I'd just let it fly over the controls and steering wheel or myself. It didn't matter. The next wave would completely wash it all away. I didn't have time to turn my head, and besides, during that hour I really didn't care.

I was getting hit hard from every side, and sometimes it even felt like the waves were coming from above me. I thought to tie myself to the captain's chair, but even a distracting thought was dangerous. My muscles were beginning to tire; I was concerned that my strength would give out soon. Another big wave picked up my boat and slammed her on the port rail, sending me flying toward open water. As I hit, I instinctively started grabbing. I thought I had been thrown overboard, but I felt the solidness of the deck beneath me. I hugged the plastic buoy that hung over the side of the rail, and I lay there for a moment. I was sliding back and forth on the deck, my face in warm salty water and foamy vomit. I now saw everything in slow motion. I was whining and growling, a strange place between begging for my life and the obstinacy of an aging prize fighter. "Not going down, not going down, keep fightin,' come on, Lee, you're not going down!

The engines were still engaged and the steering wheel looked possessed as it spun wildly back and forth on its own. Another huge wave picked us up and spun the boat around and up on her rail again. The ocean was rushing into the boat and I thought the boat was taking on water. I just thought, "Okay, I'm done. Time for a nap."

I slid to the captain's chair and grabbed the support pole amid the chaos of crashing waves. At times, the boat seemed to stand almost straight up. I pulled myself off the deck and the boat luckily was thrown in the perfect direction. I was almost pushed to the wheel. I was yelling and growling. No words now, just sounds. I had no idea where the growling came from. I didn't even know I could growl. I stabilized with a wide stance and pinned my body against the chair, locking my elbows like a steel bar, while tightly wrapping my fingers around the wheel. I fought for what seemed an eternity. I had lost my sense of time.

I was still making those bizarre, primitive growling sounds with every heave of vomit, when I realized, I was holding my own. It remained a scary, tough fight, but the waves were no longer breaking my grip. I was still being slammed into the wheel, but at least I wasn't in jeopardy of being thrown over board. The primitive growl was replaced with a primitive howl of celebration. "YEEEEEES!!"

These were not sounds I had made before or could replicate now, nor would I want to. Just to my right, I saw that I was about to cross paths with a large freighter. I was able to slip through first and narrowly avoided its tremendous wake. I was able to glance at my shaky GPS again, and saw I was seven miles from my Bimini waypoint, North Rock. I must have been fighting for a couple of hours. I tentatively reached down and picked up the buoy and put it to my waist. When I would drop into a trough between waves, I would wrap the line around me again. It took five waves to completely tie it off, and with every other trough I would slip the radio, satellite phone and spare GPS into my jacket pocket. At least then if I was thrown overboard I could call for help and give my location. With every mile, the waves seemed to decrease. My distress did not.

I was throwing up pretty often, and violently now. My belly was full of warm salt water and it would turn to foam and distend my stomach. Vomiting gave me a moment of relief before the salt water would create more of that awful foam which was all over my clothes and control panel. There were no more waves breaking over the hull to clean me, just a constant spray. In the past couple of hours, I had seen myself growl, howl, pray for salvation, and consistently and violently vomit on myself. A humbling trip so far, but it appeared I just might survive, for now.

The waves, now only two to three feet and all coming from the same direction, gave me the opportunity to pick up speed again. For a moment, I thought I saw the rise of land on the horizon ahead of me. I pushed the throttles forward and was skipping wave top to wave top at over twenty mph. It was a rough ride and I had a pounding headache, but I had to get out of this place.

I made the decision that I would stop in Bimini for the night, and then turn back for Florida in the morning when the seas were calmer. I was simply not prepared for this assault. I couldn't do it. I had survived so far, but I couldn't do it any more. I was so seasick and spent I just wanted to drown myself.

The water was becoming lighter in color, a pretty cobalt blue. It was definitely land that I saw ahead. I sprayed the console with vomit again, seawater and stomach acid make for a powerful explosive. A couple miles from land and the ocean calmed to less than a foot. The water was taking on different colors as the bottom changed and became shallower. I was now skimming across the water at forty mph. A half mile from my first waypoint and my environment became a paradise. The water was effervescent blues and greens. I had Bimini a couple hundred yards to my right and other little islands were starting to pop up into view. The water was now as smooth as in a bathtub, and I was racing into a postcard.

I was sick and exhausted, but on an adrenaline high having just gone through the toughest physical and mental challenge of my life. I changed my mind, about stopping. I was going on to Cuba.

Several miles on the other side of Bimini and I was in an area out of a surrealist painting. The sky was a brilliant blue with a few scattered clouds hanging around. The water was crystal clear. I could see the sand on the bottom, not even twenty feet below. There was an occasional deep hole in the sea floor that made the water take on an artificial aqua blue color. It was so beautiful it seemed unreal. It looked like the Ti-D-Bowl Man had been there. It was beauty and freedom all rolled into one. I could no longer see land but was able to make out a large sailboat many miles away. Even though my throat and nose were raw from so much stomach acid and my head was pounding, I knew I was blessed to have been in that spot at that moment.

Suddenly, my port motor seized up and a warning light started flashing and beeping on the system's monitor. One motor was dangerously overheated. I started to panic. With just one engine, I could only do fifteen mph. I had broken down in the middle of the ocean and had no idea how to call for help (no AAA card). Then I realized, "Ah shit, I'm going to be out here in the open ocean at night!"

I took the opportunity to stop, wash off and drink some water. I hadn't stopped throwing up, I was still full of salt water. The ocean was totally flat and probably had no current. I turned on the satellite phone and called Barry. He was as pumped as I was. We were both cussing with bravado on who was the toughest MF on the planet. I promised to call whenever, if ever, I reached Fresh Creek.

The day before Lee was to arrive in Cuba, I knew he was on the boat heading towards me. He had told me not to worry. Many of his friends take boats through these waters all the time. And there would always be a boat near him. He said it was like a popular road with many people, and there were no waves. He said it would be too easy, but still I worried for him.

I was with my mother and sister at my friend Yanela's house. We were having a celebration dinner. My mother was very sad that day. She is my best friend. But I was laughing and having fun. I knew that my life was going to be different from now on. I gave away my clothes, shoes and the books that Lee had brought me. I called some friends in Havana and said goodbye in our secret way, so they would know I was leaving now.

We were laughing and talking about America, and my sister was so upset that I was happy about leaving. I wasn't happy about leaving my family, I was happy to be free. I called a guy Yanela knew to see if he would drive us in two days. I had four other people coming with me to the Campismo-Yanela, her friend, her brother and the guy that was going to drive us. Only Yanela knew our plan.

I pulled out five life vests, put one on, and didn't take it off again while I was on the boat. The other four I tied to the rope lines on the front, back and sides of the boat, so I would have something to grab onto if I fell over. I thought about the tens of thousands of Cubans that get into that same water, 200 miles to the south, many of them doctors, lawyers and educated people that in a normal society would have a desirable life. They climb onto inner tubes and rafts, willing to die rather than live under a tyrant. Adianec knew many people that left under those conditions and were never heard from again.

I cleaned my sunglasses and put on sunscreen, I was Mr. Safety now. I saw on the console that the engine temperature had dropped. I said a quick prayer to my father, who had died about eight years earlier. "Okay, Dad, you want to redeem yourself? Now would be a good time. Please talk to whoever you can up there. I really need your help and guidance. I'm in a jam, pretty fuckin' scared. Come on, Pops, "Dead Dad of the Year Award" is in the balance here. Let's make up for lost time."

I hit the button and the engine started, that perfect Harley rumble. "That's it Dad." I cranked up the starboard engine and I was on my way. I was cruising at forty miles per hour through the Great Bahama Bank. The Bank is a giant underwater land mass that the Bahama Islands sit on top of. It surrounds all the islands. You can be sixty miles from shore and be in ten feet of water. I never saw it get much deeper than thirty feet on the Bank, and it covers about 45,000 square miles. I had a bit more than 100 of those miles straight ahead of me until my next waypoint.

The water was as smooth as glass, and I was flying over a kaleidoscope of colors. That boat was so true I just sat back in the captain's chair and every five minutes or so softly tapped the wheel with my foot to adjust us back on course. If it hadn't been for the rapidly setting sun it would have been nirvana. I didn't want to accept the fact that I was not going to make Fresh Creek before sunset. If that was the case, I was going to have to stay out in the ocean until sunrise, when I could visually make my way through the barrier reef. I started to yell at the sun to stay up. "Come on! Just a little bit longer! You can do it! Here, I offer you a sacrificial Red Bull to give you wings!" It's funny how when you're alone in nature it doesn't seem so schizophrenic to be talking to yourself or inanimate objects, like the sun.

I was doing all I could to entertain myself so I wouldn't panic. The Red

Bull didn't help the sun, though. It took a little over two hours to travel to the next waypoint. A few boats had passed in the distance here and there. The sun was on the horizon behind me and dusk was quickly setting in. I looked around for the moon, nothing. It was going to be a very dark night and I wondered if I should anchor right there where it was shallow. Once I made the turn at my next waypoint, I would head into the Tongue of the Ocean. It was 6,000 feet deep, a tad more than my anchor line.

That last two and a half hours had been incredibly relaxing. I had stopped for several minutes and set up the running lights and pole light. I organized everything I would need to find in the dark: local charts for reefs, flood light, and water. I was concerned about reading the GPS in the dark. If I kept the unit's internal light on, I would lose battery power before reaching Fresh Creek and that would be devastating. Then I remembered the tiny LED light that Jenny, Jay's mom, had given me for Christmas. It had a small clip on it to attach to the bill of a hat. I rigged it up with earthquake wax and shined it directly on the GPS screen. Without that little 1/8 inch light, I would have been flying blind. I drank a Red Bull and ate a Balance bar to keep me up for the next sixty miles. I pushed down the throttles and headed into the darkness that lay ahead of me.

The sun had set but there was still a little light, and had I not been in such dire straights, it would have been breathtaking. The Bahama Islands were now appearing all around me in the soft light. Straight ahead, I thought I could make out the lights of Nassau, and the northern tip of Andros was very clearly coming up on my right. I was feeling confident that I could make Fresh Creek. "C'mon, man, you can do this. It'll be an adventure, something to tell the grandkids. You can do this."

Within minutes, someone had flipped a switch and I was racing into total darkness. Aside from the wind, I had no sense of movement until I hit the "Tongue." Although it didn't feel dangerous, just one-foot swells, it was a weird sensation bouncing off waves I couldn't see. But in my extensive maritime career, I'd seen worse. I just kept my eye on the GPS. Continuing was an act of faith due to being blinded by the all-encompassing black canvas that was wrapped around me. After a while, I could begin to make out the dots of faraway lights in the blackness. I didn't have a sense of the distance because there was no separation of earth and sky.

Samantha, in her infinite wisdom, had set the last waypoint five miles into the Tongue, passing Andros and then back in at a twenty degree angle into Fresh Creek, creating an upside-down "V-route" instead of skimming the coast. The barrier reef on Andros notoriously jumps in and out of the coast. It can lay right offshore or pop out several miles. I looked at the chart and decided to save some time and cut a mile off my jetting out into the ocean. I canceled the next waypoint and set the GPS for Fresh Creek.

Fresh Creek has a light marker buoy at the entrance of the cut through the reef. It is a yellow light that blinks four times and then stops for several seconds. Every port along Andros has its own color and cadence. I spotted the one for Fresh Creek. It looked like it was just in front of me but that was an illusion due to the darkness. It was actually ten miles away.

Because of the difficulty in judging distance, I swept right past the light buoy when I arrived, almost hitting it. I spun back around to come up on it and stopped to look at the chart and re-familiarize myself with the route. Within seconds, the current had pushed me past the light. I had to keep spinning back in the murky darkness, as I studied the chart. The route in zigzagged through coral heads leading into the inlet for the marina. Even though I was only a half-mile off shore, it was so dark I couldn't see land and had to use my compass to know in which direction to head. The current was confusing me until I realized I was contending with two currents, the ocean and the one ripping out of Fresh Creek that the chart had warned of. I glanced at the other warning on the chart that said, "Expert visual navigators should attempt only in perfect daylight and weather conditions."

I found that amusing. I'm a seasick novice from Los Angeles, first time alone on a boat and in total darkness… Shouldn't be too much of a stretch!

I turned on my searchlight (quad zillion candle power) and sat on the rail of the boat. The boat was throttled at about two mph. I had my left hand on the wheel and the light in my right. I leaned over and shined the light into the murk below me. The light lit up an amazing world of coral, rocks, sand and beautifully colored fish.

I kept the edge of the coral just to my right. The chart was pretty accurate on when to zig or when to zag. After ten minutes, it looked like I was going to run right into the beach and then, like magic, an entrance opened up to the right. Once inside the small inlet, I could see the lights of the marina. It had about twenty-five slips with five or six boats docked. Some of the boaters were on the softly lit dock having cocktails and laughing. I could see the water rushing by me. The current was very swift, over five knots. I slowly pulled up about ten yards out from the end of the slip and made my turn in. By the time the turn was complete, I was halfway back out to the inlet. I flipped around and tried again. This time I pulled up beyond the slip. After my fifth try I had my nose in the slip and gave a little gas to head in. The current was still pushing my boat sideways and slammed the port side right into the dock, shaking the entire marina. Some drunken sailor yelled out, "Yep, that's the dock, found 'er."

I turned off the engines and smiled back at the group. "Thanks, couldn't have done it without ya."

"Ya know you were supposed to back in."

We all laughed, but under my breath I muttered, "Assholes!"

The Dockmaster showed up as I was tying her to the dock. He looked a bit bewildered and asked where I had just come from. I told him, "Miami. Why?"

I acted as if it was an easy jog over. "Alone?" he said incredulously.

I started to unpack as he spoke, hoping he would go away. "Uh huh."

"All that way alone, and then you came through the reef alone…in the dark?"

"Uh huh."

He stood staring at me with hands on his hips and mouth agape. I could tell he was trying to come up with something to say. He just shook his head and walked away. I felt happy to be making so many new friends.

I took off my weather gear and discovered that my clothes were soaked with sweat and sea water. Fresh Creek was quiet and peaceful. Aside from my new best friends. The air was still and warm. I could see across the other side of the creek, which was less than 200 yards wide, that there were several small buildings. On my side, the small "lighthouse marina" was down a grass hill from a two-story motel. On the other side of the motel, hidden from my view, was a liquor and food store. Even though Andros is the largest of the Bahama Islands, 100 x 40 miles, it is also one of the least habitable.

I walked up the short flight of stairs to the motel and into the lobby. My ears were buzzing from the sound of the engines over the past eight hours, which left me feeling somewhat disoriented and physically and emotionally drained. I asked for a room for the night. The hotel had about twenty rooms and a restaurant.

I called Barry on the satellite phone and Lisa answered. It was comforting to hear a familiar voice. She was very excited and wanted all the details. I told her to call me back on the room line. She and Barry got on the phone and we laughed for the next ten minutes at all the insane things I'd done. "Unbelievable, you are fucking unbelievable."

Lisa asked, "Well, how was it, how are you?"

"The second half was absolute heaven, well, until the sun went down and left me floundering in the dark."

Barry said it was crazy, but you could just tell he was shaking his head in amazement. Lisa was less excited. "Yeah, quite a story to tell."

Barry let me know that Bill was "shocked and happy you made it. His brother said you'd be lost or dead by now. Lucky, huh?"

Lisa never quite understood what I was trying to accomplish. "Well, you proved you could do it. Maybe you should turn back now, before it gets too bad."

Gets? "It already got. But I did get very lucky today." I knew I got lucky. I wasn't taking anything for granted. They didn't want me to take any more risks. I understood that. "Okay, well I ordered some food, so I better…I'll call on the sat phone sometime tomorrow."

"If you need anything…" Barry didn't even have to say it, but I could tell he had something else to say. "Lee? I know you don't want to hear this, but Bill said a cold front is moving in. Weather is going to get really bad. He said get in, grab her and get home."

My gut tightened. "Yeah, that's the plan, Stan. Okay, good night."

My optimistic mood plummeted. I was scared again, but I knew if I gave in to fear I was done. I had to stay positive- Get in, grab her, and get home.

After the call, I took a shower and watched CNN as I ate the dinner I'd ordered from the restaurant, a salad and fried Conch. Watching CNN was like having a friend beside me. Like a security blanket it's comforting to have something familiar when you're in strange surroundings. My ears were still ringing and my senses were shot, so I really couldn't taste the food but I needed the nourishment. I fell asleep until around 2 a.m. Sleep didn't last long due to unpleasant dreams.

I walked outside and down to the dock. The dock lights were off, but the moon had risen and was casting a glow on the whole marina. It was low in the sky, so it made very long shadows. A slight warm breeze was rustling the palm trees and a giant white bird was gliding just above the surface of the water. I thought to myself that I would like to revisit such serene beauty, on better circumstances, sometime later in my life.

Chapter twenty-seven

INTO THE UNKNOWN

I took another restless nap, and woke up at 5:30 a.m. I dressed in the dark and went outside. With the help of a small flashlight, I negotiated my way along a narrow path that led to the beach and lighthouse. I sat and meditated on the dark beach. The sun's glow was beginning to show straight ahead over the Tongue of the Ocean.

The "Tongue" is a 6,000 foot deep oceanic trench that cuts through the Bahama Islands, and is, as the name implies, shaped like a tongue. It's about 20 miles wide and over 100 miles long. It is unusual because the 6,000 foot drop can be immediate, sometimes right off shore. The average depth before the plunge is about twenty-five feet. All my charts had numerous warnings about the area, almost all due to the reefs and currents, but the most ominous was the warning about smugglers and pirates. I would be racing through that area in about five hours.

A half hour after I had sat down, the sun was beginning to break the horizon. Through the golden streaks of light, I could begin to make out the miracle I had performed the night before. The water was a sheet of glass with rocks, coral and a string of barrier reefs popping up sporadically, creating a maze in the water. Even with sunlight I couldn't see a way through it all. How I blindly stumbled my way through in the dark could only be explained by divine intervention.

I took stock of my luck from the previous day; it had been a study of contrasts. Brave and stupid, life threatening and miraculous, the most harrowing day of my life, and conversely the one most filled with beauty and peace. I was apprehensive about what lay ahead. Thinking about it and allowing the full weight of what I was doing to sink in made me start to shiver. I started to get up to go and prepare the boat, but my legs were shaking so badly, I had to sit back down. I wanted to turn around and go home. Actually, I wanted to call Bill or Phil and ask one of them to fly out and take the boat back for me. I knew what I was doing was moral. I also knew it was an act of desperation and desperate people make mistakes. I prayed, for the strength to do the right thing and to know what that was.

I wondered what Adianec was doing. I knew for certain she was worried for me. Of all the unknowns and confusing details of the whole situation, one thing I knew for sure was that that woman loved me. She had a capacity to love beyond anything I'd experienced before. It was visceral and palpable. Rescuing Adianec wasn't just the right thing to do, it was the only thing I could do. Now with the full morning light, I walked back over to the boat. I pulled around to the fuel depot and filled her up.

As I pulled away from the dock, I'd already forgotten how powerful the Boston Whaler felt. They are solid, stable and fast. Driving back out through the half-mile mine field just made me shake my head. As I hit the Tongue, I opened her up. The morning air was a bit chilly, so I put on my yellow weather gear, set the GPS and headed south for Cuba.

I was very apprehensive about the pirates, and constantly searched for boats heading my way. Spotting them would be easy…they always have the black and white skull-and-crossbones flag overhead, thank God for that. The conditions got increasingly choppier as I made my way toward the south end of Andros. This also meant that I was getting closer to the narrow cut I had to make through the barrier reef.

Five miles to the cut and I was sweating the unknown. Conditions were still good; a two-foot chop maximum. When I finally saw the cut, I laughed out loud. It was incredible! The barrier reef was probably ten-feet high at that point and the cut, which looked as wide as a hair on the chart, was easily a quarter mile. I could see the straight line where the depth went from 6,000 feet to 25, and then the water flattened out. I made a hard cut at the last second and sent a wall of water into the reef.

I headed into a replica of the previous day. I was now in the southern end of the Bahama bank. The numerous rocks that dotted the charts were visible from a half mile away in the perfectly clear water. The ocean was about twenty feet deep and although I could no longer see Andros, there were tiny islands everywhere, just a foot or two above the waterline. None were bigger than fifty feet wide, some had vegetation, others just white sand. Again I found myself in paradise. At forty-two mph I made the forty-mile trip west in under an hour. And then I hit my last waypoint. Now it was due south. Less than 100 miles to go and I'd be in Cuba.

About fifty miles from Cuba, the water depth was still quite shallow. I stopped the boat and turned off the engines. There was one small cloud in the sky west of me. The water was so calm that the boat didn't move an inch and I could see every detail of the bottom. I took the video camera off its wax base and filmed 360 degrees around. Years from now when I tell of this place, even I won't believe me. With a Lyle Lovett CD blasting through the speakers, I called Barry on the Satellite phone and described my surroundings. "Bro."

"Hey, are you in Cuba?"

When you're out on the open water by yourself, it's both comforting and odd to hear familiar voices. "No, about fifty miles north, no land in sight, nothin' but water in all directions. But get this? I can see the bottom."

"Of the ocean?"

"Yeah, I'm in the middle of the ocean and it's only twenty feet deep." It was beyond beautiful. "I'm videoing it right now. Probably be too busy being chased next time I'm here to do anything but pucker up."

"Hey, man, you need to be careful. Go over your plan again before you hit Cuba."

Plan. My plan…Shit, I didn't have a plan. "Barry?"

"Yup?"

"What's my plan?" I was joking, but not entirely. "Yeah, I know. I've been trying to account for all scenarios, 'cept for the one that will actually happen. Call you soon with 'my little friend' beside me."

He wished me good look, and I returned to the silence. I sat on the back platform, took off my deck shoes and let my feet dangle in the water. I could see the shadow of the boat on the bottom. I sat there for about thirty minutes and let it all soak in. Two days later, I wouldn't have time to enjoy this place. We would be racing to get out of Cuban waters, perhaps even being chased, and into a world new to Adianec.

Cutting through the Great Bahama channel, I had to race another freighter to our intersection point, and I beat him by half a mile. Within minutes, I could see the thin line of Cuba which brought a spring of enthusiasm with it. I had told Adianec days earlier when we last spoke that I'd call Yanela's friend from Cayo Guillermo at 2 p.m. It was now 2:30 p.m. The Bahama channel runs very close to shore there. The water did not change into the amazing Caribbean blue until I was within a mile of Cuba. I could see two, maybe three, resorts lined up on the small key. I could also see the cut where my GPS was taking me. I rode up along side a colossal catamaran party yacht. There must have been fifty Canadian and European tourists on board.

A 200-yard long, low bridge that connects Cayo Coco to Guillermo blocks access to the backside of the Keys. I turned right into the small marina. There were no docks, just boats pulled up to the seawall and tied off. There were three boats altogether. Two for fishing, one for diving, all of them owned by the Cuban government. There were many people milling around, and one guy came up to help me tie off. When he saw that I was an American, he enthusiastically shook my hand.

"You know we should be friends, our countries." He said with a huge smile. "Americano!" he announced loudly.

The crews and workers from the other boats either came over to shake my hand or waved and yelled something, which I hoped meant, "welcome."

The area was very tropical, complete with coconut palm groves all around. The water was clear and as I walked over to one of the boats to get some insight into diving areas, I saw three sharks that had been cut in half by the fisherman. There were a couple of large yachts on dry dock, and I wondered if the Cuban Coast guard had pirated them, something they are known to do. It was hot and muggy, as usual. I was tired and disoriented from having the engine noise rumble through my ears for the past six hours, but optimistic about my prospects there.

A very serious man walked over to me and asked, "What is your business in here?"

"Vacation," I said. "I'm on vacation. I've come to dive the area."

He asked for my keys, GPS and charts. He said it was standard, nothing to be concerned about, which I knew was the case for Cuba. He took them into one of the three trailers in the marina.

Chapter twenty-eight

PARTY'S OVER

I could feel our strategy unfolding smoothly and was about to plan the victory parade, I asked to use the phone and someone pointed to a shed. As I was dialing the number of a friend of Yanela's who worked at one of the resorts, I heard a large truck come down the road and pull through the guarded gate. I could hear the tires crunching rocks as it came to a squeaky stop near the shed I was in. Then the tailgate fell with a thud and the distinctive sound of boots hitting the ground echoed through my ears and into my brain. The expression "my heart sank" would be an understatement. The boots jogged over to and around the shed. I was surrounded.

My mouth went dry and I could feel my chest tighten. All the clichés of fear and shock hit me simultaneously. There was a sharp knock on the door. I just stood there. The serious man threw the door open and said "out" in a very forceful voice. I quickly thought to play innocent and no matter what, do not admit a thing. I walked into the bright sunlight to find a dozen soldiers greeting me...well, not exactly greeting.

The serious man, whom I later found out was a captain or some kind of officer for the coast guard, was very upset. He demanded, "I want to know where the other boats are. Where are the other boats?"

Other boats? Lucky me, I didn't have to play innocent for that one. I asked him, "What boats?"

He didn't like my answer and quickly lost his patience. He threw open my charts of the Cuban coast. Laying them on the concrete, he pointed to three other waypoint markings that Sam had made on the map. She had given me other options of travel in case the passage was blocked with too many rocks.

"What do you mean other boats?" I asked.

"The landing party," he yelled. He was getting more agitated by the second.

"Sir, I don't know what you're talking about."

And I didn't. "The invasion, when does it start?" he screamed in my face.

I burst out laughing at the ridiculousness of what he had said. He must have thought I was the advance team for a U.S. invasion. Forty years of vigilance and training was about to pay off for them. I tried to explain to him that nobody knew the hazards in the area I was boating through, and I needed to be prepared with other options for safety. I tried to reason with him, "Look at the other destinations, all the other marinas. Do the Marines come in through the front door? Look. See what I brought here?"

I stood up to go to the boat to show him all the care packages I'd brought. When I did, he pulled the bundle of papers out of my back pocket. Now he had *the* papers, with all of Adianec's information. Her return ticket and her email with details of our rendezvous. I had no time or even the ability to think right then. He demanded I stay right there amongst the solders and he went inside for about thirty minutes. I remembered a book I'd read on the internet about a year earlier about how to survive in different situations; Rhino attacks, snake bite, getting lost in a blizzard, and my favorite one was how to amputate your own limb. But the one I needed to recall now was how to survive a hostage situation.

First, make some kind of contact and let them recognize that you are human. Next is to truly understand their intentions and find a non-condescending way to let them know you get it. Then have them discover you, who you are, so they can gain some empathy for you.

Some man called for me at Yanela's neighbor's house. It was very strange. The man asked if I knew Lee and said he needed my full name so Lee could rent a car. It made me very worried. I knew there was something wrong. He didn't need my name to rent a car. But I was also relieved that Lee had made it across the sea.

After the man hung up, I called right back at the number on the caller ID. It was the marina in Cayo Guillermo, so I asked to speak with the American man. Lee came to the phone. He sounded so beautiful. But there was something wrong. I could hear it in his voice. I said I know something is wrong, he said "No, I'm just making friends."

He told me there was a slight confusion about the plane ticket he had for his friend "Adianec" in Miami. Then I knew what was happening. Lee was letting me know they were on to our plan. I am very aware of what my government is capable of, so I begged Lee to be careful with his temper. I hoped they wouldn't push him too hard.

The officer came back out of the office looking very troubled. I showed him the food and medicine I'd brought with me for the Cuban people. Invading armies don't come bearing gifts. Someone from one of the trailers opened the door and yelled something. "You have a phone call," he said with irritation.

It was Adianec. She was very upset and wanted to know why I was being held in the marina. I played it down and told her I would call soon, and to wait for me there. In other words, don't come. "Do you remember my friend in Miami, Adianec Ibarra, the girl with the exact name as you?"

"*Si.*" She said hesitantly.

"You know, when I get back to Miami she is flying home with me for a few weeks. They found her ticket and want to know who she is. That's all, that's why I'm still here."

I wanted to get as much information to her as possible in case she got caught. I also knew they were listening so I had to be cautious. I felt a little relief knowing that she knew I was safe and had been warned to stay away.

But now, what of me? I walked back outside and the officer pointed to a chair someone had placed outside in the direct sunlight next to the shed. I took that as an invitation to sit. It also gave me an opportunity to think of answers for any questions they may have. Certainly they would ask about the airline ticket with Adianec's name, why was I there, why did I come by boat, who was she to me, and why was I alone. My mind was racing so fast I didn't know if my story would be convincing or pathetic. I was trying to focus on my breathing and not think of the consequences. I was getting nauseous and could feel the burning of bile rising into my throat. I knew that under no circumstances should I show any fear, which would be difficult because that was all I felt.

As I sat there with two guards standing over me, I remembered Adianec's California driver's license that was in my pocket. I had picked one up in downtown L.A. several weeks earlier. I thought it would come in handy once she was on the boat. It would help her pass for an American if we had gotten stopped. If the guards found that, it would be over. It had her picture on it, and there would be no way to pass it off as someone else's. After an hour, I stood up to stretch. My guards motioned me back down. I refused, with a smile. They were perplexed as to their options. The way I saw it, I was not yet under arrest and the chair was offered, not necessarily ordered. I walked in circles looking for a place to discard the license.

Two hours must have gone by sitting in that heat. The guys working on the government boats would sneak a smile or look of sympathy my way every so often. Then I was ordered to go into the shed. My two bodyguards followed me in. The shed was similar to a small construction office I've often used on job sites. Inside was a steel desk with a chair behind it and one folding chair in front, with one leg shorter than the other three. It was stifling in there and eerie, with only one fluorescent tube for light. The only window had been covered with cardboard, so that prevented any chance of cross-ventilation when the door opened.

My two guards and I stood there for about ten minutes. As I had been doing for the past couple hours, on occasion I would make eye contact and smile. I could tell I was wearing down their stoicism, their demeanor was softening. An older man with a crisp but ill-fitting brown uniform walked in and was saluted by my guards. I gave a friendly smile and said hello. A tall, frail gentleman in plain clothes, who had brought in another chair and placed it next to me, followed him in. He introduced himself. "Hello, I am your interpreter."

Now the long process of interrogation began in earnest. Things started very simply: my name, where I was from, and what did I do. The "what did I do" was my opportunity to start the bonding process. I've had a few friends who had become celebrities and I was an acquaintance of a few more. I knew the privilege it brought or at the very least, curiosity. I decided to make that my trump card. I had nothing else.

Government offices have access to the internet in Cuba so I knew any information I gave them of my acting resume could easily be confirmed. If I was going to play this game, I had to be general in the things I said. Distraction was the only tool I had to direct the outcome.

"I'm an actor." I could see a quick flash in my interpreter's eyes; he looked as if he wanted to ask some personal questions of his own. When he asked why I had come to Cuba, I went into a diatribe of the unfairness of the embargo and how the American people love Cuba and feel shame due to the embargo. I couldn't tell them the truth, which was that Cuba isn't even on most Americans radar.

I looked down and paused for a moment to bring an emotional connection to the situation. Then I looked up, and told him, "It is my conviction to do all I can to help the Cuban people."

This was actually true, that was why I had all the food and medicine in the boat. I then went into a complete embellishment of my living conditions in L.A. I spoke, uninterrupted, of all my cars and homes. I said, "I always feel guilty when I come to visit my friends in Cuba who have so little while I'm swimming in such incredible wealth in America."

I could see they were transfixed. Now, my conviction to help my friends in Cuba was true. Speaking of all my wealth and privilege in L.A. was a complete embellishment, but it was working. Soon we were talking like old pals, and I kept them laughing. Every time I would speak, my guards and interrogator would lean in expectantly as my interpreter would translate my jokes. They "got" my sarcasm. "You say you have friends waiting for you in the Bahamas?"

"Yeah, and are they gonna be pissed they missed all this fun."

But of course, all too soon the interrogator realized we had gotten off track again. He wanted to know why the boat and not a plane. "I told you, I was scuba diving in the Bahamas with a few buddies, and when I realized how close I was to Cuba, I shot on down. That reminds me of a story George Clooney once told me."

They stopped me, immediately forgetting why we were there.

"*The* George Clooney? The movie star?" Though it was part of my plan, I was still a little surprised that communist officials on a segregated island were gushing over him.

I gave them a look like yeah what's the big deal. "George and I play basketball together."

Another embellishment. Many years ago, before George was "*The George Clooney*," we played basketball together at the Hollywood "Y" or Hollywood Athletic Club (can't remember, it was so unimportant at the time), two or three times, and I'm not sure if we had ever said more than hello to each other. Back then I was on TV about as much as George...had I only known.

Every time the interrogator would get back on track, I would ramble on about my incredible life. I told them, "You want to make sure to catch my next film, *Sideways,* which is opening in Havana next month."

That was true. One of my guards forgot himself and said in Spanish, "You're a movie star too?"

The interrogator quickly reprimanded him, and I acted a little insulted. I made them feel like they were out of touch. "You don't know me, seriously? My movie just won an Academy Award."

They seemed like good guys, I could see that in their eyes and I hated to play this game with them, but if I lost, it could be my freedom or worse. They apologized, saying that I did look familiar. "No, it's okay, really. It's refreshing not to be hounded," I said, waving them off. "I'm actually better known in Europe, because I do more independent films."

I couldn't tell them the truth, which was that nobody in America, including my own mother, knew who I was. But when they looked up my name online, which I knew they would, they would see my name attached to many high-profile shows. What it wouldn't say was that I was always the supporting role, somebody's husband or boyfriend. Never the "*somebody.*" I thought it interesting that the power of celebrity, which had always eluded me, might now save my life. The officer finally lost his will to continue, and walked out…smiling.

I knew that word of my worldly importance would spread and maybe end this thing quickly. My translator had left with the officer, leaving the two guards and me alone again. This time they were much more receptive to me. They were trying to ask questions in Spanish. I repeated some lessons from my seventh grade Spanish class with Senor Watson, which made no sense under the circumstances, but I acted them out and had my guards laughing…the sillier I was, the better.

I was trying to maintain my open approach, but I was getting more anxious as the day wore on. I was also getting weak, physically. All I had had to eat that day was a sandwich in the Bahamas, a few Balance bars and two Red Bulls. I knew I was playing my cards right, I just didn't know how much longer I could keep it up. After an hour, my interpreter walked back in and my guards took their previous, serious stance. As the door opened, I could see it was getting dark outside. The wind was picking up. It must have been that cold front. It brought a nice, but all-too-temporary breeze into our little sweat box. My original nemesis, Señor Serious, was next to come in. My interpreter boasted, "This man is very important. You need to listen to him."

Even though he spoke English, he let the interpreter translate for him. This made me nervous. No doubt that was his plan. It was easier to distract the interrogator before, because so much got lost in translation and I could play dumb to questions I didn't want to answer. He asked, "So tell me again about the charts and why you have decided to come to Cuba?"

I started to tell him my story about scuba diving. He put his hand up to silence me. "Yes, I heard the fabricated version and now want the truth."

I thought I better try a new angle with him. Whatever it was, I had to keep talking and try to control the agenda. "So I'm your enemy and everything I say is a lie?" Actually, it was. "This is insane, I am not here to cause problems."

It was easy to act sincere because I really did believe what I was saying. I also knew that it was the dream of almost every Cuban for our countries to be friends. "Really," I said, "I am not an enemy of the Cuban people…or of you."

He responded immediately, "Yes. I know you are a friend of Cuba. But I also know that you are lying."

We went back and forth for about thirty minutes when he asked me what President Bush thought about my visits to Cuba. "Bush is a pendejo," I blurted out.

We all froze. None of us, including myself, knew how to respond to that.

In Cuba, saying that in public about Castro is a guaranteed prison sentence. I just kept looking him in the eye and after a few moments we both broke into laughter, followed by the guards and interpreter. I silently congratulated myself for finding the chink in his armor. I was in a fight for my life and if the President had to take one for the team, so be it. I don't think they saw the subtleties of what just happened. Say that in Cuba about Castro, you go to jail. Say that in the U.S. you're just practicing your civil rights. They asked me if my government knew I was there. I told them, "They don't tell me what countries they're going to invade, I don't tell them what embargos I'm going to break."

That was their favorite line.

We spent the next ten minutes talking politics, mostly anti-war stuff. He left frustrated and angry, telling me to wait there. These guys were not stupid, and I knew I wasn't convincing them of anything. I was just wearing them down. Their goal was, without a doubt, to throw me in prison. If that did happen, they'd be throwing in a corpse, because I wasn't going without a fight.

I didn't have a clue how this was going to turn out, although I couldn't imagine they were going to just let me go. Then I remembered Adianec's driver's license again, and asked to use the bathroom. They took me over to one of the larger trailers. Stepping out of my cramped shed and into the cool night air was an absolute pleasure, I took a deep breath of the clean air. The marina was quiet and peaceful. Most of the soldiers had left, replaced by two uniformed cops. Once in the bathroom, I took her license out and slid it behind a sheet of paneling that had come loose. When I walked out of there, a lady was typing at her desk. She was pretty and about thirty years old. She said I could stay in the air-conditioning with her until they came and got me. Her name was Mariean. As we talked, the phone rang. It was Adianec. "Amore, why are you still there?" she asked tearfully.

I told her everything was okay, that they had just asked a few questions. "Lee, please leave now."

I did think about jumping back in the boat, except that they had my keys, my charts and my GPS. I was trying to calm her down, as she was in a panic. I told her, "Listen. I'll call you when I get to my room. Okay? I promise. I'll call, but you have to stay where you are."

After I hung up, Mariean and I spoke for about fifteen minutes. She already seemed to know a lot about me. I don't think she knew the bad shape I was in though. I had not stopped sweating since the interrogations began and I could feel the effects of dehydration. My body was shutting down. I needed food and water, both of which I had on the boat. I walked out of the trailer, my legs wobbly and weak. But I came out with a smile, like nothing was wrong. My boat was only fifty yards away and I started casually to walk over to it. Señor Serious had a fit, telling me I was not to go near that boat until it was searched. I stood there for a second, thinking what would an innocent person do? "Is this the way your country always treats tourists coming in to dock?" I asked defiantly.

As before, he and I kept our eyes locked on each other. "This is normal. Everything is normal." He replied.

I asked if I could just get a bottle of water and some food. He said no, and asked me to go back into the shed. I told him that I'd like to check into a hotel and again he told me no. I had to wait for immigration, and they were on their way. After the seven feet of concrete sidewalk that was part of the seawall, there was ten feet of grass before the trailers. I walked over and sat down on the grass. I had no desire or intention of going back into that shed. Next thing I knew, I was being woken up by one of my guards. He handed me a yellow plastic cup with putrid smelling water inside. Not that thirsty, thank you. I said *gracias* and put it aside. Several minutes later, a woman appeared with a plate of food for us. They all grabbed at what appeared to be sandwiches, and my new friend motioned for me to come over and eat. I went over, but the flies got to the plate before me. It appeared to be raw pork and dry bread. I felt my stomach start to churn, so I quickly walked to the side of the trailer and threw up.

"My boat, under guard 24/7, at the Cayo Guillermo marina"

I was exhausted. Luckily, an increasingly strong, cool breeze had pushed out the heat. I went back over to the grassy area and fell asleep. When I woke up, it was late and very quiet. The only people I saw were the two policemen. "Hey," I said smiling. Then with as much confidence as I could muster, I said, "I'm gonna grab some water."

They were nonplussed. I jumped on the boat and grabbed my large bottle of water and a bag of trail mix. It could not have been more satisfying.

Around midnight, a large van came across the bridge and everybody came out of the trailers. The van pulled up, filled with uniformed officers. I felt like I was about to get sick again. They all gathered in one of the trailers and I was left with the police and my two guards. The longer they stayed inside, the more I was convinced I was going to prison right then and there. Thirty minutes later, they all came out and walked to the boat. About that time, a car came down the road and over the bridge. Someone said something in Spanish. The only word I understood was *perro*, dog.

Señor Serious told me that if the dog got a drug hit, they would take the boat. Now I couldn't breathe. They have a zero-tolerance policy. I panicked, thinking that certainly someone who had rented the boat recently could have smoked a joint on board. They could also fake a hit as an excuse to take my boat. At any rate, I knew the boat was history. I had been warned that modern day pirating is a common and well-known practice of the Cuban Coast Guard, and now I was going to be a statistic.

All my bags started coming off the boat and I was told to unpack everything. I was a zombie, barely able to function. My mind was spinning and I started to have an anxiety attack. If I lost control, it was over. At least now I was keeping them at bay with my bullshit. As I laid everything out, the dog was brought in to sniff around. Someone saw the satellite phone and freaked out, leaving Señor Serious embarrassed that he hadn't found it first. I whispered to him that I had other GPS units and a cell phone and a radio. He gave me a look of gratitude and I pointed with my head to their location on the boat. He found them and was saved from another humiliation. He nodded and smiled as he climbed out of the boat. There was no downside to that. They would have found them, anyway.

They were all very curious about the eleven care bags. They were filled with shampoo, deodorant, razor blades, tooth paste, candies, and more. Each bag had about fifty items. Señor Serious explained to them in Spanish what they were for. I could tell by the way he put his hand on my shoulder that it was a favorable accounting. I opened one of the bags and spilled the contents on the ground. Curious, they all gathered round to look. Finally they were ignoring the dog, which really had no interest in my personal things anyway. One of the officers said something and they all laughed. Then one looked over at me and nodded. Now it was time to put the dog on the boat. I was certain he was going to get a hit.

He didn't.

With that done, they all said their goodbyes and left. I began to repack all my things, thinking it was over. By the time I stowed everything back on the boat, it was 2 a.m. Señor Serious called me back into the shed. I sat down and the interrogation started all over again! He said, "I want to fill in the many holes. First, who is Adianec?"

I was ready for that question. "Which one?" He threw his hands up in disgust and stared at me. "Which one? The one in Miami or the one in Cuba?" I asked again.

"There is no Adianec in Miami." He said angrily.

"Well you should tell her parents that. They would be surprised."

"You expect us to believe that you have a friend in Miami and Havana with the same name."

"Yeah, well, I'm not the sharpest guy, so I tend to have friends with the same name to avoid confusing myself."

We went back and forth on many issues. I had lost the energy to be funny or clever, so I just denied everything. After about a half hour, I was delirious and put my head on the table, continuing to answer his questions with my eyes closed. He knew there was nothing to accomplish by continuing. He called the front desk of the closest resort and explained to me how to get there. "Thank you, I'll be leaving first thing in the morning."

"No, you're not!" And he handed me all my papers.

Even though there was a beautiful moon out that night, it was pitch black because there were so many clouds moving in and blocking the moon's light. As I walked to the resort, I felt the relaxed energy that I always feel in the air there. On my right was a military barracks behind a grove of palm trees. I said hello to the guard, and he just stared. I could see lights through a forest of dense brush and trees, so I took the first path I came to. It led me to a long driveway which was lined with short palm trees. I walked into the open lobby. As was the case since I had met Adianec, my feet were in two different worlds. I had just survived being interrogated by a communist regime. And now I was in a resort with drunken Canadians laughing and singing out by one of the pools.

The girl behind the desk knew who I was and had the paperwork ready for me. I was so tired I couldn't read the information card. I just wrote my name on top and handed her the cash. I couldn't use credit cards because U.S. cards are not honored in Cuba. She explained in broken English how to get to my room. The hotel had many separate two-story, barrack-style buildings. Four lined up in a row with at least three rows heading off in different directions. I thought I must have passed my room because the last building didn't have any lights on. And was obviously unoccupied. After searching the other buildings for my room number, I walked over to the last one, and sure enough they had put me in the last room of the last building. I guess they were trying to keep me away from the other guests. Another surprise as I was putting my key in the lock was that I saw the glow of a cigarette being smoked behind a palm tree. I was being watched.

Almost as soon as I got inside, the phone rang. It was Adianec. Her voice sounded so good, I hungered to touch her. She sounded worn out and I assumed she had been crying. I told her everything was fine, that we were all good friends at the marina. She convinced me to let her and her friends continue their plan to come to Cayo Coco. I had no energy left to fight. She said if they didn't come it would appear too suspicious. The whole time the phone popped and crackled.

"Fidel is in our lives," I told her. Which meant the phone was tapped.

"I don't care. *Tu eres mi vida*, (you are my life)," she whispered to me.

After we said goodnight, I dragged myself into the bathroom to take a shower. As I slid the shower curtain open, a handful of roaches scattered and dove into the open drain, and up the wall. I was too tired to care. The water pressure was as I remembered...just a cold drizzle. The hotel towels were missing, so I had to dry off with a pair of jeans. The room smelled musty. As I fell onto the bed, which seemed to be made of lumpy cardboard with polyester sheets, I started to wonder if they had done all this on purpose but I passed out before I came to a conclusion. Sleep was an escape. Once I woke up, I slowly became conscious of what was happening to me. I awoke thinking that I might be entering the most dangerous day of my life. Every fiber in my body ached from stress. I needed help and wanted to call someone, but I was on my own.

We left Yanela's house at 5 a.m. My mother was there and she started to cry. I said, "Mommy, I am here. Don't cry now. If I make it to America, you can cry then."

I had a bad feeling, but I had to go. Lee was there.

When we got to the check point at the beginning of the bridge, they took our ID's as usual, but after twenty minutes, I knew something was wrong. After an hour, they came to our car and apologized that there was a computer issue. We would be able to leave soon. I asked to use the bathroom. The policeman said there is a baños in the other building. Walking by an open door, I saw many policemen and immigration officers talking quietly. I came back to the car and whispered to Yanela that we had been caught. They came back out and said we could continue, but I knew this was bad. I started shaking. I thought about Lee and wondered where he was. Certainly he was going to prison for this. My heart sank.

As we pulled into the Campismo, a police car came up to us with lights and sirens. They made Yanela's brother get out and put him into the police car as a policeman got into the front seat of our car. Our driver was told to follow the police car to the station. Everyone was so scared. I had two credit cards that Lee had given me last time he was here, in my name, in case we got separated on the escape to America. I quietly ripped open the side panel of the door and pushed the cards and seven hundred American dollars into the door. I whispered to Yanela not to worry, just say she knew nothing about it. I didn't want her to go to jail, too.

When we got to the station, we were told to leave everything in the car. And immediately, they began to search it with dogs. We were put in separate rooms for interrogations, and left there alone for hours. During that time, many people, immigration officers and secret police, would come in and stare at me, to intimidate me with large files. Then they would leave without saying a word.

I was in a bizarre predicament. I was free to roam around the resort, but not free to leave. I guess it was like house arrest, only my house was a narrow, several mile long key. I went to the front desk and asked about a restaurant. The hotel was filled mostly with Canadians, which made me feel somewhat at home. Watching them in the pools, laughing with their families caused a deep ache in my soul. Just beyond the boundaries of this resort was so much suffering and oppression, and they were unknowingly helping to finance it. In my ignorance, so had I. Maybe I was wrong to break the embargo as I had, but now it was too late, I had friends here that relied on me.

I was happy to discover that the resort was all-inclusive. There was fresh fruit and vegetables. Everything substantial missing in the rest of Cuba is funneled to the tourist resorts. They even had chicken breasts. The jobs in these resorts are highly prized by Cubans. But the price they pay emotionally must be unsettling. Daily they witness the incredible inequities of freedoms and lifestyles. They then suffer another humiliation at the end of their shift, as they line up for the bus that will take them through Cayo Coco and across the bridge to the mainland where they live. They are each thoroughly searched and then tagged as they board the bus. If anything is found on them, even a phone number, they lose their jobs and can be arrested.

After breakfast, I walked to my boat to get fresh clothes and some food. I had told Adianec that I'd meet her on the road near the bridge around noon. I took a shower and put on some clean clothes. I noticed that I had lost a significant amount of weight and my pants were loose. I went through the papers that Senor had given back to me the night before. I had to get rid of the incriminating ones. The difficulty was that I was being followed, and not all that discreetly.

As I walked past the laundry room, a separate cinder block structure, I noticed the floor drain didn't have a cover. I turned around as if I'd forgotten something, and came to face my followers. They had to quickly turn down another path to avoid contact with me (it was actually comical). I slipped quietly into the room while two ladies talked as they ironed. It was very noisy so they didn't hear me walk in and shove the papers into the drain. I walked out and back to my room, everyone oblivious to my actions.

I took a side excursion to the pools before meeting Adianec. The grounds were not well kept but had a worn, natural beauty. Chickens and roosters roamed freely, even around the pools. The water and the beach were like a picture postcard. The wind was blowing strong, about twenty five knots. The water was a light, bluish green with whitecaps as far out as I could see. Even though it had a raw beauty, it was devastating for me. There was no way that my boat or I would ever survive these strong winds and seas. Even if they released me, the cold front had now arrived and I wouldn't be able to leave for at least four days. Yet, I also had not and could not give up hope that I could get Adianec out of Cuba.

I walked past the marina to the main road. Right next to the bridge was a boat concession. I walked over and saw Mariean in one of the offices. She was one of those people that I felt comfortable with immediately. The available boat rentals for the tourists were two-seater speed boats. They could take them through the jungle waterways and into the interior wetlands. Mariean came out and spoke with me for awhile as I waited for Adianec. "Have you spoken with her again?"

"No, not today. But I'm waiting for her. She should be arriving soon."

I could see that Mariean wanted to say something. She just pursed her lips and got up from the rock we were sitting on. She touched my hand. "Lee, you seem like such a good man. I want you to have luck today."

As she walked away, her cryptic words gave me the chills.

Chapter twenty-nine

The Cuban secret police

Around noon, after everyone else had been interrogated, they took me into a very large stark room with only a desk in the middle. The windows were blocked with green curtains which made me even more nervous. There were many men around the room. Some police, some immigration, and a man from the secret police. He was sitting at the desk. He was a short, heavy mean man, but I knew how they play their communist game and I said to myself, "Okay, I am ready to fight you." He was very mean with me, slamming his fist on the desk and telling me everyone had already confessed and I had better tell him the truth.

"Well, if everyone already told you the truth, then you know the truth and you don't need me."

He showed me a copy of Lee's passport and asked if I knew that man. I got very scared for him and asked where Lee was. He slammed his fist down again. "He is no longer your concern. He has been arrested and sent to jail. You can see him in nine years." He screamed.

I put my hands under my legs so he could not see them shaking and kept my eyes on his. I begged to please tell me what Lee had done. He said, "Aside from helping you and your friends to leave the country illegally, he brought many drugs into this country."

"That is impossible, that is not Lee, he doesn't even drink." I pleaded.

"You obviously don't know this man." And he sneered at me.

Stealing Castro's daughter

He showed me Lee's file. They knew everything about him, every time he was in Cuba. Then the other men in the room started to throw questions at me. They wanted to know what was in the plastic bags on his boat. "It is probably soap, shampoo, medicine for my mom and maybe clothes and shoes for me. I'm not really sure, but that is what he always brings me and similar things for people he meets." I told them. "He is very concerned for the Cuban people and he tries to help."

I didn't tell him we were in love, but just that we were friends. And since he was in the Bahamas with his boat and I was in Camaquey, we decided to meet. I told them I had not seen him in four months. Then they sent me back to my small room for many hours.

It was melting hot on the rock, even with the gale force winds. I'm not good at sitting around, but I couldn't take the chance of missing her. Thinking of her was the only thing that could make me smile at that point. Every time a car came over the bridge, which was not that often, I would get up, see that it wasn't her, then I'd sit back down with disappointment. I walked up on the bridge. It had two lanes and a large sidewalk on both sides. The water below was shades of blue, depending on the depth. The deep holes were cobalt blue and the shallows were almost fluorescent.

A police car was waiting at the other end. I approached the center of the bridge, which was also the highest point for miles around. As I walked toward the other side, two policemen got out of the car and motioned me back. Any doubts I'd had about whether or not I was being held had now vanished. I also knew that Adianec would not be coming to see me. I went back to my room. I turned on the T.V. and watched CNN until I fell asleep.

Around dusk, there was a knock at my door. It was my interpreter and one of the guards from the day before. The interpreter told me that I was to pack my things and come with him. They were both strangely silent. I tried to make small talk but he said, "It is best if you said nothing."

I stopped as we were making our way through a grove of coconut palms. Nervously I said, "I need to know what is going on."

He looked at the guard before he spoke. "You have broken our laws and you will not come forward with the truth. I am sorry. We all like you but they are taking you to prison. They have said it is nine years."

I felt like I'd been hit by a truck. I fell over, my breath exploding out of my lungs. I put my hands on my knees to keep from falling down and I watched as saliva poured out of my mouth. I was about to throw up, again. My interpreter patted me on the back and said we had to get moving. I couldn't walk. I stood up to get my bearings. The moon was on the horizon. It was falling too far behind the sun, I was thinking. There were birds chirping, funny that I hadn't noticed that before. There were birds on Cayo Guillermo.

181

Lee Brooks

"Small shed in the marina where I was interrogated"

I didn't realize it, but we had started walking and we were almost at the marina. I thought about knocking them out and running, but to where? This Key was water-locked. As we passed the boat, I thought to myself, "Shit, how am I going to pay for that nine years from now?" The next thing I knew I was in the shed. I sat there, isolated with my confusion and one guard.

My mind was going a bit wacky. I knew that I had been naive, thinking this escape plan was a game. I just wanted to go home. I was imagining my living conditions for the next nine years. The scenario turned into a John Waters musical. My jail mate was a 300 pound transvestite named Jose-phina. I started thinking up prison soap jokes in my head. I was making myself laugh out loud. It raised my spirits and I started thinking, I'm not going to prison for nine years. I'm not a brainwashed Cuban who acquiesces to authority. I'm a freakin' American. Who do they think they are? God won't permit this, I was certain of that. Some laws are meant to be broken, and these laws that I'd broken were anti-human. Fuck them, I thought to myself, I am not going to prison.

After an hour or more, a weathered, old gentleman, black and very thin, walked in and sat next to me. He introduced himself. "I am your new translator. The officer coming in is very important."

I smiled, having heard this before. The officer came in, very professionally, and took his seat. He asked very detailed questions, all of which I'd answered before. He never argued with me or tried to trap me. He just wanted details and he wrote down every response. How much did it cost to rent the boat? What are the names of my friends in the Bahamas? Many particulars of my "friend" Adianec in Miami. This went on for about thirty minutes and then he just got up and left.

I had been stuck in the room alone for many hours. I called the mean one over to find out what was going on.

"Why are you holding me, what is the problem? You said I am not arrested. If that is true then I need to go."

"Come with me," he commanded.

He took me back to the interrogation room. Then he yelled at me. "Do you think I'm playing here? I'm not playing, because of you I have not slept in thirty-six hours. And since you won't help us figure out what is going on, you are now arrested."

He really scared me, but I couldn't let him know. I tried to sound brave. "You cannot arrest me. I was not on his boat. He knows I don't want to leave this country, especially on a boat, I can't swim. Besides, I am a revolutionary. You are making a big mistake about him, because he cares about the Cuban people. He hates the way his government treats the Cuban people."

The other men in the room started to question me again, all at the same time. They were trying to confuse me. They were saying that we contradicted each other, so one of us must be lying. The mean guy got in my face. "You cannot intimidate me by not eating" (I had refused all food they had offered.) "You do not intimidate me, I am stronger than you. I have been doing this for many years. Do you have any idea who we are?"

I knew I couldn't back down, though he scared me. I looked him in the eye, trying not to shake. "Yes, I know who you are, do you know who my step-father is?" I told him his name and his rank. "My mother's husband is very important in the communist party and he will protect me."

He got very quiet. I continued, "Where are my friends?"

"Your friends have been sent to jail, because of you. When you cooperate with us, maybe they can go home." He paused for a moment and smiled "We know how you girls meet these tourists in Havana."

I had taken too many insults from him, now I was upset and forgot I was scared. I jumped from my chair and went up to him. "Be very careful and give thought to what you say. I was educated by this revolution and know what my rights are. Nobody can decide your feelings for you. I fell in love with this man. That is the real truth here. And now with the way you are acting, you are the one who is wrong. You're the bad guy here, nobody else."

He went crazy and came after me. "Watch your mouth, you are out of line. My patience has gone past its limits."

I knew I was in trouble. The nice one stepped in quickly and told him to leave the room. Then he sat me down and spoke to me very calmly. He asked me to please eat the ice cream he put in front of me.

"Let's try this again. This time please tell me the truth so we can clear all this up."

It was just the same information we had been going over. They wanted me to admit that Lee came in the boat to take me off the island. But if I even suggested that, Lee would go to jail for many years. He probably would anyway. After a while with no change in my story, he said, "Let's go for a ride."

I knew we were going to Cayo Guillermo. The mean guy told me to get in his car but the nice one said, "No, she is riding with me."

In the ride over in the car he was talking to the other men. He asked me again about the other girl in Miami, the one with the same name as me. They didn't believe me. I noticed how bad the weather had gotten and then I saw the ocean. It was very angry. I started to cry. I knew Lee so well and if he got angry he would do the opposite of what they wanted and walk away. He wouldn't care. He would sail into the dangerous sea and hurt himself. The nice officer asked me what was wrong.

"Please don't make Lee angry. I know him, he won't care. He will fight you and maybe die. Please, Lee is a very good man, but his temper will make him do things."

The nice officer was very sincere and promised to take care of Lee and to make sure he wouldn't do anything that might get him hurt. When we arrived at the marina, the man pointed out Lee's boat to me. I knew he was close and it made the pain of not seeing him even worse. They put me in a room with the driver and a guard, and they told me they were going over to deal with Lee.

An hour had passed and we were still waiting for the next round or the inevitable sentencing. After a while, there was a knock at the door and a lady stepped in and put a plate of that same raw pork sandwiches on the table. I could feel that she was acutely aware of me but made a conscious effort not to look my way. It didn't take long for all the flies in our shed to discover the delicacy. The wind was picking up outside, and every so often the shed would shake as it got hit with a strong gust. I wanted something to happen. The not knowing was driving me nuts. When the door opened and sent in a strong cool breeze, it woke us up. The new interpreter walked in and again tried to make this new guy seem even more important than the last. I looked at my guards. "At this rate, I'm expecting Jesus to walk through the door."

When the translator repeated what I had said, in Spanish, they laughed and nodded.

One of the guards said something to my interpreter. When he responded, I could see the look on my guards' faces fall. It was a phrase I'd heard before…"*Seguridad del estado*" "the Cuban secret police!" The man walked in casually, dressed in plainclothes, and stepped over to shake my hand. It was like meeting someone for a dinner meeting. He was very polite and friendly.

"So," he said smiling as he sat down. "Why don't we tie up all these loose ends so we can end all this, yes?"

I nodded. As he began, he reverted to Spanish. This guy was too nice and spoke perfect English. It really unsettled me. His calm demeanor had the opposite effect on me. I was tired, scared and weak. Just like the day before when I had had an interrogator that spoke English, this guy understood the translation. So I couldn't stall for time by playing dumb with the translation. I would just tell him I needed to think for a second because I didn't want to be misunderstood. He would press me hard and make me repeat things often but he never lost his cool. His first question was about "this girl Adianec."

"Which one?" I asked.

"Ahh, very good, okay. Is she your girlfriend?"

"No, neither of them are."

He got a quizzical look on his face, as if he knew something I didn't and was about to hit me with it. "Hmm, I see. Then why the boat?"

"You guys should compare notes. The others asked me the same questions."

He didn't laugh, but my sarcasm didn't make him angry, either. "How do you know we're not comparing notes?"

"Ahh, true. Do you think I mean to do this country harm?"

"No, I don't believe you do. Why the boat?"

That was where he was going and wouldn't be distracted. "Since you've already read the other's notes, you know I was in the Bahamas with friends, so I shot down to see my friends here."

"What are their names?"

"Manny, Moe and Jack. The Pep Boys."

"Your friends in Cuba?"

"Oh, sorry, no ahh." A quick spontaneous laugh to myself. "Mostly it's that girl Adianec, and then any people I may meet."

He nodded, and asked. "How did you come to meet this Adianec?"

"Cubamatch.com."

"The what?"

"Nothing. It was a joke, or maybe not. We met in Havana at her school."

"Name?"

"Uuuhhmm…Adianec?"

"The school?"

"Oh, I, no, I don't know."

"Is she going for a boat ride with you?"

"She doesn't swim."

"I see."

And so it went.

He remained very pleasant, never got upset and almost convinced me he was on my side. When he knew I was not being honest he would just smile and say, "Hmmm, I see."

After an hour, he stood up and told me how nice it was meeting me. Then he shook my hand. I knew I was being set up. They were certainly two steps ahead of me, I just couldn't figure out where they were going. I would rather he slam me against the wall than smile and be polite. He opened the door and I could see it was starting to rain. A storm was coming. Quite a metaphor, I thought.

There was little doubt this was all leading up to something. Even my guards felt the tension. When the interpreter reappeared thirty minutes later, he wouldn't even look at me. Seconds later the door burst open. I could see the wind was now gale force, blowing the palm trees almost to the side, but the little bit of breeze trickling into the shed was a relief. The weather was really getting bad. This would make escaping near impossible…*then he walked in.*

I could tell by the nervous reaction of my guards and interpreter that this new interrogator truly was more important than the others. My interpreter's hands were actually shaking. This guy really caught my attention. He was at most 5` 6`` tall, and about the same in width, but he moved swiftly and with authority. Sweat beaded up on his ruddy face. He was wearing street clothing instead of that one-size-fits-all, drab green or brown uniform. I assumed that he, like the nice guy, was with the Cuban secret police. This could not be good for me. He walked in without acknowledging anyone in the room and nonchalantly dropped a heavy file on the table. I knew it was to get my attention. He said something in Spanish under his breath and the two guards ran out, almost bowing as they left. My interpreter rose half way, not quite knowing what to do. The interrogator stared at my interpreter in a superior way over the top of his glasses, obviously very irritated that he was still there. My interpreter, not quite getting the hint, looked back and forth at my chubby interrogator and me. Finally, after having been stared down, he slowly backed out of the door…

Now, it was my turn.

There's a lack of due process in this richly beautiful Caribbean island.

With a communist dictator at the helm, an accusation is a conviction. I was acutely aware of the fact, that people disappear here.

He sat there with a perma-frown scrunching up his wet chubby face. Arms folded, he stared at my file with an occasional deep sigh. He was trying to convey that he was contemplating my fate. He contemplated well. After a few minutes he finally looked up at me, with the same air of superiority, glancing over the top of his chipped glasses. I tried to maintain eye contact to assure him I had nothing to hide, but he was so intense. I was certain he knew I was lying.

"Señor Brooks, we're getting quite tired of your little *bullsheet* story."

He spoke in almost perfect English and I was worried I wouldn't be able to get anything by this guy. This short, sweaty chunk of banana republic paranoia seemed very intelligent. I reminded myself, this is not the principal's office and he's not going to send me home with a note.

I didn't respond to the "bullsheet" comment. I just tried to look concerned and confused like I had no idea what he was referring to.

"Señor Brooks," he said again as if I wasn't listening. "I'm growing tired of your bullsheet. Your story, it rings bells in my head."

More "bull-sheet." I smiled, rather charmingly I thought, trying to be helpful and said "You mean it sets off alarms?"

He just stared. I've seen that look before, when my attempts at being witty fail to charm people.

He opened the thick file, my file, and pointed to a page. "You come to Cuba often." I nodded. "You always fly in through Mexico, except once you decided to come from Canada."

I was so stunned my mouth must have dropped. "Yes, Señor, we are not the bumbling bobos you think we are."

Bumbling bobos? "You've got the wrong guy, that's not what I think."

I sincerely protested. Not that I even knew what a "bumbling bobo" was. He started flipping through my file, nodding and making single worded comments.

"You seem to appreciate the big pool at the Copa." He looked up with a sarcastic smile. "Ah, El Aljibe, good food?"

I knew I shouldn't go toe to toe with this guy. No doubt he could snap his fingers and I would disappear. But if it was over it was over, and I had no more energy to kiss ass. Besides, he was obviously a bully and they don't respect weakness.

"Yes, I guess you wouldn't know; too expensive for a Cuban." He gave me a cold stare. "So you know a little about me. It just proves that you are part of a paranoid, closed society. Congratulations, you have proven the point of all your detractors."

"Okay, sir, no more niceties, is that it for you?" As he stood up and leaned forward in a threatening manner, I knew I had pushed my luck too far. So I took a breath and sat back in my chair.

He wanted to know why I would come to Cuba on a boat that costs over $500 a day, versus a flight which is thousands cheaper. I reminded him, "Don't forget the cost of gasoline for the boat which makes it an even bigger disparity."

If he was going to dig a trap I was going to jump right in and take him with me. "So, you think this is about money?" I had to get us back together, somehow connect with him. I leaned in and said very sincerely. "I know you make about $12.00 a month. You know how much I make? Add three zeros. Is that fair? Don't you think I feel guilty about that every time I come to Cuba?"

He sat silently. I knew that their whole system was based on equality.

"So, I have money. Fair or not, I can afford this little adventure many times over and not even feel the pinch." I was thinking, feel it? It's going to put me into bankruptcy. "This is a romantic adventure, like Ernest Hemingway." Ernest Hemingway is the most famous American in Cuba, an old friend of Fidel. He has the status of a legend.

"Uh huh," he said, thinking he caught me. "It is about romance."

"No sir, not a love romance, romances of adventure of the open sea."

That got him back on Adianec. We discussed my relationship with her for thirty minutes. I used the "I'm a movie star" thing on him. He had obviously read my resume on the internet because he nodded and said, "Si, we know who you are."

"And you don't think I have beautiful women crawling through my window every night?...I wish." I replied. He kinda chuckled at that. "Why would I risk all I have for one girl?"

He pulled out a picture of us walking down the street together. "A very beautiful one," he noted.

My protectiveness of her burst out. "You must be very proud of how your country has to spy on its own people...afraid of something?"

Several times over the next two hours he would slam his fist down, in anger, as he got up and leaned over the table to intimidate me. At one point, he closed the file and said, "In your attempt to smuggle five people off this island, you have put us in a very difficult position in our relationship with the *Norte Americano* government."

I was concerned this was it and that he was about to lower the boom. I had to keep talking and redirect this conversation. I had one more risky hand to play.

I laughed sarcastically, "Your relationship? What relationship?"

Now it was time to convince him we were comrades. "You're not talking about my government, the one that contributes to starvation in your country. The one that takes over a sovereign country by having a military base within its borders, have you heard of Guantanamo?" He was listening, and seemingly buying it. "This same country that attacks Iraq without provocation and slaughters tens of thousands of innocent women and children." The Iraq war was Fidel's new party favor he brought out daily as proof of U.S. imperialism. "And you expect me to believe you care about that relationship."

We got into a twenty minute diatribe on why I would still live in the U.S. I explained to him the attributes of democracy and the greatness of the United States, compared to the oppression of Communism. I tried to reason with him about why we're so successful. I explained how I have the ability to travel around the world, the freedom to express my opinion and the constitutional right to elect a new leader every four years, freedoms denied to Cubans. I told him, "I may not appreciate all the policies all the time, but I love my country and her people. And one day the U.S. and Cuba will be partners. I guarantee you that."

He lit up, but just said, "*Si*, maybe."

I pushed my luck a bit when I told him, "I have the right, the duty, in my country to stand up and speak out when something is wrong. President Bush would defend my right to disagree with him. What would happen if you disagreed with Castro?"

He went ballistic. "I don't need to hear anymore from you. This is complete. Your five friends have already told us the truth."

It didn't occur to me until that moment that Adianec had been arrested too. My tired brain struggled to make sense of this new information. Did she really tell them our plan? If so, what did she tell them? What have they done to her, to make her confess? I feared that they had beaten or raped her. But then I didn't think that probable by the men that had interrogated me so far.

Then I realized what he said…("Smuggle five people.")"You've seen her?" I asked.

I was very excited thinking that she might be close. He started packing up. "I've been with her all day."

I knew he was bluffing about the confessions. Why would they admit to something that was not true? I was not smuggling five people, just one. Although in Cuba, it's not necessary to have any evidence for a conviction.

I decided to play into his bluff, convince him I was not in love with her, and then hopefully play my final card. "Are you going to see her again?" He looked up and nodded. "Give her a message!" I angrily demanded. He grunted. For the first time, I raised my voice. "Tell that fucking bitch to go to hell. Are you fucking kidding me? I was coming here to bring medicine for her mother, clothes, shoes and all kinds of fucking shit for the whole god damn family. And this is how she pays me back. She thinks she can just sneak her entire fuckin' neighborhood onto my boat without my permission?"

I was now yelling at the top of my lungs, which like my energy was dropping by the minute.

My sudden burst of anger threw him.

"Señor, señor *por favor*. No need to get upset."

"No need to get upset? No fuckin' need, are you fucking loco!? Do you think I've enjoyed coming here to this shit hole, every few months? Do you really think I was shitting you about my life in the U.S.?"

He seemed to be in a bit of a quandary now. Perfect. Last card. One way or another, it was now over. "And you! Do you really think you can put me away for more than two months? Have you lost your mind?! The public outcry will shatter Fidel's ears. Next week, my friend, when I don't come home, my agent will call CNN. And what is going to happen to your precious tourism when vacationers hear you put me, a movie star, in prison on bullshit charges?"

Tourism is Cuba's top contributor to their Gross National product. If they lose tourism, they will feel it on a national basis.

I was counting on Cuba's communist paranoia to scare him into saving his own skin. He kept trying to calm me down and I kept getting louder, although now I was so weak I had to hold onto the desk.

"So in two months, yes, I'm in a shitload of trouble with my country, but I'm free. I'm free, you idiot, because you cannot just lock up one of America's biggest stars and not get the attention of Canada and Europe. My movie opens in Havana next month (that was true) and you will be the one they point to. My movie will be playing here while I'm in prison…Think about it! Tourists will be scared out of their fucking minds. And what happens to you, the one who caused all this international upheaval? You're whacking weeds around Guantanamo!"

I grabbed my chair to throw it across the room. But I barely had the strength to pick it up, so I threw it straight down. The room started spinning and I knew I was finished. I slowly picked the chair up and sat down before I fell down, and proclaimed, "I'm done talking to you."

And I was. I had played my last card. I was sure they weren't convinced I was innocent. But maybe I gave them a reason to let it go.

"Señor, this is all not necessary, no quick decisions, we have much to discuss. This girl she is close, she worries for you."

"No, I don't ever want to see that bitch again. Do you understand what she tried to do to me? She lied to me, deceived and manipulated me."

Then he said, as if he hadn't had the thought before, "You're saying you were not going to take these five people with you?"

Finally, I get a chance to be honest. I pulled myself up and looked him straight in the eye. "I swear to you, I promise you with every fiber of my being, with every thing I hold sacred, I had no plan nor even knew of a plan to take five people off this island or anywhere near my boat."

And that was the truth, it was only one person.

I felt the tide changing with this guy for the first time and I wasn't going to let this opportunity pass.

"I have a bunch of guys waiting for me in the Bahamas, what do you think they would say if I showed up with five Cubans on board so we could all smuggle them into the U.S.?" I said almost as if I was confiding in him. He was clearly following me now. "And how do I get an overloaded boat through the U.S. Coast Guard? You know they have better technology than you, and I couldn't even do that here."

He left quietly, and for the first time in over two hours, I could breathe. I didn't care anymore what was going to happen. I was done. I didn't want to, nor could I, lie anymore. It took too much out of me. Thirty minutes later, the nice guy walked in. Now I got it. Good cop, bad cop, and again good cop. He sat down, with my file. "No more, I'm finished with your questions." I told him, completely exhausted.

"Mr. Brooks, you have to understand we have a job to do. Your story has many holes and our job is to fill them. We know you are in love with this woman. I'll tell you something," and I believed he was being sincere, "The love she has for you is very rare. But you have broken our laws. If it happens again, you will certainly go to prison for a very long time. If you want to be together, get married and move here."

Still not knowing if this was a trick I said, "I don't love her or want her to come to America. I have too much to lose."

He smiled, "Well, you tell her that tomorrow. Now, it is very late. Everybody needs rest"

"Is she okay?" I couldn't hide my concern for her.

"Yes, she is in no trouble. This will not go on anyone's permanent record. And you are welcome to come back to Cuba, by plane, whenever you'd like." He wasn't being completely honest. Nine months later, both Yanela and her friend lost their jobs for "plotting to leave the island illegally."

I shuffled outside. It was so refreshing; the cool wind and rain. I walked over to "bad cop" and apologized for causing so many problems and promised to never return on a boat. He laughed and put his hand on my shoulder, and we spoke for a few moments. "So you know that guy, George?" he questioned.

"I do, and I will give him your regards."

He took one last friendly dig. "So, he is much more famous than you."

I just shook my head, "You have no idea."

We laughed and I walked in the driving rain, back to my room in exhausted amazement. I hoped that was the last time I needed to embellish. I was beginning to confuse myself.

Chapter thirty

I LOVE YOU

It was well past 2 a.m. when I got to my room. I was starving. I ate a Balance Bar took a shower and turned on the T.V. I didn't so much fall asleep as pass out. The phone awakened me several hours later. It was Adianec's mother, she was crying hysterically. She hadn't heard from Adianec nor had Yanela's mom. I told her not to worry, I had just left the authorities and Adianec would be home soon. It wasn't until I hung up that I realized I had spoken to her completely in Spanish and she understood. It was an interesting surprise. I speak Spanish.

I couldn't fall back asleep, so I walked outside. The heavy rain had stopped and there were holes in the blanket of clouds where the moon's light poured through. The wind was pretty fierce, blowing the palms completely to one side. I walked down to the beach. It was dreamlike on the edge of the dark, deserted resort. I must have been the only one awake, with the exception of the man following me. The white caps on the water were translucent and the ocean was a moving art board. In my exhaustion, the night seemed like a hallucination.

I could hear my phone ringing as I approached the room. I ran to the phone knowing and hoping it was Adianec. She sounded completely wiped out. I asked her if she thought it was over, but she didn't know. We made plans to meet that morning in a place called Ciego de Avila. It was about an hour inland from Cayo Coco. I laid back in my bed and became very angry that this could happen. That a government could think it had the right to control and pen up people like sheep. What gives them the right to decide whom she can love and where she can live? I finally admitted to myself that Adianec was the most important person in my life. In fact, she had become my life. In some strange way, we had grown to be a family. This was no longer a good deed, or an unselfish act. I knew I was in love with her.

I went back to the boat early that morning to pack up some things for the next few days or until the weather broke. Mariean came out from her trailer and asked if I could give her a ride to the mainland so she could spend time with her daughter. I said that would be great, she could be my navigator. She actually knew the place where Adianec wanted to meet. She also said she would find a car for me to rent. By the time I finished on the boat, she had found a car and also a place for us to stay. She said the car wouldn't be available for a couple hours, though. What I didn't realize at the time was that we were being set up and manipulated so they could follow our every move. I don't blame Mariean. She has a daughter to take care of and has to do what she is told. Besides, who was I to her but some American who came to her country and broke its laws?

I felt relieved to be at least somewhat free. In retrospect, I felt bad for Mariean, even though she was there to spy on me. I never stopped talking the entire two hour drive. I hope she got hazard pay for that. We talked a lot about the current relationship between our two countries. She thought President Bush was a warmonger, and feared that he would order an attack on her country. I think I convinced her that she misunderstood the rhetoric.

She did get to slip in a word here or there. Her most personal question was, "Do you really knew George Clooney?"

"Well, I did. But I don't really know him any more." She seemed disappointed. "But I still know a couple of people who may be able to get his autograph."

It amazed me that a guy I played basketball with a few times many years ago had helped pave my way out of a communist prison. I doubted, though, that I'd be able to get her that autograph.

When we arrived at the town center, I thought it interesting that Mariean saw Adianec before I did, since supposedly she had never seen Adianec before. Adianec was standing in the shade of a Cuban version of a fast food restaurant, sans the fast food. We walked up to each other very slowly, silently communicating the whole time. I pulled her in and held her tightly in my arms, and I could feel the pounding of her heart against my chest. Her body began to quiver and I took her face into my hands and kissed her deeply. I knew I was doing the right thing, although I failed this time. This relationship was real. It was not an illusion created by an environment of vacation and adventure. We fit together, as crazy as it seemed. With vastly different backgrounds, we just fit, seamlessly. I couldn't deny it anymore and I told her, "I love you."

As we walked back to the car, I kissed her cheek and whispered, "Trust me, and play along."

When we got within hearing range of the car, I acted like we were in the middle of a heated conversation. "Amore, that makes no sense, then why would they say it?"

Smart girl, she just played her hand. *"Amore, no se."*

We got in the car and I continued, bringing Mariean into the conversation. I knew whatever Mariean heard or saw would get back to the Cuban officials.

"Mariean, my interrogators told me that Adianec was planning to get on my boat. I was very upset about that. Now she tells me it's not true, she never said it."

I could see the empathy in her eyes but she had to hold the party line, and also the car was most certainly bugged. Her every word was being recorded. "Please don't let it come between you two. I'm sure it was just something that got lost in translation."

She seemed a bit embarrassed, sympathetic, but unable to help.

Ciego de Avila was an interesting town, located in the western province of Camagüey, near where Adianec was born. The houses were pushed together in an eclectic display. Some very run down, slum-like, while others had fresh paint and were well maintained. We drove around the block. Mariean wasn't sure where her "friend's" house was.

We continued on, passing some very old buildings and churches. It reminded me of Barcelona, Spain. The streets were filled with people and old horse-drawn carts. Adianec and Mariean were chatting away and laughing about something. I think they were amused by my frustrated reaction of trying to drive with people walking down the center of the narrow road.

We pulled up to our new home, a two-story rectangular building set 100 feet from the road. The front area was for parking. The house was pretty by any standard, but there were bars on the patio windows, which surprised me. There was brightly colored Bougainvillea growing freely, and the house had an upper and lower balcony. The upper balcony was for our room.

We were accompanied up to our room and left there as Mariean and the landlady went down to talk. When they came back up, I spoke to the lady for the first time and told her that we liked it. "How much?" I asked.

She was very abrupt, and I quickly realized I did not like her. It's very unusual for me not to like someone, but on that rare occasion where it does happen, I don't or can't pretend otherwise. I handed her three days rent and she left without saying a word.

For the first time, Adianec and I were alone. We sat on the bed and held each other. I apologized often over the next hour. I honestly felt that my arrogance almost got us imprisoned. I told her, "Baby, I'm so sorry I put you in this situation, I just want you to live and experience a better life."

"I know you do. You are not to blame here. My government is bad, controlling, that is not for you to be blamed."

"I tell you though there is a silver lining here" She didn't know what I meant. "Uhh, something good out of this bad situation. Do you think they have really let us go?"

She started laughing, and whispered, "No, *mi amore*, they have ears in this room." She paused, and then realized I hadn't explained yet. "What is good with this?"

"Uh, yeah. I realized when I was being questioned and about to go to jail for nine years that the only thing I cared about was you. To quote my best friend, my love for you is crazy."

"Si it's true? I know, I always knowed."

"I've always known."

"You did?"

"No, no, I mean, no I didn't. But I was telling you how to say it correctly. But I do, you know. I want you in my life. I want a life with you now. Always. I love you."

Then she showered me with kisses. We discovered that the radio, T.V. and shower were all in non-working condition. Our landlady, Little Miss Sunshine, just shrugged it off. "*Que lastima*," what a pity.

I told Adianec to tell her the room is half price until it is a complete room. Everything was fixed by evening.

Since there was no water, Adianec boiled some water downstairs and gave me a sponge bath in the shower. I fell asleep in a chair reading and woke up to her ironing my clothes on the bed. It felt so natural to let her take care of me that way, something I was never accustomed to doing in relationships with women. Besides, whenever she ironed, all she wore was one of my shirts. She gives homemaker a sexy edge.

We spoke in mostly sign language all night in case our room was bugged. If they wanted to listen in on us making love, that was their business. We decided to not let it subdue us. Lucky them. We were both drained and not in the right space to ask, "what now?" We had a few days at least before the weather let up, and I could leave. I quietly told her about my interrogation and how lucky we were that my movie was opening in Havana. I was whispering and laughing about how I convinced them I was famous, and that they had to let us go or it would affect their tourism. "You know your boyfriend is brilliant."

"*Si,* I know. Why do you?"

"Well, I mean the way I bullshitted them into thinking I was famous, so they would let us go. I even had myself convinced."

She shot me down, and told me, in a somewhat condescending way, "You know, my love, they have no way to tell, they don't watch your TV." She believed something much more powerful was at hand, beyond my b.s. "But *mi amore*, it was our love that saved us. The man, he saw how much we love and it touches his heart."

Was she serious? These guys were hardcore commies. Nothing touches their hearts. "Come on, baby, you didn't see my performance in there, it was a game of chess and your boy took the queen. I really had them convinced that putting me in jail would affect their careers. Honey, what you're saying makes no sense."

"What is it you say? Tomato, tomahh-toe?"

She was throwing Cole Porter lyrics at me. "You're just not going to give this one to me are you? I'm right, you know I'm right. Babe, you cannot romanticize this. I was a trophy for them little missy, you don't just throw one away due to empathy."

"Potato, potah-toe!"

Silly girl. I hope one day when Cuba is free to have an opportunity to sit down and ask them why they looked the other way. I think it may have been a combination of self-preservation and compassion. Several months later two unarmed men in a boat tried the same thing. They were both gunned down. This happens often.

Lee had this idea that we were released because he worried them with his false stories. But I knew it was the passion and depth of our love that they saw and found compassion for. After they had released us, the nice man was very sympathetic and had offered advice on how Lee and I could be together legally. Sometimes Lee has a very healthy ego, but that is one reason why I love him so much.

At 6 a.m., we were jolted awake by what sounded like a baby being torn apart. It was the most harrowing sound I have ever heard. I jumped out of bed. It sounded like a murder was taking place thirty feet from our window, in the house next door. I frantically tried to get out through the locked balcony door while Adianec tried to calm me down.

"*Amore*, honey, it's a pig." I didn't comprehend what she was saying. She said, "Yes, a pig, for *comida*, food." They were slaughtering a pig at 6 a.m. in the middle of the city. It sounded like a human baby screaming. The terror in its raspy pleading voice was horrifying. I thought I heard it use words crying out for help. I am sure it said, "No please, help." The dogs in the neighborhood went into hysterics. The pleading of the dying animal got quieter and weaker over the next three minutes as the blood was drained from the single slice to its neck, while it hung upside down by its feet. My heart was pounding and I knew I would never eat pork again. It seemed human.

When we woke up later, Adianec explained that most people couldn't afford to buy meat so they would raise a pig and share it with the neighbors. It was something she had witnessed many times and for a Cuban, it was their only source of protein. This was not a part of her I was ready to embrace. She saw my reaction and teased me on the proper way to break a chicken's neck. She really was a country girl, a beautiful, graceful and sophisticated country girl. And I loved her. But it didn't mean I'd ever eat pork again.

I was groggy when I stepped into the newly-working shower and touched the live current on the shower head. The neighbors must have thought we were killing another pig by the way I screamed. I put on a pair of jeans that Adianec had ironed the night before. (Not only did she iron my jeans, she always folded my socks and underwear as she packed my suitcases.) As I put on my freshly ironed jeans, they slipped down. At first, I thought I had taken someone else's jeans, but when I tried on a pair of shorts, the same thing happened. I realized I had lost a great deal of weight.

There was a sense of dread hanging over our heads, but we did our best not to let it interfere with the short time we had together. We drove over to the town center to use a public phone in one of the hotels. As we were looking for a place to park, I slowed down to look around to see if I could find a space. A cop pulled me over and gave me a ticket for illegal parking. I had had enough of this place and their asinine laws. I wouldn't sign the ticket. I explained to him in very colorful language that he was a moron and the idea of an illegal parking ticket is if people actually park. We had never slowed to less than 5 mph. I didn't raise my voice and Adianec didn't translate, so he was clueless. I never paid the ticket.

I called Barry on an antiquated public phone. I was due home that day and nobody had heard from me. Through the static and crackling reception, I let him know, "Yeah, things went bad. I'll fill in you in later."

"You probably don't want to hear that Bill's research shows treacherous weather for the foreseeable future. Cold fronts are lining up back to back."

I just could not digest what Barry had just told me. How the hell was I going to get out of Cuba, and how much longer would my limited cash last…I decided to not think about it.

Chapter thirty-one

Adianec's childhood

We spent the day sitting by a nice lake with the far shore barely visible. The wind had picked up even more and the water was very choppy. It made me sick wondering how big the ocean would get. We sat up on a little bluff shaded by a clump of pine and palm trees. The grass had a strong earthy smell that I found intoxicating. We felt safe and protected there, and pretty confident that the trees were not bugged. Though we were trying to ignore the predicament we were in, I could not shake the heavy sense of dread that enveloped us. At any moment we expected to be re-arrested and sent to prison.

I sat there for hours, mesmerized by stories of her youth. I didn't say a word, I was so taken by her, I could have held that moment for a lifetime. She shared with me the difficulties of getting an education. The school was six miles away and there was no bus, so the kids had to walk. And with every new school year the group walking would have fewer kids as the boys went to work in the fields and the girls began to get pregnant and married, starting at age thirteen. Many years she had no shoes or just a pair her grandmother had handmade for her. After the Soviet collapse and until they allowed tourism, there was very little food, a small amount of rice and maybe a piece of fish, if her dad had caught one. Often they would only have one meal a day.

"Where Adianec grew up"

"I bet Fidel never missed a meal. Did you have soap and toothpaste?" She said if they did, they would have eaten it. "Hon, how'd you get through all that?"

"Together, amore. You do things alone in your country, but here we do all things together. We laugh together and we suffer together. My father would break glass on the rock outside and my mother and I would use it to shave our legs." She talked of her family, especially her mother and sister. She told me about how her mother would stay up all night with her during an asthma attack. When Adianec was a child. Her mother would never leave her, making a fan out of a piece of paper and fanning her face all night to bring Adianec more air. She told me how she always pushed her sister to stay in school so she could become a doctor.

"Oh, yeah, God forbid you had have hairy legs while you died of malnutrition."

She laughed. It was good to hear her laugh, even when talking about such a difficult situation. "Amore, no. What I mean is, life has to go on. You have to find normality. Normalcy."

"That's a big word...I'm very proud of you, you know. I feel lucky to have met you. Really I, I'm amazed by this love I have for you. I wish I had known you then. It makes me feel guilty that I wasn't there to protect you."

After graduating from high school, it was assumed she would go to work, but she wanted to get a master's degree in psychology. She had to deal with family members and neighbors who felt she thought too much of herself. The stories she told me of how she not only survived with barely the basics, but achieved her goal of becoming a teacher of children with special needs, elevated her even higher in my eyes. I felt blessed to know her and the most fortunate guy in the world to be loved by her. After university, she worked for a while near her hometown and then transferred to Havana and lived with Sol. She had been there for a year when some American guy began to stalk her.

She asked if Americans were forbidden from all communist countries. I hadn't thought about that. But no, Cuba was it. Even with our obvious enemies Iran and North Korea who are actively procuring WMD's and have threatened to annihilate us, still there is no law against traveling there. But Cuba, who doesn't have the ability to invade Burbank and does not threaten us physically, is considered far too menacing for us to visit. I could see that she was hurt by my answer. She asked me why my government hates them. I explained to her that it was politics. The Cuban-Americans are a small but powerful political community and they demand we isolate Fidel.

I told Adianec how the Cuban Americans had their lives and livelihoods ripped away from them and about their forced exodus to a foreign country. The annihilation of the entire middle and upper class of Cubans during the revolution isn't a subject taught in Cuban schools. But I agreed they should come up with something better than a failed embargo and create something that subdues or destroys the government of Castro but not the Cuban people. It seems to me that everyone is right and everyone is wrong and as usual, the innocent are the ones that suffer. It gave me some consolation to think that some day I would take one name off that list.

"You have to understand how much I love my family and how difficult it will be to leave them. I wouldn't leave them to just embrace freedom, I do it to be with you, no other reason."

I didn't know what to say. I still don't.

Even though we had always been taught that America is evil, most people know it's not true. Almost all Cubans want a better relationship with the American people. We are very curious about the American culture. We hear about America everyday and we wonder if Americans think about us. We know the U.S. government does not like us and that keeps us scared. What have we ever done? We just want to be friends. We have always heard that all Americans are very rich and we always talk about what it must be like to be American. When Lee told me that he can travel to all countries but mine, it was impossible not to be sad.

Lee told me things about the revolution that I had never heard before. They certainly would never teach this in school. I had no idea that Castro had stolen so much and destroyed an entire class of our society. We had been told that the Cuban-Americans had abandoned our country and had taken millions of dollars with them. The truth was very sad to hear. But it still does not justify an embargo that only hurts us. The Cubans that left, or were forced out in the 60',s have little or no family left here, so they don't have to care if this embargo hurts those of us that are still here. Certainly Fidel Castro does not care.

As we drove back to our apartment, we saw hundreds of square miles of incredibly rich soil and potential farmland overgrown and untouched since the revolution. Every few miles there was a billboard to remind Cubans how lucky they are not to be capitalists. God forbid they would actually be able to have three meals a day. Every time we were in the car, we would send a hello to the people eavesdropping on us. We would have over-the-top conversations, talking about how much we loved "Papa Fidel." The more I was exposed to Communism and Castro, the more disgusted I was by both. I explained to Adianec that capitalism can be exclusionary, cruel and sometimes devastating due to corporate greed, but it was the best system that humans have come up with so far.

The next morning, we called Barry again. Bill had told him that the second cold front seemed to stall, and gave me Thursday as a possible window to get through. I told Adianec, who nodded and smiled but I could see her sadness. I didn't know it at the time but she and Yanela had agreed that I probably would not ever come back to Cuba after this. Adianec felt that these were our last few days together.

We drove to Yanela's house, about an hour away. She lived in a remote farm town, though not much farming was being done there now. The home was in a long, nondescript, rectangular barn-like structure, split into four separate homes. It was a small community of about twelve families. It depressed me that people had to live in these conditions. As we walked into Yanela's home two things stood out; the simplicity and the cleanliness. The floor was concrete and cracked in some areas, but so clean it looked polished. You could literally see your reflection. The furniture was plain but comfortable, and there were little *tchotchkes* with plastic flowers on the bookshelves, along with all the books I had brought Adianec over the past eighteen months.

I was torn between feelings of empathy for their living conditions and admiration for their warmth and sense of family. They seemed to embrace life in the moment. The house did not have a finished ceiling, just painted roof rafters. I videotaped them as they all talked and laughed. I had brought in two "care" bags from the car and handed one to Yanela. Yanela loved the U.S. more than any other person I had ever met, including Americans. Adianec told me that Yanela had always wanted to go to America. She was like a love-struck school girl. She knew more about the geography and history of the U.S. than most Americans. I told Yanela to try the Reese's Peanut Butter Cup, to get a taste of America. She took the smallest bite possible, which I found strange until I realized why. She loved the taste, then she shared a small bite with her mom and they both giggled. She folded it up and put it away until her brother arrived. Then she jumped up, retrieved the candy and gave him a small bite. Then she laughed with him. She wrapped it up again to save the last small bite for her other brother who was coming home in a few days. I was so impressed by her generosity. She had to share the candy with her family to get the full benefit for herself.

We said goodbye and headed back to our place. As I started up the car, Adianec decided that she wanted to learn how to drive. She had never driven a car before. "Why not? The car is owned by the government right? Which, according to Fidel means it belongs to the people. So, it's your car."

Technically, I let her drive her own car. She was doing okay on the country road until a tractor came toward us in the middle of the road, putting us in a shallow ditch.

This was going to be our last night together, maybe forever. The next day I would have to get back to prepare my boat and gas up, then head out just before dawn on Thursday for a 460-mile one day sprint. The only stop would be Fresh Creek for gas. If all went well, I would be in Miami by 8 p.m., Thursday night. We called Barry that night. I asked if Bill was sure that Thursday was a good day. I didn't like Barry's answer. Reluctantly he said, "I wouldn't say it's going to be good. In fact, it will be rough. But you have no choice, Friday is impossible."

Barry was becoming the bearer of bad tidings. I felt a sense of dread. The last thing I wanted to do was get back on that boat alone. I knew how lucky I had been on the first half.

On Wednesday morning, we went down for breakfast and to settle our bill. The lady added a two dollar a day surcharge for parking. What irritated me was that she told us where to park and never mentioned that my car had to pay rent as well. We had also learned the day before that she was letting the secret police into our room every time we were gone. I'm rarely rude to people, but I had taken enough shit the past week. I placed the money on the floor and walked away. If she wanted the money, she'd have to get on her knees.

The lady whose house we stayed in had not been very nice to us. I found out why as we were leaving. She told me the secret police had been searching her house everyday after we left in the morning, which put her in a very dangerous position. If they had found any contraband, food, or anything out of place, she could be sent to prison and lose her home. She told me to be very careful with whatever we were doing and good luck. Then she told me she was glad we were leaving.

Putting Adianec in a taxi tore me apart. She always put on a strong front, but this time I could see the pain in her eyes. She couldn't hide it. She was afraid of my boat ride home, something I wasn't ready to deal with at that moment either. I wanted another day with her, even an hour. I wanted to tell her how much I loved her, to convince her of it.

The way she looked up at me as she got into the car, I could see she was scared. I knew I would do anything for this woman. Obviously, I would die for her. "I promise I'll call tomorrow night as soon as I pull up to the dock."

She stepped out of the car and hugged me one last time. I couldn't seem to let go of her, I felt paralyzed in the moment. Then she pulled away without looking up, jumped into the car covering her face, and drove off.

When we said goodbye, I knew it could be the last time and I cried all the way home. Lee said the water was easy. But I knew, because my father had been in the coast guard, that the water around Cuba is very dangerous and Lee could easily disappear. The thought that I would never hear from him again compressed my heart. Even if he made it home, I could not expect him to continue to help me. It had become too much.

I felt that I never had the opportunity for Lee to really get to know me, because of our language barrier. How could he know that my love for him was unconditional? I was not using him nor did I want anything from him, except his love.

I picked up a few hitchhikers along the way back to my boat. I thought about the stories Adianec had told me of having to walk back and forth to school. When I saw the young girls on the side of the road walking to the university, I had to stop. They were shocked and animated that they were picked up by an American way out there. Communication was very limited, but they kept erupting into giggle fits every five minutes. For the next twenty miles I felt, in a weird way, that I had helped Adianec in her youth.

Just before I got to the long bridge that would take me to Cayo Coco, I was stopped and searched thoroughly. They had me empty the trunk and open the hood. They even crawled under the car, just to make absolutely sure Adianec was not in the car. I got another ticket in Cayo Coco for going the wrong way into a turnabout. This time I deserved the ticket. The police officer and I talked for fifteen minutes after he wrote the ticket and marked my rental slip. He was curious about my friend Jay and wanted to know what it was like being a cop in L.A. I don't know if I really convinced him that it was not a war zone with police in constant riot gear, but we did laugh quite a bit. As I got back into the car to drive away, he ripped up my ticket, threw it on the ground and smiled as he got back on his motorcycle. I guess professional courtesy to Jay.

After I checked into the hotel, I went to see Mariean to let her know I was leaving at six in the morning. I needed gas and all my things that had been confiscated. I was concerned about the price of gas. I was sure they were going to gouge me and I had spent most of my cash, leaving $800 to cover gas and another night's stay. When the man came to fill my tanks, he made sure that every drop was accounted for. He had to make several trips with a fifty gallon drum in the trunk of a car. The gas was over near the jungle speedboats and my boat wouldn't fit under the bridge, so it had to come by land. The final bill was the cheapest per gallon price that I had paid for gas in over a year.

Chapter thirty-two

CURSE OF THE BERMUDA TRIANGLE

I hoped that the new day would bring calmer winds. I woke up at 5:00 a.m., opened my door and stared out into wet, pitch blackness. The weather is usually calmer in the morning, but not that morning. I walked to the boat at 5:30 a.m. in the misty rain, which seemed much worse because of the strong wind. The marina was empty except for the two guards. I prepared my boat, and put on a sweater and my foul weather gear for the wet day ahead of me. Mariean showed up at six and said, "I'm sorry. You cannot leave yet. Immigration wants to talk to you."

I felt that familiar chill run through my body, even though most of my nerve endings were shot at this point. I was holding my pants up with one hand. They were now at least two sizes too big. The sun was breaking through the horizon in pieces between the storm clouds. It was shooting long golden arrows across the sky. I found it interesting how nature could still express itself with such beauty as an individual's world was simultaneously falling apart.

The immigration guys showed up at seven, searched my boat one last time and had me fill out some paperwork. I hugged Mariean goodbye and promised to email. Since she runs the government marina business, she has Internet access. A crowd of no less than ten people gathered in the rain to see me off. One of the captains gave me some last minute advice on the squalls forming in the area. He said the seas had not calmed yet, and were too heavy for his boat. He explained to me at what angle to hit them and how to ease off the throttles when I caught air. Also, I should try to get as far north as I could before noon. As I pulled away from the dock, I felt as if a huge weight had been lifted from my shoulders. I was going home.

I rounded the corner of the marina and turned around to wave goodbye. Then I looked straight ahead at my destination. If I hadn't had to go through it, I would have been mesmerized by its furious splendor. The waves coming off the Old Bahama Channel were crashing down on the reef a half-mile out. These were even bigger than the nightmare of the Gulf Stream. But I had no choice, I had to go home. I went up a bit further to where I could hear and almost feel them slam onto the reef. I put the satellite phone and spare GPS into my pocket and tied myself to the captain's chair. I hoped I'd had enough rest to recover physically from the first leg.

The first hit really shook me to the core. After I got about a mile out, I realized that even though the waves were bigger than the Gulf Stream; nine to eleven feet according to the internet. They all came from the same direction and didn't break on top of the boat. The ride was no picnic to be sure, but it was manageable. My speed really took a hit, maybe 10 miles per hour, but I was able to remain on course. I also felt a little safer knowing what this boat could do. It was a weird sensation coming up high over a ten foot wave and having the boat simply drop into the air, hitting the deep trough below. Then I would be in this shadowy, wet narrow world for a second with towering walls of water to my front and back. According to what Bill had told me, these waves were going in the perfect direction for the course I set. I wasn't hitting them straight on, but at a slight angle, like surfing, only uphill. I was trying to make a sport out of it to control my fear.

I started to feel the symptoms of nausea but was able to hold it down for about fifteen minutes. Then out of nowhere, the wind turned wicked and the rain blinded me at the top of the waves. I had hit one of the squalls the Cuban captain had told me about. The wind sounded deep, even evil, and would nearly pull my boat out of the water when I was exposed at the top of the waves. It would whip under my Bimini-top, feeling like it was going to rip off the boat. The ripping and cracking noises almost drove me insane. The rain was hitting me like tiny darts, leaving welts all over. I was tied in, so I knew it was just about being cold, wet and miserable. It didn't take long for my stomach to start its upheaval. Twenty minutes later, as quickly as the storm came, it left. I really wanted to pull over and find a motel for the rest of the day.

Aside from throwing up and dealing with the headache that was creeping in, it was quite interesting to watch how this boat took a wave. There were times when I went into the wave too directly and the boat almost stood on end and gave me a direct view of the clouded sky. The boat didn't actually go over the top of the wave, but got about three-quarters of the way up, then snapped down and fell through the wave. Sometimes it would drench me with warm salt water, but it would almost always drop into thin air on the other side and slam into the trough below. My solar plexus got reacquainted with the steering knob. Whenever the propellers hit air, they would scream into uncontrolled RPMs. But, if I was in sync, I would have the power pulled back. It was a bit like a dance, everything was in the timing. I was still getting tossed about and it was a constant up and down, in extreme. I figured if I was supposed to die, the Reaper had had plenty of chances already.

After an hour, my seasickness had drained all my energy. I was in a miserable routine of letting my eyes close and taking two second naps. Then, on one of the snaps into the trough, I felt a pop in my left shoulder. I didn't feel a tremendous amount of pain, unless I tried to use it. So I tucked my arm inside my life vest and drove with one hand, which effectively ended my ability to power up and down.

The intensity of the waves dropped off quickly as I made it through the Bahama Channel and slipped into the Bahama Bank. The seas were significantly smaller, maybe three and a half feet, but still violent. It was like driving at high speed across a row of deep ditches. I pushed the throttles down as far as I could stand the intense vibration and shoulder pain. Although I couldn't see the bottom due to the boiling conditions, I had some comfort knowing the bottom was no more than thirty feet down. I was playing hide and seek from the stinging rain by ducking behind the windshield and popping up for a second to make sure I wasn't heading into one of many rock and sand obstacles in the area.

Up ahead, I could see the darkness of another squall heading my way. I looked at the charts and saw that a large rock was just to my right. It gave me a reason to shout and my spirits rebounded when I was able to fine this shelter in the middle of the ocean. It almost gave the impression that I knew what I was doing. She stood about ten feet above the water, approximately one hundred yards long.

I tucked in and put the small island between the storm and my boat. Then I threw the anchor over board. I knew there was a rule on how to set an anchor in regards to wind, current and land, I just didn't know what it was. I tilted up the engines as the squall hit to keep from losing my props on the rocks. The fury of the storm rolled over and around me. But aside from the rain, I was untouched. It gave me a moment to reflect emotionally on what had happened the past week. My arrogance had put Adianec's life in jeopardy. This insanity of thinking that I could do anything, charm my way into or out of any situation, almost cost the woman I loved her life. It humbled me, hopefully a lasting change.

After the storm passed, I sat there dazed, wet and shivering, as another

Elton John song finished on the CD player. I drank my last Red Bull and walked out on the back platform to relieve myself. As I kneeled down to steady myself against the engine hood, a young porpoise popped his head up four feet from mine. I yelled from surprise and fell back. I think he did the same. I just lay there, laughing at my situation, and crawled back over to have a talk with the young mammal, but he had already gone.

The closer I got to Andros, the more certain I was that they weren't coming after me. The seas were just over two feet there. The water was churning pretty violently, but not enough to make me sicker, just enough to keep me rattled. Keeping up my energy was a minute-to-minute affair. The clouds were thinning out as I made my last turn east, less than forty miles from the Tongue of the Ocean. I was concerned about the conditions at the cut through the barrier reef. I knew the boat could handle it. It was my legs and shoulder that worried me. An hour and a half later, I saw the cut ahead. I knew for certain that the Cubans had let me go, and the nightmare was over. Even though Cuba is ninety miles away, they consider the southern tip of Andros and the miles of water in-between to be Cuban territory.

I hit the cut with less respect than I should have and got drenched in the upheaval of 6,000 feet of water coming up into a twenty-five foot deep shelf. The Tongue was rough but no more than four feet. I was hitting patches of sun here and there and I took it as a good omen. I knew that civilization lay less than sixty miles north. It gave me a reserve of strength, even as the cold, wet, wind and vomit were zapping it. Though the signs were obvious that I was going to make it home, feelings of despair saturated me. In my wildest imagination, I could not have predicted that I would be alone at this point of the journey. I missed Adianec and I was embarrassed. I knew that a deep depression was going to hit me when I got home. This was the biggest failure of my life. I felt impotent in my ability to fulfill her greatest need… freedom.

About ten miles ahead of me, I could see it. It seemed to form out of nowhere. Another squall was heading straight down the middle of the tongue, and this one was a monster. I said to myself, "Shit, this could hurt. Not good, it's just not good." I asked the old man for one more favor, "Come on dad, need you again."

The leading edge of the storm was curling up under itself with black and green clouds taking a prominent lead. I had never seen dark green clouds before. Had I not been heading straight into it, I would have been morbidly curious. We were closing together faster than I would have liked. I had no protection from this storm and was miles from a cut through the barrier reef just to my left. I would also have to maneuver through a gauntlet of lightening bolts. I could see Andros five miles deeper beyond the reef.

Since the storm decided to take up the middle of the twenty-foot wide tongue, I was hoping to pass it with minimal damage by staying as far left as I could without hitting the reef. The Barrier reef juts out and back sharply in this area. I wouldn't need the GPS for another eighty miles, as I could stay on course visually until I got to the top of Andros. This storm worried me. It looked quite fierce and I felt anything but.

There was no gradual introduction. The winds hit like a wall, lifting my boat up by the Bimini top, and left me with little ability to steer. The temperature that accompanied the storm dropped sharply and left me aching and shivering. I was watching the color of the water, trying to stay as close to the reef as I could without hitting it. Driving the boat felt more like a weight-shifting exercise than using a steering wheel. Control was more of an illusion. With my face frozen, the driving rain had me cursing in pain.

Without warning or a gradual change in color, through a deluge of rain I saw the light blue of shallow water just beyond me. I turned the wheel sharply to the right but the wind denied even the thought of it. I threw the throttles into reverse as I hit the reef. I must have been thrown over the center console because I found myself on my back, in the front of the boat, looking straight up at the sky. I was breathing heavily and the rain was coming down so hard it kept choking me. I thought I'd just lay there and wait to get hit by the lightening that was striking all around me, or until the boat sank. I didn't have the energy or desire to save myself. "What a mess you've made with your life, pal. It's over. Your life is over."

I knew I wasn't going to die, but my life was over. I had ruined the life of the woman I loved and now I had wrecked a hundred and fifty thousand dollar boat. The shore was three or four miles away, but I knew even with a bum shoulder that I could make that swim in the shallows. Then I remembered what both Bill and Phil said. "It's a Boston Whaler. They are unsinkable, stay with the boat no matter what." So I lay there and listened to the boat grind across the reef while being battered by wind and wave.

I started to whimper like a pathetic dog, blaming God for all that had befallen me in the past week. The storm had passed in less than forty minutes leaving nothing but blue sky and sunshine behind it. I thought about my option of calling the owner of the boat and telling him the quadrants of where to pick up the wreck. I would just stay in the Bahamas and teach scuba diving. No more worries, bills or hassles. I would make my life one of leisure, and suppress any goals and expectations. The idea of having to face what would definitely be lawsuits and bankruptcy did not appeal to me. I was of no use to Adianec any longer, so there was no need to go home and be responsible.

The intensity of the sun heated me up quickly. With my soaking wet clothes under the rubber weather gear I was wearing, I began to steam. "Good," I thought, "Burst into flames and end this misery."

I was getting too hot to pity myself any longer, so I pulled myself up on the boat rail and looked over into the water.

I had never seen anything so beautiful. I didn't want to recognize it because my burden in life had just gotten too heavy to bear. Seeing any beauty right now would give me a grain of hope and I didn't want any. I let go, flopped back to the deck of my wreck and screamed out loud at God for several minutes. All I wanted to do was help another human being and for that, he took away everything. I crawled around the console to lay in the shade and took off all my clothes. If this is what He wants, here I am, naked, nothing left to give, and that's what I told him. "Hey! Here I am, if this is what you want. I tried to reason with you, but you weren't having any of that. No? Fine. Then take it. Take it all. Me? My life. I don't want it. I don't want any of it. None of it. Take it all. All of it. Just save her, that's all I'm asking. Just, please, have some decency and save her. Please."

I was spent. With an aching stiff shoulder and wobbly legs, I climbed up to the chair and sat. I looked again off to Andros. I was being played. How could it look so beautiful when I had been thrown into hell? A gentle breeze was blowing and the water was not of this world. I could see the bottom. The coral reefs were deep shades of reds and greens soaking in blue water so brilliant there was no name for its color.

I realized I was at a crossroads, but I didn't want that. I didn't want an option on how to feel. I was miserable and I deserved to wallow in it. I had made sacrifices but still, the thought kept banging into my brain. I had a choice to recognize that there is always beauty, always hope. If I chose to not become overwhelmed with self-pity, this was a beginning. Boy that really sounded like bullshit! Could I use this as an opportunity for personal growth? It would never get this bad again. And if I embraced this moment like a lesson and walked into it, eyes wide open, I would never have a challenge this severe again. I knew this was a bad sign to be talking to myself, so I dove into the water. It was warm and refreshing. I took a deep breath and dove down about eight feet to the bottom, scattering brightly colored fish. I wedged my good arm into a hole in the reef, closed my eyes and let myself hang weightless for a couple minutes until I needed air. It felt so relaxing that I did it a few more times. Being naked out in the open was freeing. I knew there were no people within forty miles.

On my last dive, I looked over at my boat from under water. I couldn't see any severe damage. I didn't trust my eyes. This was unbelievable. I had heard and felt the crash, there was no mistaking it. I swam closer but all I saw were superficial scratches, no gaping holes. I jumped up into the boat and raised the engines to check to see how damaged they were. Nothing. One small dime-sized chip on the fin below the propeller was all I could see. I wasn't ready to claim a miracle. But, I did hit that reef at close to twenty mph. The boat did stop dead in its tracks and I was thrown to the front of the boat, so where was the damage?

Then I noticed that I was drifting, I was freed from the reef. When I raised the props off the rocks, a small wave washed me inside the barrier reef. I lowered the engines and prayed. I pushed the port starter and heard the rumble, same with the starboard. I was so amazed that I even began to doubt that I had run aground. When I put the engines into gear I was brought back to reality. The props didn't spin, they had been stripped! Still, the damage should have been so much worse. I noticed that if I kept the engines between 400 and 550 rpm they would stay engaged. It was only about three mph, but it gave me the ability to steer while riding the current.

I was about forty miles from Fresh Creek. At this speed, I would arrive in thirteen hours. I couldn't see a break in the barrier reef so I had to stay inside, which was filled with land mines of sand shallows and a maze of reefs. I remained naked for some unknown reason. It seemed to keep me from falling into despair. Occasionally I would have to get into the water and manually guide the boat through tight spaces. I was about two hours into this exercise when I noticed a boat up ahead in the shallows. All I had on was deck shoes and a sunburn, so I slipped on a pair of shorts to prepare for company.

Chapter thirty-three

SAVED BY JESUS

Two Bahamians on a flat bottom boat cruised over to me. I was a bit sun blinded, so they appeared to be just dark, featureless figures with large smiles and deep, calm voices. "Where you at Mon?"

"I believe I'm in hell, sir."

"Ya mon." They both laughed.

"I hit the barrier reef, spun the props, and now I'm just getting a slow tan."

"Ya mon." More laughter.

"Trying to get to Fresh Creek. Can you help?"

I was ready and willing to be taken advantage of, I just wanted out. "Take this line Mon, close yer eyes and get yerself a nap dere. We'll wake you in time, mon."

They went into shore and back out many times, following an unseen route up the island. They seemed to know every inch of these waters. Every so often I found myself relaxing and enjoying the moment. The moment was perfect. My situation was another story.

Within a couple of hours, we were at Fresh Creek. I asked what I owed them and they said, "The rope."

So I threw it to them and limped into the marina. I went straight to the fuel depot and pulled in without incident. I tied up and ran to the front desk, tripping over my now oversized shorts. I needed a mechanic fast.

The man at the desk said the only mechanic on the island was Junior but he didn't have his number. He started calling around for anybody who had Junior's number. He found it and called, but no answer. I ran back out to the boat to raise the engines and take a look at the props, as he continued to try to locate Junior. I was worthless as a boat mechanic so I went back inside. I asked if there was anybody on another island that could help. We called a marina in Nassau; the desk clerk explained my situation. The man in Nassau said he could send someone out, but not for few days. I took the phone.

"I will pay double his overtime, his flight and a surcharge on the parts. But I need him on the next and last flight of the day, leaving in forty-five minutes."

"Well, I is really busy after work."

"You live on an island, how busy can you be?" My voice was getting louder.

The desk clerk laughed and nodded. I was getting frustrated. "Listen, please don't go anywhere yet, I'll call back in a few minutes." Now I was back in panic mode, I looked up at the desk clerk and pleaded with him. "Do you know any other way of locating Junior?"

"This is the only number, but I'll keep trying."

I went back to the boat. There was now an old beat up station wagon parked near the fuel depot. I jumped on the boat to open the gas cap. Someone in the car said, "Hey mon, you need some help?"

"Nope, I'm fine." Needless to say, my mind was preoccupied.

"Okay, I'm here if ya need me Mon."

He kept trying to engage me in conversation but I was too filled with anxiety to make friends. I ran back up to the front desk. No luck locating Junior. I called Nassau again, and the man asked for the model of the engines. Again, I ran back out to the boat, my shorts kept falling down the whole time, tripping me up.

My new friend in the car said, "If ya need anyting, I'm yer mon, mon."

I kinda snapped at him, "Listen dude, I'm a bit overwhelmed right now, can you see that?"

He laughed, my insult washed right over him. "Sorry for yer problems, mon."

I felt like an insensitive idiot. So I walked over and shook his hand. "Sorry man, I'm just having a really bad day."

"I know you is, Mon, I'm here."

"Yes, you are, what's your name?"

"Me name's Junior, mon"

"JUNIOR! You're Junior? The mechanic, Junior?"

He let out that deep calm laugh again. "Ya Mon, that Junior."

I couldn't believe it. "I've been looking for you!"

"Here I is."

"Why didn't you say anything?"

"I did Mon, I said I'm yer Mon, Mon!"

With that, Junior got out of the car to look at the props. He was a very big man, maybe six foot four, with skin as dark and pure as Doctora Rosi. He told me what parts to order and began to pull the boat over toward a break in the sea wall, where you could walk down to the water's edge. I ran back inside and told the desk clerk the conversation I had just had with Junior. We laughed and called the guy in Nassau. I asked to please have the parts on the next flight. He wouldn't make any promises, he had things to do.

When I returned to the boat, Junior had it tied off about ten feet from shore with the engines raised. He appeared to be standing on the surface of deep water at the back of the boat, pulling the props off. The sunlight was reflecting brightly off the water where he stood. It wasn't until I got to the water's edge that I could see he had piled up rocks and a wooden crate to use as a platform just below the surface which he was standing on. I told him about the illusion from the sea wall and I thought he was walking on water. "Maybe I should call you Jesus."

He laughed so hard he almost fell into the water. He liked the idea of me calling him Jesus. I said, "Perform a miracle on this boat and I'll always call you Jesus."

The parts were due in on the 4:45 p.m. flight. Junior said he'd be back at 5:30 p.m. sharp. He had to fix a friend's boat. I asked, "Is that 5:30 p.m. sharp real time or Bahama time?"

He laughed again. "Real time, mon." I got back from the airport with the parts at 5:35 p.m. Junior stepped out of the lobby, smiling. "Real time, mon!"

He brought along his friend, Harold who was even taller then Junior but quiet. Harold and I stood on shore harassing him the whole time. "Jesus" was one of the best-natured guys I'd ever met. It was actually the norm in the Bahamas. Very large, and so friendly, you'd think they were Canadians. Within thirty minutes he said, "Let's go for a ride."

I handed him the keys and he looked at me astonished. I said, "Not for keeps."

"No, Mon, but you gonna let me drive?"

"Absolutely."

The sun was going down fast. We had maybe twenty minutes of light left. They loved the boat, and its speed. When we were out in the Tongue, I thought he said, "That was where we found you." Above the roar of the engines I asked if that was him. He smiled, nodded and pointed to Harold. With all the wind and engine noise, I was never sure if that is what he said and I have always forgotten to ask. But I liked the idea that "Jesus" had saved me.

We came back into the marina in the dark. He didn't need a light or chart. He could have made it through blindfolded. We sat on the dock throughout the night, drinking and talking. Harold was a bit of a mystery and I said something in reference to that. Junior laughed and began to tease Harold about his secret "runs." It soon became evident that Harold's secret was that he was a smuggler. He had a couple of fastboats and made midnight runs. My heart raced at the thought of that. They felt comfortable with me and began to open up. Harold ran both drugs and people. Playing dumb, I said, "Oh, people. That could only be Haiti, huh?"

And then I heard the music. Harold said, "And Cuba."

I joked around with him, wanting more information before I came clean.

I told them my story. I could feel Junior's empathy. He turned to Harold and said, "You got to help our Mon."

Harold just nodded. I changed the subject, not wanting to sound as desperate as I was. We talked about the weather the next day. Evidently, the next cold front had stalled until late the following morning. I asked them about the smooth 100 mile area between the Tongue and Bimini. They told me they called it "The Lake." They often go to the beach there. A group of boats go and hang out in less than a foot of calm water, on a sandbar, in the middle of the ocean. As we said goodnight I took both of their numbers. I asked Harold how much the rescue would cost me. He said, "Maybe $2,000, expenses only."

I got up at 5 a.m. and was in the boat warming up the engines by 5:30 a.m. It was dark when I headed out, but Junior had showed me how to get out in the dark using the inlet and beacon. I don't remember much of the trip until I got to Bimini and the idea of re-crossing the Gulf Stream made me very uneasy. I called Barry, "So, I'm making the crossing. Expect a call in two hours, Any longer than that, there's a problem and you should call for help."

It was rough but not nearly as bad as the week before. Finally seeing the skyline of Miami almost brought tears to my eyes. I called Barry from my cell phone as I entered the inlet. no need for the Satellite phone, anymore.

I made the crossing in an hour. It was almost noon. I had a hard time believing it was over but here I was, pulling into Miami harbor fifteen pounds lighter with a bum shoulder and a wrecked boat. Bad trip, however, I finally had that 31" waist.

As I pulled up to the dock to fuel and unload, the manager came out and said, "Your sister just called. She is very worried."

Barry had called him several days earlier to tell him we were having such a good time in the keys we wanted the boat a few more days. The manager said he told my sister that, but she wanted me to call home immediately. I did, and told her I would call back from the hotel and explain everything. She asked to speak to Adianec, but I just muttered, "Not possible."

As we did the checkout on the boat, I actually got sad. I was going to miss that boat. We had been through a lot together. The manager noticed the divot on the prop fin and asked, "How did that happen?"

"I have no idea, just charge me for it."

He waved his hand. "Naw, looks like you took good care of her."

Truth is, she took good care of me. Without question, had I taken any boat other than the Boston Whaler, I would not have made it.

I checked into "our" hotel and went up to the room. That was when it really hit me that I had failed and might never get Adianec to America. I was devastated. Maybe it just wasn't meant to be. But there was a problem; she was a part of me now. Perhaps she was the part of me that I had always felt missing. I tried calling her to let her know I was okay, but the lines to Cuba were busy.

The pizza and Coke I'd ordered arrived. As I stood by the window looking out over Miami, I took a sip of Coke and the skyline began to spin. I don't know how long I was out but when I came to, the table was turned over, I had a small bump on my forehead and my pizza was all over the carpet. My body had finally given out. I took the pizza to bed and watched CNN, which had become my habit, since Cuba. After a two hour nap I got up, did my laundry and began to call friends and tell them my story. Jay and I made up a MasterCard commercial:

"Trying to smuggle your girlfriend off a communist island: $58,780.
Bringing the rescue boat home four days late: $1,250.
Losing 15 pounds in a Cuban prison…Priceless!"

I was going crazy worrying about Lee. He had told me he'd call when he got to Miami, but I had not heard from him. So I called Barry and he told me that Lee was stuck in the Bahamas. I was so desperate to speak to him. He called me late the night he arrived in Miami. His voice was sad and very tired. He told me he couldn't explain what happened until the next day when he got home. I was so relieved he was alive. I will never allow him to do anything that dangerous for me again. I would rather spend all my life under Fidel than hurt Lee.

I flew home early the next day. First thing I did was rip down the "Welcome Home Adianec" banner stretched across my living room. I walked to the beach and took account of almost two years of my life. I had drained all my savings and was over $20,000 in credit card debt. I had spent almost $60,000 and offered up my very existence several times with nothing to show for it.

Over the next few weeks when I would call Adianec, there was a distance between us. I don't think either of us knew how to face the truth, that maybe she was trapped in Cuba. In the beginning, I put the Harold option out of my mind. I'm not even sure that I mentioned it to her at first. I was out of money. All my friends were totally entertained by the story of my failure. It was a kind of Don Quixote-like adventure that made their testosterone rumble and momentarily forget they were opposed to the whole affair. As news spread, I was getting calls from Hollywood producers wanting to buy our story. I had no interest, not without a happy ending.

During this time I ran into Yoga Girl again. We went out to dinner a few times but she was seeing someone else and I was beginning to realize that regardless of my indecision, I was in a relationship. I joked with Kevin that the reason I had tried to rescue so many women was practice for the big one.

About a month after the fiasco, Harold called and asked if we were going to do this thing. I was financially, emotionally, physically and spiritually broke. During the past two years, I had spent almost all of my money on her and due to all the travel and distractions; my annual income had dropped to less than half of what it was. I had to ask myself if this was even a possibility and at what stage of ruining my life should I throw in the towel? Yet I couldn't walk away and abandon her with one more opportunity floating about, or if ever. How do you give up on family?

I half-heartedly told Adianec about Harold, though I was just too spent to take anything serious. I did run it by Barry, briefly, and he agreed I couldn't just slam the door. Adianec also mentioned to me about some guy that had approached her after hearing our story. He said he could get her to Antigua on an exchange program. I looked at the map. It was a thumbnail off the coast of Venezuela. That meant I would have another very long boat ride. Absolutely, no way would I ever captain another boat alone. I just brushed that idea off.

Harold called again and said it was a go, but he needed the money to buy gas and pay the guys. I knew it was not the best business move to give a smuggler $2,000 but I had no choice. I sent the money to my nephew Michael in Orlando. Harold was making a run to Miami and he could run up to Orlando and pick it up. After Michael met with Harold he called and asked, "Uncle Lee, do you trust this guy?"

"Michael, he smuggles drugs and human cargo, of course I don't trust him. But we're out of options and besides, I'll be on the boat."

Harold called me several days later and said he was at the airport heading to Cuba to scout things out, and he would call me in four days. Adianec kept bringing up the other guy that has gotten Cubans to Antigua. I said "Darlin', it might as well be the dark side of the moon. It's ten times the distance from the U.S. as Cuba is."

She said something about it being close to the U.S. Virgin Islands. I got a little irritated with her and said it was not the U.S., it was just U.S. territory. She swore it meant the same thing with political asylum. So I called a law firm on St. Thomas and said very matter of factly. "If I wanted to smuggle someone from Cuba to the U.S., could I use St. Thomas as a dry-foot welcome-mat?"

The lawyer chuckled at my lack of tact and said "In a word...Yes. Just like landing in Miami."

I checked out the map, still 200 miles of desolate open ocean between Antigua and the Virgin Islands. I checked the Internet, average wave height; six to eight feet, with the occasional thirty-foot rouge wave. The waves come straight from Africa with nothing to slow them down along the way. No, that was not going to happen. I got lucky the first time, and besides, this guy was no doubt a con man just like everyone else. Still Adianec kept bringing it up every time we spoke.

I called Harold back about a week after he took the flight to Cuba, and I left a message. This went on for a week before he called me back and said, "There is a problem in Cuba. I'll have an answer in a week, mon."

Blah, blah, blah. This scenario went back and forth for six more weeks until he disappeared with my $2,000 and the last bit of hope I had left. Harold Laflear from Fresh Creek, Andros Island in the Bahamas is a thief.

At this point I was becoming negative and was regularly in a foul mood. I wasn't even all that pleasant with Adianec anymore. She begged me to consider the Antiguan option. I finally said, "Okay, fine, but I need to speak with this con man first. If I like what he says, I'll do further research."

Chapter thirty-four

Antigua

The very next day I got a call from Antigua. The man's name was Jose. He was from the Dominican Republic and spoke primarily Spanish. His English on a long distance line was too much work so I put him on the phone with Luis, my foreman, to translate. I was in negotiations with another smuggler, but this time, the game was going to be played by my rules.

I let him know immediately that I didn't trust him; he would have to earn it. To sweeten the deal and make it safer for Adianec, I told him she was the first of four I wanted to get out. I knew that if he was going to take a shot at me he would wait to do it on the last person. I no longer felt the defenseless desperation I had in the past. I realized that the smugglers I'd been dealing with lived by a different code, then the rest of civilized world. They recognized and respected strength and greed over human decency. I told him, "On this first one, no money up front. When she lands in Antigua, I'll be standing beside you, money in hand."

I was no longer nice and naïve in the ways of the world's underground. Trust no one and lie to everyone. That was a motto I would have to learn to live by until Adianec was safe.

With Jose's nature of never telling the whole truth and having some things get lost in Luis's translation, I was not entirely sure of how this was going to be done. What I gathered was that Cuba and Antigua had an exchange of energy and resources, ideas and people, flowing back and forth. They would let groups of Cubans go over to exchange energy efficient light bulbs.

I couldn't figure out why people in Antigua couldn't change their own light bulbs. He said, "We will have to bribe some ministry official in Cuba to get her freed from her university commitments."

Castro speaks so triumphantly about free education. The truth is a bit different. Adianec was forced to work in the fields throughout her time at the university and then full-time in the summers. Then, like most Cubans, she would be enslaved for many years in order to pay off her "free education." Once we eliminated her obligations, we had to give another bribe for an exit visa. In most countries you need a visa to enter. In Cuba, you need a precious and rare visa to exit. Adianec paid both the education "fees" and exit visa fee.

We now had to figure out how to get her from Antigua to the U.S. Virgin Islands. I checked the British Virgin Island immigration website and read about the process to get her a visa to Tortola. Since they were a British Commonwealth, my friend David in London could invite her to Tortola. From there it was a three to four-hour boat ride to St. Thomas and freedom. I had that much of a boat ride in me. Looking at the map, I would be cruising near many islands, and we would always be in sight of land.

I had to let Barry in on the plan, though I was a bit embarrassed to admit I was setting myself up again. I was taken aback by his reaction. He and Lisa were completely supportive of the plan. They came up with a thousand things that could turn south and how to be prepared. Aside from that, they were very enthusiastic. Several days later Barry called and said, "Sit back, the cavalry is coming."

Bill and Barry's friend Herb wanted to help with the actual introduction to freedom. Herb suggested he charter a 100-foot yacht, captain, crew and chef. Adianec would come to America in decadence. I had already checked out the legal ramifications. Bringing her into the country would not be considered illegal as long as we didn't profit from the task. Safe there, since Herb was financing the entire operation.

Barry's brother, Steve, called me and asked if I needed any help, financially or with logistics. With Steve part of the team, success was inevitable. Steve, to me, is a demi-God. Most people see Steve as a 5'6" nice little Jewish boy from Culver City that made good. But for me, Steve is 7' tall with cojones the size of two swinging Volkswagens. When he walks into a room, he is the Alpha Dog. Several years earlier, Steve and Barry had given me another option in life besides acting by setting me up in business. Steve was fearless and that he was offering to be involved in Adianec's rescue made it that much more attainable. If I could just get Adianec to Antigua, it would take an act of God for us to fail and I was certain He was with us.

Within six weeks of that original call from Jose, everything was falling into place. Adianec had purchased her plane tickets and sent them in with the papers requesting an exit visa. She was told to expect a response in two to three weeks. With Adianec's flight booked only five weeks away, we were sweating every day. We had decided to make Herb's yacht the back-up plan. Getting her a visa to Tortola would be our primary goal. The least amount of people involved the better, though everyone in this so far could hardly contain their excitement over the prospect of what was happening.

After all we had been through I was not going to allow my expectations to take over my life. For some reason I had a strong feeling everything was going to work this time. Trying to get a visa to leave my country is very difficult, due to so many things that can go wrong. Maybe even the person that is supposed to stamp it could be in a bad mood. I was so nervous when I went to immigration to see if it had been approved. I turned in my ID with everyone else, and the lady began to call names. When she had finished my name had not been called. I waited twenty minutes before I could gather the courage to go up and ask for my ID. She rudely (it is the way of government people in Cuba) told me to sit and she would check. I went back up an hour later to remind her. She slapped my passport on the counter. I opened it up and there was my exit visa. I felt numb.

I went outside and sat on the curb for a while. My legs were shaking too badly to walk. After a while when I assured myself it was true, I called Lee. It took me a moment to convince him. For the next few days certain realizations came to me. I was leaving my family and might not see them for several years, but I didn't want to think about the negative implications. I wanted to think about finally getting out and seeing the world through my own eyes. I could actually see myself sitting next to Lee in his car. I started to smell him and imagine him next to me when I woke up every morning. It began to feel real.

I will never forget the day she called me. It was less than two weeks after she sent in her application. She excitedly told me, "Baby, reserve your flight to Antigua! I have my exit visa in my hand."

It was good for sixty days and then she was expected to return, though of course she would not.

Every time I called her, she seemed more nervous. There was nothing to do but wait for the departure date and hope our Cayo Coco deal didn't get reported in the meantime. If so, she would get stopped by immigration at the departure gate. We still spoke in code. I was getting concerned now about little things in our relationship. I reiterated again that she did not have to come to L.A., that I would still take care of her in Miami. She flew into her passionate Ricky Ricardo persona, and although I didn't understand one word, I got the point. I suggested instead that we should not decide on a commitment until one year after her arrival. She agreed.

Two days before Adianec's departure, a tropical storm was churning in the Atlantic and heading for Cuba. She was already very anxious about her first plane ride and having to make a connection in Jamaica and Barbados. Now, with the possibility of having to fly in bad weather, she was not to be calmed. "Honey, what if it rains? How will the plane fly in the bad weather?"

"No, Adianec, I fly in rain all the time. If it's too bad, they won't take off until the weather clears."

That only brought another fear, how she would find me. I assured her I would find her. "Amore, the important thing is to get off that island. Once you're in a foreign country, we have options. Get on that plane! Do you understand? No matter what, get out. I will find you. You have Barry's number memorized?" She was too scared and couldn't remember it. "Baby, you have to trust me. You remember everything I told you about the plane?"

Everything about planes scared her. All she knew was what she had seen on television a couple of times. She worried if the plane was late, that she would miss her connection. "Many things can go wrong, I don't want to get lost or crash."

"Okay now, listen. You need to calm down. We both have to focus the next few days. Please honey, don't make me worry about you."

But I was worried. With the storm coming, how would I know if and when she left? Adianec had two connecting flights in English speaking countries. All of our conversations still required us to have dictionaries on hand, and when she got emotional her English was nonexistent. Any small deviation from the plan and she could be lost. Even though Adianec was a grown woman she was very naïve to things of the outside world. Things I took for granted, like transferring planes at an airport, were a very complex and frightening ordeal for her.

I had to leave for Antigua the next day so I could be there when she got off the flight and also so I could set up our rental house. Again, there would be a communication blackout for two days. I told her, "I love you. The next time we're together, you'll be a semi-free woman."

We were finally close to achieving the goal we had worked so long and hard for, but two things could still go wrong. The tropical storm was due to hit Havana with forty mile per hour winds within an hour of Adianec's departure and could delay her flight, causing her to miss her connections in two different countries. We were also concerned about whether or not our recent escape attempt had been recorded yet. If so, would the bribes we paid hold it off?

As I boarded the red eye at LAX, I knew in my heart that everything would work out and I would see her the next day in Antigua. But I still worried about the storm and her anxiety. She would be alone and if there was any deviation from the plan, I was concerned that she would get lost. Her English was still strained, and she was leaving Spanish speaking countries behind.

The past couple of weeks, I had been busy setting up a place to stay through a foreign boyfriend of Adianec's schoolmate. He was a fisherman and sold his catch a few times a month to a buyer in Antigua. His buyer was a crazy Syrian national, Sam, who had immigrated to the island several years earlier. Every time we spoke, he had me doubled over in laughter. It wasn't what he said, as much as it was how he said it. Always very loud, he talked very fast, a strange, pidgin English. He didn't have a clue as to how funny he was. He had recently married and had just rented a house on a private beach. The day after we were to arrive, he was supposed to take his family home to Syria for a few months, which was perfect timing for us.

"I have brand new home on the beach. It is yours, my brother."

"Is it secluded?"

"Ahhh" less a word than an exercise in exhalation – "Perfect for you on a private beach, my brother." Sounded perfect. I told him that I'd take it and asked how much it was. "Oh, you my brother, very good price, just what I pay, no more."

"Okay, how much do you pay?"

"How long will you be here?" I really couldn't say. Two weeks, maybe a month, hopefully no longer than that. "$500 is good."

Five hundred was good, very good. I told him, "See you tomorrow, my brother."

Time-wise, everything was up in the air once Adianec got to Antigua. Although with Barry, Steve, Bill and Herb as very enthusiastic members of the team, I didn't consider failure an option. I think my last rescue attempt, although universally accepted as insane, had pumped up everybody's imagination. Even though they were all highly successful and respected in their careers they were still, after all, just boys at heart.

After a short layover in Miami that morning, I had a less than three-hour flight to Antigua. I was to arrive at 10 a.m., fifteen minutes before Adianec was to take off from Havana. Antigua is part of the Lesser Antilles, in the middle of a chain of islands that run in a semi-circle from Venezuela to Cuba. As we flew in across the island to line up with the runway, I could see the entire island from end to end. It's not that big, 29 by 18 miles. From the plane it looked enchanted. The island is smothered with rich green palm trees and tropical foliage. As I was nearing the door to walk off the plane, I could hear the excited chatter of the passengers walking out into the heat. It was like stepping into an oven, but strangely, it wasn't a burning sensation. It went deeper, a radiant heat. Antigua is only 100 miles from the equator.

Walking across the tarmac to the terminal, I couldn't help but smile, knowing that Adianec would be making the very same walk and almost be a free woman in about ten hours. The airport grounds in Antigua are very beautiful, with lush grass and bright flowers. The airport is very active with commuter prop planes, landing and taking off every few minutes.

The line for immigration was long, slow and hot. But nothing could cast a shadow over that day on which Adianec and I would, I hoped, begin our life together. She had become the best part of me and I wondered if this was the only way I could have made a commitment to a partner. We had gone through so much together that the commitment made itself. God works in mysterious ways. I thought about all the personal changes I'd have to make, but with her by my side in Los Angeles, I was looking forward to each and every challenge. The way I had it planned, we would be arriving in L.A. in about three weeks.

I arrived at the airport with my sister an hour before my flight took off. I was very nervous and excited that my life was about to change. It was raining hard from the tropical storm, so we were not surprised when we heard the flight was delayed for three hours. In a way I was relieved because I was able to put off saying goodbye to Laura. She has been by my side since she was born and she was not as ready to let me go as much as I was ready to start a new life with Lee.

Laura was upset because I wasn't sad. I wished I could have been sad for her but I was going to see Lee in the airport of a free country in several hours. Where can sadness hide when your heart is exploding with joy? I also knew from watching other Cubans checking in that I was probably not alone traveling to Antigua.

I was nervous getting on the plane, it was so small inside. In the movies it always looked bigger. I hadn't eaten or had any water the whole day because I was afraid to use the bathroom on the plane. They asked me if I wanted headphones I said no. They offered food and drink but I still said no. I just wanted to disappear until we arrived in Jamaica.

Sam, the crazy Syrian, showed up shortly after I arrived. His cell phone glued to his ear while he discussed fish poundage, he shook my hand, and helped throw my luggage into his truck. He didn't have much of an indoor voice. The decibel level of his normal speaking voice could hit the bleachers at Yankee stadium. He had a constant smile and was on the Darwin side of hairy. Driving with him was like going on an E-ticket ride. His focus was divided between our conversation, the person on the other end of the phone call, writing up an order and his insane driving. The road from the airport (not quite two lanes) to his house wound along the crystal blue Caribbean Sea. I don't believe we ever slowed down below fifty on those curves, even with cars coming in the opposite direction. We came so close to colliding with other cars, if his truck had had one more coat of paint, we'd have hit them. As we passed by one nicely manicured area, he pointed to an island a couple hundred yards off shore and proudly told me that that was where Oprah Winfrey lived.

Sam's house was actually a hurricane shelter, white and perfectly square. It had sixteen-inch concrete walls and roof. The half-inch fixed glass windows were placed in the middle of the walls when the concrete was poured. The walls had one-inch holes two inches above the floor to let the sea water out when the tide rose above the house and flooded it. No hot water, though. Most unsettling was the fact that there was no AC, and the only windows that opened were on one side of the house. It was relatively spacious inside, with a dining room, living room, kitchen, bath and two bedrooms.

The beach was private and tropical, shared with only two other homes. The sand was black from the area's volcanoes, and just fifty yards off shore, I could see the water softly breaking over a coral reef. The water in this small cove was very gentle, and the waves never seemed to go above a few inches. The neighbors to the left had a newly built, concrete L-shaped dock that went out just past the reef. To the right, our French neighbors gave me a déjà vu. Anchored just inside the coral reef was their twenty-seven-foot Boston Whaler, just to remind me that we were still in the middle of a rescue.

After a quick tour to make sure I felt at home, Sam let me know that, "you are family now" and he took off for the fish market. I had noticed this embracing before in Arab men. If you're a friend, then you're family. I wandered around what would be Adianec's first home in the new world. I was hoping that the enchanting location made up for the lack of charm in our temporary home. The view from every room was extraordinary. The windows on the north side had a full view of the ocean and beach, and on the south side the kitchen and bath windows looked into a tropical jungle. I called Luis to make sure everything was okay at work and then called Jose. "I'll have the money at the airport tonight."

When we arrived in Jamaica, we realized that twelve of us were getting on the same plane to Barbados, but we didn't know what to do. Finally, some Cuban nurses saw our confusion and showed us to our plane. As soon as we boarded, the plane took off, no time to be nervous. All I thought about was every minute that went by, I was closer to Lee.

The heat was really pervasive. I couldn't nap, so I snorkeled on the reef for a while. The reef was small but perfect for being right off our private beach. My thought for the next two weeks, while we waited for Adianec's visa to Tortola to come through, was to treat this as a vacation in paradise, the alternative was to wallow in anxiety. I had reserved a place in Jolly Harbor Beach to get her Scuba certification. I wanted to introduce her to everything wondrous on the planet. She has spent her life taking air through a straw and now I planned to feed her pure oxygen.

Overcoming Sam's objections, we arrived at the airport thirty minutes early. I didn't want to take any chance of her plane arriving early and having her panic that I was not there. I was sure that this was a very stressful day for her. Her flee to freedom would be filled with more fear and angst than relief. I watched on the outdoor screen to see that the 9 p.m. flight from Barbados had landed, so I walked over to the immigration arrival area. I couldn't stop smiling.

Thirty minutes later, no more people were coming through the gate. I asked one of the guards to go back and check to see how many more people were still coming through immigration. She came back and said immigration was empty. I couldn't breathe. My mind went to all the dark possibilities. She missed her flight in Havana because of the storm, or something happened to her in Jamaica or Barbados. Whatever had happened to her, wherever she was, she was alone.

I ran down to the Caribbean Air counter to ask if another flight was due to arrive. The girl behind the desk just shrugged.

"What does that mean?" No response.

"Excuse me, my girlfriend is missing. Do you work here?"

She took a quick moment to look up at me, as if to say, "What do you think?" and then a deep sigh and back to her magazine. "Are you kidding me? Hey! Is that the last flight?" Another deep sigh and without looking up from her magazine, she pointed to the flight board.

"I don't...what are you saying?" That must have been some magazine article. "Miss, please, I need some information, does anybody normal work here?" In hindsight it was probably not the best question I could have come up with. Not surprisingly, I was ignored with another deep sigh.

I came back over to the immigration gate in a panic. All the while, Sam was telling me. "Calm down my brother. Everything will be okay."

None of that calmed me down, but then I noticed a small group of people seemingly in a panic not far from me. They were speaking Cuban Spanish, so I asked if they were expecting people from Cuba. They said yes, and we confirmed that they were all on the same Havana flight. It felt like a thousand pounds had been lifted off of me, at least she was not alone. They told me that the flight had been delayed in Havana but it did take off. I had told Adianec no matter what to get on that flight and get out of Cuba. Any problems in a third country we would deal with later. An older woman was on the phone with relatives in Miami who were the contact for the group. They said that the group had missed the connecting flight in Barbados and had tried to get on a later flight, which was all they knew. We traded cell numbers and before I made it home they called and said, "The group has been arrested in Barbados!"

Before we landed in Barbados, we knew we had missed our flight to Antigua. I was very confused. I didn't know if I had to pay for another flight or if they would even let us into the country.

I told some lady in a uniform, with my bad English, that we should be on the Antigua flight. She laughed at me and pointed into the sky as she walked away. We knew it had taken off. We just didn't know what to do now. No one in our group had ever been on a plane before. One man came up, took all our passports and tickets, and put us in a small room with a few chairs and locked the door.

We were left in that room for five or six hours without any explanation. I was desperate. I had no way to contact Lee and I just wanted to cry.

Finally, at 12:30 that night, they took us to jail and said we would fly out in the morning. A lady in the group began to complain loudly that we had had no food all day. Sometime after, I was able to take a shower, when they brought us chicken and Coke, I noticed one of the guards had a cell phone. I offered him $50 to call Lee in Antigua. I was crying when Lee picked up the phone, his voice was so close and calm. He kept telling me that it was all okay now. We would be together soon. I felt a little better and fell asleep for a short time.

I tried calling the airline to book the first morning flight to Barbados but they were closed. I was in familiar territory now. She was in trouble and I was unable to help her. Sam had told me he knew people that knew people who could help, and he reminded me again that I was family. There would be no sleep that night, so I walked out onto the end of the neighbor's dock and laid down to look at the enormous stars. Even though I was wearing just my bathing suit, I was very comfortable with a warm tropical breeze flowing over me.

I spoke to Adianec as if she were beside me. I whispered, "Don't worry. I'm your protector; I'll be on my way first thing in the morning to bring you to safety. I promise, no matter what, that you and I will be together soon, sleeping in our own bed in Santa Monica. But I need you to be calm tonight. Just be calm and know that I'm coming. Trust me."

I then evoked God to keep all His promises of caring for even the lowliest creatures. In my mind, I would only allow thoughts of her smiling, cuddled up beside me on our couch back home, eating Dominos' Pizza and watching Monday Night Football. That was the only outcome I would allow.

I must have fallen asleep on the concrete dock. In the distance, the ringing of my cell phone back inside the house woke me up. Luckily, I had a full moon to light my running path through the large green plants and hole in the fence. The call went to voicemail before I reached it. I looked at the time, it was 2:30 a.m. The phone rang again thirty seconds later. It was Laura, needing to hear her sister's voice. I told her Adianec had a layover in Barbados and would arrive in the morning. She wasn't fooled and began to cry. They had been inseparable their entire lives. *"Lee, Lee, dondé ésta Tata?"* She was so upset she forgot to speak English. I tried to tell her that Adianec was okay. *"Habla, por favor, habla."*

"No, Laura, Adianec is not *aqui.*"

I could hear how desperate she was. *"Ahh, Lee, mi hermana, donde?"*

"Barbados, honey. *Mañana*, I promise. I'll go get her *mañana.*"

This wasn't helping her. She was crying very hard now. "Lee, *por favor, mi hermana. Si*, Lee, yo' understand, pleeze Lee, pleeze *importante.*"

"I know honey, I know. I will find her, do you understand? Can you understand me? I promise."

She begged me to do something. I assured her I would head out first thing in the morning and bring her sister back.

I was filled with nervous energy, so I took a quick swim to calm down. As I sunk into the warm, moonlit water, the phone rang again. I ran inside and had to catch my emotions as I heard Adianec's beautiful voice. She sounded tired and scared, but she was okay. She couldn't talk long. She had borrowed a cell phone from a man in the group. She said, "I'm in a plane to Antigua, *manana. Yo estoy preocupada*, they won't give me into the country, I'm late mi amore. Lo siento, I sorry my love."

I laughed and explained to her that it didn't work that way. She said they were being treated very poorly by the Barbados officials. I just couldn't deal with that right then. I told her to think of our future together. "Honey, you're free, you're out of Cuba."

She said, "*Si, amore, por favor* be at the airport. They take me to Cuba, I need to kiss you first."

I got very stern and told her she would never return to Cuba unless it was on her terms. But, because she had no experience with travel she thought of herself as a second-class citizen since she was Cuban. I felt relieved when we hung up knowing that we had hit a speed bump, not a dead-end.

Chapter thirty-five

FREEDOM...SORT OF

Not wanting to bother Sam, I walked down the beach to a resort at first light and grabbed a cab to the airport. I got there before the airport opened. With every flight from Barbados I ran up to the observation deck on the roof to watch passengers walk off the plane and across the tarmac; four flights, no Adianec. My phone rang. It was Jose, demanding to know where his money was. I really wasn't in the mood for his tough guy shit. I told him, "I'm here. Meet me at the bottom of the observation deck."

It was not hard to pick him out. He was about 5'4" with two intimidating "bodyguards" flanking him. As big as they were, I was bigger and just for that moment, badder. I walked up to Jose and told him, "Look, if you play any games with her freedom, you're gonna lose. The money is in my pocket and I'll pay you the moment she's in my arms." I bent down to his ear and whispered, "But if you even pretend to delay her release through immigration, I will go ape shit on you and your two hairy girlfriends."

I wasn't bluffing, I was in a corner ready to fight and he knew it. Mutt and Jeff backed down and Jose softened considerably. He knew the flight she was on and said, "The flight will arrive in twenty minutes. Don't worry."

He obviously had connections in both countries' immigration offices. It occurred to me that was why he was a no-show the previous night. He knew she had been arrested.

The feelings rushing up inside me as I saw Adianec step off that plane and onto the tarmac are as fresh today in memory as they were at that moment.

Just then, an ocean breeze blew the heat off the tarmac up and over the terminal, and the heavy white clouds that gave a moment or two of relief from the burning sun moved along. In my life, I've never wanted anything more than her freedom. Her first step onto Antiguan soil was both an accumulation of two years of ongoing sacrifice and proof that anything is possible. Though I was aware that we had a challenge or two ahead of us, at that moment she was free from Castro's grip. Above the noise of the airplanes warming up, I yelled down to her in Spanish, "You are a free woman. What took you so long?"

She kept her head down but I could still see the smile and tears.

As I came down the stairs, I saw Sam pull up at the curb. I guess family is always there for you. I walked over to his truck and told him she was coming through now. "See my brother, everything worked out," he said laughing.

When someone opened the arrival door, I could see her being checked through customs, so I called Jose over to pay him. Not knowing if Adianec and I would need him again to help get her to Tortola, I wanted to keep the deal looking sweet from his end. I told him we still had more people in Cuba to get out and we should talk when I get back to L.A. I then stood back in the mass of people milling about and watched Jose signal (nod) to a man in an immigration uniform. It's only about money with these guys.

When I got off the plane in Antigua, I could hear Lee yelling at me from the roof. I was so exhausted from the past twenty four hours I wasn't as animated as I had dreamed I would be, considering it was a moment Lee and I had waited two years for.

She looked exhausted as she came through the door. I was the happiest I had been since the day we met. We piled into Sam's truck and she gave me a look when she realized the ride home was going to be a bit life-threatening. The more I got to know her, the more I saw a saucy side to her. She bluntly told Sam to slow down. He did. Sam disappeared shortly after congratulating Adianec on her escape and welcoming her to his home. We showered and laid down for a few hours. The ocean breeze, if I left the front door open, drifted through the bedroom curtains and across our bodies giving just a thought of coolness. After making love, we laughed about our life ahead. I told her, "The rest of our lives will be like this. Nobody can ever keep us apart." Adianec said she needed just one more day to believe me. I asked her how it felt to be free.

"I don't feel free yet, amore." She would, though. "Tell me we'll be in L.A. soon."

"Soon, *mi amore*. Tomorrow we'll start the process. We'll be home soon."

We both fell asleep and slept deeply for an hour. I woke up and stared at her sleeping for a few moments before waking her. I told her I had a special lunch in store for her.

We walked down the coastal road for about a mile, with a beautiful hilltop view of a windy, raw ocean the whole way. Antigua has an unprocessed feel, like it's new to the earth. It seemed untouched and far from home. I guess it's almost a dangerous sensation, not from people but from a rawness of nature. It is literally in the middle of nowhere, and you're always aware of it. The Blue Waters Resort is on the Northwest tip of the island, and it deserves every one of its four stars. The grounds are laid out perfectly, with tropical plants surrounding every path. The dining room was open on three sides, with big king-sized cushioned chairs. We picked out a table near a small pool with palms dipping into its cool shaded water.

"Adianec's first meal as a free woman (Blue Water, Antigua)"

I dramatically pulled out Adianec's chair, and she reciprocated by curtsying in return. Our table was facing the ocean with some coconut palms and white sandy beach between us and the water. When the food arrived, the variety and amount seemed to confuse and almost overwhelm her. She looked at me and the other diners. I think she wondered if it was a community plate. I told her it was all for her, but I had to clear off half of the food so she could make sense of it all. There was not one item she was familiar with. I looked back at her but I was too late to stop her from putting a large spoonful of sour radish into her mouth. She stopped chewing immediately and looked at me with full eyes. I said, "No Amore, not like that."

She swallowed hard and laughed until tears came. I didn't have much of an appetite that day. I was just so incredibly grateful for her meal. It was one that I had waited for.

We had a perfect afternoon lying on our private beach, making love on the warm sand, swimming and snorkeling. She was in awe of all the colors and life on our small reef. Her life was changing in a flash. Sam came by and took us to the grocery store. Yet another eye-opener for her. Twelve aisles all filled with food she had only seen on T.V., or had no knowledge of at all. We only made it through half the aisles before she said, "Lo seinto. I have this pain in my head, I'll go to the car. I'm sorry."

Later, she confided that it was all just too much, too soon.

That night, I baked lasagna and chocolate chip cookies. As she cleaned up, I spoke with Luis about how to resolve some issues that had come up that day. While I was on the phone, I pointed to the leftover lasagna and the box of Reynolds Wrap and then I motioned to put them in the refrigerator. In others words, wrap the lasagna and put it away. Later that night, I went to get the two of us some ice cream as we watched one of the DVDs I'd brought. In the refrigerator, I saw the pan of lasagna, uncovered. I looked all over the counter and in all the cabinets for the Reynolds Wrap, couldn't find it. I called her in. "Amore, do you know where the Reynolds Wrap is? The, uh, Reynolds, the aluminum, um…"

She had no idea what I was talking about. We played charades for several minutes, since I didn't have the Spanish word for aluminum foil. Finally she understood, "ahh, *si, yo comprende*. Oh I mean, I understand."

She reached into the refrigerator and innocently pulled out the carton of Reynolds Wrap, not knowing what it was. She had done exactly what I had asked her to do, Put the lasagna and foil in the refrigerator. We fell into each other's arms laughing after I showed her what I had intended for her to do.

The following morning, Sam picked us up and drove us to the embassy for Adianec's visa to Tortola. One moment we were in sunshine, the next in the middle of a tropical deluge. Oddly the rain water was almost hot, so much so that it was startling. Sam smiled and said it took some getting used to. At the embassy, I gave them the letter of invitation from my friend David in London, the application, and Adianec's Cuban passport. Hopefully, they would approve her visa to visit Tortola. From there, we would rent a boat and sail to St. Thomas, U.S. Virgin Islands, and freedom. The lady informed us the application would have to go to Barbados for approval, and we should have an answer in two to four weeks. Sam then took us to meet his cousin in the town of St. John.

The town of St. John is a congested, one square mile, semi-shanty town. The narrow roads have deep, concrete lined open drainage ditches on each side. It has an interesting character about it as some of the shops seem to be made of salvaged building material. It also has an incredible amount of commerce and a very irritating rush hour, twice a day. The building conditions improve dramatically the closer you get toward the port, where the cruise ships dock. Several times a week, the ships come in and drop off passengers on the island for a few hours. The nice area is filled with jewelry stores that have incredible deals on diamonds and gold. One afternoon, Adianec and I did some window shopping and met the owner of the biggest jewelry store in the port area. It was easy to see that he had an eye for Adianec. He proudly brought out his prize, a five and a half carat, nearly flawless diamond. I asked Adianec if that was the biggest she had ever seen. She looked at me like I was crazy. "Amore, it is the only one!"

Lee was very excited about our new situation and he kept asking me what it felt like to be free now. I didn't know what to say, I didn't feel any different, not like I thought I would. Obviously I could move around and do things that I couldn't do in Cuba, but I was not comfortable yet with the concept of being free. I was also very nervous being even further away from America. I trusted Lee, but not our situation.

Sam's cousin, Francis, had a clothing store with his father across from the farmers' market. It was situated along a very busy street with so much pedestrian traffic that, traveling in a car, you could go no faster than the people walking. There was a large fan at the back of the store blowing out the hot stagnant air and billowing clouds of cigarette smoke. Francis was young, maybe twenty, and very friendly. Since we were with Sam, we were considered family. He offered us cigarettes and coffee. "You must drink, Syrian coffee is the best in the world."

He then took Adianec by the hand and started to give her a pile of clothing, shampoo and perfume. I was very taken by the warmth of the Syrian community during our stay in Antigua. After an hour or so, Sam gave me the keys to his truck, and said please give it back to Francis when you leave. This guy, a stranger to us, gave us his truck to use while he was gone. He said he was leaving that night and he wished us a safe journey and congratulated Adianec again, telling her, "Your life in America will be blessed by God."

On the drive back to our home, we noticed that the Cuban embassy was in our neighborhood. I suggested to Adianec that, as a neighborly gesture, we should invite the diplomats over for a cup of tea. It saddened me the control they still had on her. She would always tense up whenever we drove by.

Early the next morning, we found an internet café in St. John. She was able to send an email to someone in Cuba who would forward it to her family. As we left, the guy behind the counter, who spoke Spanish, told Adianec that they had direct phone service to Cuba. She made a thirty minute call to a very relieved family. ("Mami, mami, its Adianec.")

You could hear her mother's scream on the other end. ("Ahhh, my baby!") She assured her mother that she was okay, and was with me. ("You're in Miami?")

("No, Mami, but soon. Mami, I can't talk long")

("I'm so worried for you. We saw the plane lift off. I couldn't think that my baby was in that thing way up in the air.") They were both laughing now. Even talking about how great the food was. ("*Mija*, when will you be in Miami?")

She told her, ("Maybe two weeks,") which is what we hoped. I assured her that she could call her family every other day. ("I miss you, Mami, I kiss you many times.")

("I love you, *mija*. Kisses.")

Twenty miles south of our place, and on the other side of St. John, is a marina and bay called Jolly Harbor. This was where Adianec was scheduled to take her Scuba class, and I had read in travel books that it was very beautiful. Words and pictures in books did not prepare us for the ethereal scene that we entered into that afternoon. Jolly Harbor is as visually close to "Ahhh" as one can find. The mouth of the Bay is maybe a mile across, with lush green mountains pushing up from the sea and guarding the entrance of water so blue and calm it defies logic. As the land begins its half moon curve, the mountains evaporate into pure, white, powdery soft sand. From the northern end, there are a few houses, then a beach side open-air restaurant before Paul's Jolly Harbor dive shop. After Paul's place, the rest of the area is a resort until it all ends at the southern side.

I had called Paul a few weeks earlier when I was in Los Angeles, and after a few lengthy conversations, I felt like I had known him for years. When we walked up to his thatched-roof dive hut that sits on the sand fifty yards from the water's edge, he greeted us like old friends. Paul is about 6'1'', lean, late fifties. Like many transplants on Caribbean islands, he has a colorful past, some of which he is running from and some he weaves into his non-stop jaw-dropping stories. If one reads between the lines, Paul has seen and done all there is to do on the high seas. He counts as his friends millionaires, prime ministers, smugglers and pirates, many of whom we met during our nighttime outings with Paul. It was great to meet him and we embraced as if we had known each other a lifetime. "Paul?"

"Lee, man."

"Yep."

"And this must be your lovely bride."

Paul had full knowledge of our situation from the second time we spoke. I confided in him, partly because I trusted him immediately, and also, I knew we needed someone watching our backs on the island. Paul, who spoke Spanish, pulled Adianec into an embrace and treated her as his own daughter from that moment on. "*Buenos dias* my sweet beauty."

"Good morning, Paul."

"That's mighty fine English for a beautiful Cuban refugee. Now, Lee told me your name, but please tell me again."

"It's Adianec."

"Huh. Well, that'll take some practice, my sweet beauty."

Paul had a woman working for him, Diane, who controls most of his life and business affairs. He called her the "den mother." Diane is originally from Canada. Diane has been Paul's scuba instructor for many years, and she is also a non-stop chain smoker. Paul swore he saw her smoke under water while diving. Diane is the responsible one and I constantly wondered how he would survive without her. He spends many nights drinking and carousing while she does his books and plans the next day. His daily routine captured my imagination; he lives a pirate's life.

During those first few days, Diane really had her hands full trying to teach Adianec the scuba handbook. Adianec could not understand one word Diane said, and poor Diane is not known for her patience. She didn't so much speak to me as she did bark out orders, and whenever she told me to jump, I did. It didn't even cross my mind to be obnoxious with her. Our days were spent at the beach, with Adianec learning to dive in the pool and me out on the afternoon dive boat, trying to not get too nauseous on the way back to shore. Most nights we went out with Paul, eating, drinking too much and meeting his friends that ran the island.

Late one morning when Adianec had the day off diving, we had breakfast in St. John. Then we drove around the back of the island to see English Harbor. Driving around the island with Adianec made me feel like we had been together forever. I had no doubts about her love for me, and by this time, about my love for her; yet it must have been incredibly challenging for her during that time. I had put her in the middle of the ocean, far from everything and everyone she loved. Though we had no specific way out, I could see in her eyes an unquestioning faith that I would protect her. I felt like I was at an emotional crossroads. I was evolving from a guy who had had a devil-may-care attitude, to someone who took his responsibilities in life seriously. Adianec's life was literally in my hands and I wanted to be a consistent source of strength and stability for her. For that reason, I never told her it was a fly-by-the-seat-of-our-pants situation. If the visa did not get approved for Tortola, we only had one other option. Knowing that the "Boys" were standing in the wings did help. But there still was no guarantee of success…When smuggling through distant shores options are a good thing.

Coming up over the top of the mountain, the view looking down on English Harbor was breathtaking. Descending levels of palm-covered green mountains flowing down to side-by-side, deep blue, secure harbors. We wove our way down the mountainside into the harbor area and walked through the old fortress' stone gates. We climbed to the top of a bluff several hundred feet above the ocean, with waves crashing into the rocks below. We sat under a tree on the bluff and talked about life in the U.S. She was concerned that I was too close to the edge of the cliff. I was, and it was comforting to know that I had someone watching out for me now. "Baby, get away from the cliff."

"I'm good darlin', it's just a 200-foot drop and then some water." She made that face that meant she didn't approve of something I'd said.

"*Ay, dios.*"

"So, now we're a couple. Weird, huh?"

"What does it mean for you?"

I really didn't know. I knew I loved her, but the truth was I still was concerned about my old patterns of behavior and how they'd led to the demise of all my past relationships. But still, this was very different. She asked if I thought I would always love her. That was easy. "I do, I will, I'm sure. I just never saw myself in this situation."

"Situation?"

Probably not the best word. "You know what I mean. I don't know about commitment. One day at a time, yes, but to package up the next fifty years, I'm a bit unsure. It'll just take some work, but I'm willing."

We were able to suspend our worries and enjoy walking around the old fort, looking at the yachts moored in the bay, and swimming in the warm, calm waters. We spent the rest of the day, until past dark, discovering postcard-ready beaches in the remote areas of Antigua.

The next morning, I called the consulate in Barbados as Adianec took her final pool dive test. The lady I spoke with just happened to be the person in charge of approving visas and she said, "I will finish it up later that week. I see no problems, enjoy your vacation."

I ran over and pulled Adianec out of the water and told her that we would be in L.A. the next weekend. Jose had called a few days earlier to offer his services again. For $8,000, he would pass her off to smugglers in Tortola. I told him we could handle it ourselves.

I wasn't too thrilled with the idea of going under water. Since I cannot swim, I didn't see how it was possible. But I continued the difficult lessons so Lee and I could have something to do together. However, once I went under I was amazed. The world I knew disappeared with all its problems. I wanted to stay in this new world and let it envelope me. The color of the fish and their curiosity of us entranced me. I could look into their eyes and see something there; they had expression and life. I was floating effortlessly just above the seafloor sixty feet underwater, but it felt incredibly natural. I wanted to touch and study every detail of every plant, coral and fish. We saw sharks, morays, sponges and beautiful plants that looked like Spanish fans.

The next day Adianec had her open water dive. She loved it. She came up out of the water with a big smile. She had seen a piece of this world that would never have been possible in Cuba. While we were diving, we saw beautiful coral, a turtle, several manta rays, and a small shark. She was fun to watch, like a child, her eyes wide open as she touched bright red fan coral and sponges. She was looking back at me with an expression of, "Can you believe this?"

Drying off on the boat after our second dive, the airlines courier called and said I had a package from Barbados. I almost jumped off the boat to swim to shore. "Paul, please, get us to shore A.S.A.P."

He did just that, and we got to the courier office just as they were about to close. We opened the package and there was her passport stamped with the visa to Tortola. It was finally over. We were heading home.

Chapter thirty-six

BETRAYED

I called Barry and Steve, and told them the news. Steve got on the phone and said he was going to fly to St. Thomas and charter a boat to come pick us up in Tortola. I told Adianec that I now had complete confidence in the last leg of our trip. With Steve involved, I didn't feel anything could stand in our way. We would get to spend a few days alone with Steve and his girlfriend, Erika, living on a chartered yacht, diving and swimming in beautiful desolate coves.

Two days later, after having said goodbye and thank you to Francis, Paul and Diane, we boarded our flight to Tortola. We were one step closer to Adianec's new life in America. On the flight, I could see she was apprehensive. She said, "Something doesn't feel right."

I told her, "Baby, you're just imagining things because we're almost home. Listen to me, nothing could go wrong. We have a legal visa to enter, they can't deny you."

Well, that would have been true if the Tortola officials hadn't been corrupt.

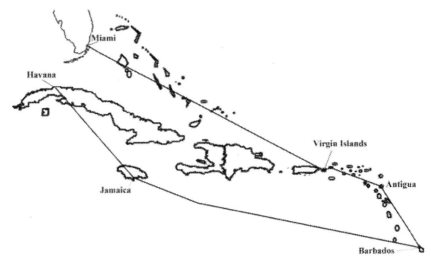

"Adianec's escape route"

At Tortola's airport there was only one immigration window open. We decided that I should go first. The man behind the counter, I quickly realized, was going to be a problem. He looked up and gave me a sarcastic snort, then proceeded to drill me on my itinerary. I had made up a back story in advance, but I knew something was up. He was too much of a jerk. After all we had been through and now with the last step, we had a problem. He asked if Adianec was with me. I said, "I'm just helping her. She's meeting friends from London."

Finally, he looked up at me and sarcastically asked, "Is that the story you want to go with?" Then he snorted again and told me, "Proceed to customs."

I looked back at Adianec as she walked up to the administrative cretin. He didn't even look at her papers and told her to stand aside as he processed the other passengers. I stood about twenty feet away, by the luggage carousel. Another plane came and he processed them as well. At one point he looked over at me and grinned. I knew right then we were in trouble. This asshole was going to screw us. One of the custom officials told me I had to leave the secure area. I told him, "I'm waiting for a friend."

He politely told me to wait outside. We were so close, she just had to pass through one more door and that would be the last one. The only thing that stood in our way was a corrupt asshole with an axe to grind. I knew why immediately. This ingrate was on the take and someone must have tipped him off that we were coming and he didn't get his bribe money. This is one of the new routes for Cubans to get to freedom and he wanted a piece of everyone that went through it. We had circumvented the process and he was going to punish us. I thought, or at least hoped, that eventually he would have to let her pass. She had a legal visa.

I woke up that morning and put on my new clothes, trying to look like an American girl. I was watching every move Lee made that morning. I needed him by my side. When we arrived in Tortola, I had a bad feeling about this man behind the counter. The way he looked at me, I knew it was trouble. He was very rude with me, making me stand next to his counter as he let two plane loads of people go through. After an hour he put me in a back room, refusing to explain what was happening.

Over the next five hours, he wouldn't allow me to use the bathroom or let the other people there give me water. I had overheard two ladies speaking. My English was still not that great, but they were standing very close to me, so I could hear everything they said. One lady looked at my passport and said to the other that everything looked good, so why was he holding me. She whispered something and the other made a face like she was upset and they left. I watched all these Americans going through and wondered what was wrong. I had a legal visa. At one point, he came in when I was crying. He started to make fun of me.

"Why are you crying? Are you crying because you're a Cuban? And now after all this you are going back to Cuba?"

I was thinking I was lost, I would never see Lee again. I couldn't breathe or stop shaking and crying. Every time that man would look over at me he would smile, he was so disgusting.

As I walked out the door into the arrivals area, Steve called and said they were running late. I explained, "Look, we have a big problem. We're not going to be meeting at our agreed time."

I started making calls to Antigua to some of the politicians, businessmen and, of course, minions of the underground we had met. A "cousin" of Francis made a few calls to people he knew at Antigua immigration and was told that someone at the airport had called Jose and he, in turn, called the corrupt asshole in Tortola to keep us out and send Adianec back to Cuba. By this time, a couple hours had passed and the asshole walked out of the secure area and headed for a lunch truck.

With him out of the way, I knocked on the glass doors and asked if I could speak with my friend. The look on the woman's face was one of total compassion. She smiled and told me to hurry. Adianec was in a large room, sobbing. She said he had been tormenting her, saying that, now, after all this, she was going back to Cuba. She was inconsolable, telling me that she knew she would never see me again. I tried comforting her, "Baby, look at me. NOTHING can keep us apart. We are going back to Antigua to continue our romantic vacation a little longer. I love you, we are a family now, and nobody can separate us."

I told her I was in contact with all our new friends and they were working on getting her released. As I walked out, the asshole came back and pinned me against the wall with his massive belly spewing his vile breath all over me. "You wanna make fool of me again, man? This is my game. Go home, you won't see her again, man."

I thought about head butting him, grabbing her and running, but there were too many cops in the airport. To this day, I fear what I would do to that miserable pile if I ever saw him again.

In the interim, someone, I think it was Paul, had called the Antiguan Prime Minister's office to ask for assistance. A call was made to Tortola, demanding she be sent back to Antigua, her last port of departure. Steve had called several times. I could tell he was itching to get into this fight but I knew that even Steve was incapable of helping. They were still sailing over, and not making very good time.

Four or five torturous hours after we had landed, the same kind woman came out and whispered to me, "She will be on the 4:10 p.m. flight back to Antigua."

I ran over to the counter and bought my ticket. I was relieved she was safe and I would be with her soon. That done and with nothing to do but wait, I walked outside. I keep finding myself in these dichotomies. My life was again falling apart. I was under so much stress that I thought my mind was going to snap. But as I looked around me, I was in paradise. The natural beauty was overwhelming. I thought it incredible that such a disgusting man with a rotting soul could live here. I called Steve and told him we were heading back to Antigua. I asked him to follow us over, and he said they would be there in a couple of days.

When I saw Lee walk into the room, I thought he was there to take me with him. I just wanted everything to disappear so we could be together. That's all we ever wanted, just to be together. I told him I was going back to Cuba. He took my face in his hands and told me that would never happen. He was always so confident, but this time I knew it was out of his control. The man from immigration for some reason hated me. Lee said for me to know we were together now and our new friends were more powerful than this man. He left quickly and I didn't see him again until he got on the plane.

I watched out the window of the departing area as Adianec was escorted like a criminal to the plane. I had never seen her so upset. She was crying the entire flight back, certain that immigration in Antigua would send her back to Cuba, like the jackass had told her. I tried to explain to her that the prime minister's office had demanded her return, but my Spanish wasn't that good. After we landed, she was whisked through immigration and then skipped customs. She made it through faster than I did. Waiting outside was Francis to take us home. Adianec had once again been treated like a criminal because she was Cuban, even though I had told her it would never happen again once she was free.

Francis took us to his favorite Syrian restaurant but we couldn't get her to eat. It felt good to have her safe again, but that man and his cruel taunting had really affected her. He had convinced her she would never see America or me again. Steve called and I filled him in. He told me, "Tell her I promise we'll all help. She is not alone."

For Adianec, that meant nothing. For me, it took the weight of the world off my shoulders.

I cooked a chicken dinner with corn on the cob and garlic bread. We also opened a nice bottle of wine. I tried to make things as normal as possible, but that bastard had really done a number on her. She was completely traumatized and spent the entire sweltering night tucked in beside me.

Francis came by early and gave us his car to drive because he needed Sam's truck. We drove out to Jolly Harbor. Paul saw us walk up and he could see on our faces that something had gone very wrong. He gave her a hug and told her the good news was we got to spend more time diving with him. We spent the rest of day driving around the island, exploring an abandoned sugar mill and roads that went deep into the tropical forest. I was doing all I could to nurture her.

We had dinner with Paul that night at our favorite restaurant in Antigua. Burt, the owner, was always a great host and had a heavy hand on the cocktails that he would pour personally for us. Bert was a big German ex-patriot who had come to Antigua twenty years ago, married a beautiful local girl and raised a family. Just one of Burt's mixers was too much of a drink for me, and that night before dinner, I had two. I was feeling a little fuzzy when I looked down and saw a fist-sized tarantula crawling toward my sandaled foot. I actually screamed like a little girl and jumped up on the table. I hate spiders. They all, Adianec included, paid no attention to the spider but were extremely amused by my fear of them. Adianec even teased me by putting her foot in front of it to steer it back to me. I spent the rest of the evening with my feet up off the ground. At least she was laughing for a moment.

Late the next morning, we picked Steve and Erika up from the airport. I knew it would be interesting watching Adianec's reaction to Erika. She was a stereotype of a Southern California girl, tall, blonde, pretty and always ready to have fun. Her carefree attitude immediately brought Adianec to life and had her laughing again before we made it to their hotel. Adianec had never met another woman like her. She was mesmerized by Erika's confidence and attitude. We had eight hours of sun left, so we drove to the other side of the island. We stood high on a mountain cliff overlooking English Harbor, amazed that this place just got more beautiful with every discovery. Suddenly Steve said, "I've been here before."

Steve travels so often to exotic locations that he hadn't realized that he had visited Antigua a few years earlier, and had stood in that exact spot. We all teased him about that, especially when he tried to explain. He was on a private jet traveling from somewhere, he couldn't remember where, and they spontaneously stopped on Antigua. He just hadn't known or cared where he was. He even described the centuries-old restaurant behind us. We all went inside to see. Even Steve was curious to see if he was right. He was. "The life of being Steve."

Steve and Erika were the first friends of Lee's that I had met. I wanted to make a good impression for Lee, even though I was very sad. I felt insecure because of my English, but I wanted to enjoy their animated conversation. They laughed all the time. But I still had heavy emotions from Tortola. Steve tried to speak to me in Spanish, which made me feel more welcome. The way Lee had described him to me, I was expecting a tall, white, rich American, like I've seen in the movies. Steve was just a little taller than me, with darker skin and hair. It was funny to see Lee with him. Steve was the leader. Wherever Steve went, we all just followed, including Lee. It was the first and last time I saw Lee like that. It was interesting. I just watched Erika. Everything about her was different. She was so nice to me, she made me feel part of the group. I didn't expect that from an American girl. I could see that Lee was upset when they left, but I felt a little closer to going home with him after that.

We called Barry that night and almost convinced him and Lisa to fly out the next day, but they both had parental duties. We came by Steve and Erika's hotel pretty early, and Steve was already up and complaining about the quality of the resort. It was not up to his standards. Personally, I thought it was great. They had free food and several pools; that's my kind of heaven. We drove along the coast checking out the more posh resorts, $2000 and up per night. I've stayed in some nice places but these were insane. They had split-level suites with private beaches and butler service. Erika had Adianec back to normal very quickly. They were laughing and ogling over the interior designs. In every one of these places, there were tropical waterfalls and people walking around with trays of fruit water. There was not a piece of gravel or palm leaf out of place. Still, nothing seemed to please Steve. He asked the women what they thought. "Girls, what do ya think, which place do you like?"

Erika, like the rest of us said, "Oh God, I loved all of them."

Steve couldn't pronounce Adianec's name, so he called her amore. "Amore, where would you like to stay?"

"*No se*, Steve...Santa Monica."

That was actually pretty funny. "Whatever it takes, amore, that's gonna happen. Now, where would you like to stay tonight?"

Considering that Adianec had never seen a waterfall in a building before, and they both had one, she was pretty flexible.

Driving back to Jolly Harbor, I saw a private road that led to some cliffside bungalows we had driven by as the dive boat went out. This place was right out of a boyhood fantasy, like *Swiss Family Robinson*. The bungalows, about twenty of them, were built right into the side of a mountain that jutted out into the sea. The resort had water on two sides, and jungle on the other two. It also had a restaurant that hung off the cliff directly above the ocean. The girl at the desk, ill-tempered, impatiently sighed and mumbled, "No vacancies."

Steve told her, "We just saw two people check out. Of course you have a vacancy." She shrugged and blankly stared at us. I almost asked her if she had a cousin that worked at the airport counter. We tried a little sign language.

Finally she had to admit, "Yeah, we have three vacancies, but it is past 3 p.m."

She left it at that for us to figure out what that had to do with checking in. I walked away in awe. Steve, who does not give up easily, told me to get the luggage, he would have the rooms ready. I don't know exactly what he promised her but in exchange, she had to get the rooms cleaned and smile every time she saw us. She smiled, and we were in our rooms within thirty minutes.

Our bungalow was incredible. It had a large bed with a lace mosquito net draped over it and hand-hued wooden floors. It was sultry, dark and very romantic. We had two showers, one in the oversized bathroom and the other, more of a warm waterfall, on the balcony which hung about a hundred feet over our private cove and swimming pool. There is something about showering outside that feels freeing, and this one was grand enough for two or more, if you're so inclined.

The next day, Steve told us they were leaving the next morning. I felt the inevitable thud of being brought back to earth. At least with Steve around, I could relax and let him take over for a while. I was tired and needed help getting Adianec to American soil. Steve told Adianec not to worry, that we would find a way to get her home. It was sad to take them to the airport. Steve mentioned he felt like he was abandoning her. "Lee, after meeting Adianec, I understand why you've done all that you have."

Chapter thirty-seven

DANCE WITH THE DEVIL

We went back to our home with no hot water, sixteen-inch concrete walls and no cross-ventilation. I couldn't help but feel a bit desperate. Having Steve and Erika there was a nice respite, but now it was back to the task of getting Adianec across the Caribbean Sea. I called Barry and asked if he'd call Herb and Bill, and try to get a new rescue plan on-line. He called back and gave me the website showing the boat Herb wanted to rent. It was a beautiful 100-foot yacht complete with crew. Herb would be available in two weeks, but we also had to contend with the weather. We were in the middle of hurricane season, so we were getting a lot of squalls running through often, and the seas remained very rough. If we didn't do something soon, I would have to leave Adianec there alone. I was out of money and my credit cards were tapped out.

I didn't want to broach the subject of leaving her, so I ignored the issue as long as I could. We spent the next week scuba diving and exploring the island. With every dive session you could find Adianec leaning over the rail, face to the water, offering up her breakfast to the fish. Paul would always yell words of encouragement. "That's it, my sweet beauty, just let it go. You didn't need that breakfast."

One day, we had a boatful of divers from a cruise ship that had landed that morning. In between the first and second dive, a strong squall snuck up on Paul and hit us pretty hard. Everybody was tucked in under the canvas to avoid being stung by the rain shooting at us sideways, and hitting with so much force we could not see more that two feet past the boat. The scary part was the wind, along with the waves it generated. It had created a dizzying ride. As soon as it blew through, Adianec was in her favorite position, leaning over the rail. Five minutes later, I was right beside her, heaving away. Paul yelled out, "See there folks, that is true love, he rescues her from Cuba and now won't let her get sick alone."

After our mutual vomit session, everyone wanted to hear our story. Sensing a spotlight, my seasickness vanished. I had a captive audience.

In my desperation, I even called Jose and set up a meeting. Although I knew he was responsible for our situation, sometimes you have to sleep with your enemies. He took us to a house in the island's interior to show he was indeed successful at this. He had twenty Cubans stuffed into a two-bedroom house. They all had an apprehensive hopefulness on their faces. At any given moment, they could get the word and off they would fly to Tortola and then on to St. Thomas and finally Miami. The people seemed very excited that an American was there. Adianec struck up a conversation with an older woman and she gave Adianec her sister's number in Miami. They both had information on Jose to share with the other. I kept coy about how desperate I felt, telling Jose, "Yeah, we have a few other solid options but they're a month out, and I need her with me in L.A. now."

In a bizarre way, Jose and I actually got along. For some reason, he wanted to impress me with his connections and future plans, which went beyond the business at hand. He confided in me his dream of buying a large container ship and expanding his smuggling operation (he showed me his professional business plan all drawn out). He even explained in minute detail how drugs, and to a lesser degree people, are smuggled throughout the Caribbean. He told me that two large cocaine shipments come through the Caribbean, on the same flights using the same airline every week. There is a network of immigration and customs officers on Barbados, Antigua, and Tortola that control the movement and protection of the shipment (luggage). In Tortola the shipment is split between the U.S. and Europe. The U.S. shipment, with a link Jose was unsure of, flows to the Bahamas and then by boat to Georgia. I wondered if my "friend" Harold Laflear was in that chain. There is very little chance of getting caught because the network is run by the top officers (including the guy I saw get the nod from Jose at the airport), with some of the profits sprinkled into the judicial system. It seems to be a very tight and closely guarded fraternity. Though he didn't say it out right, I knew that was why Adianec had gotten arrested in Tortola, with a valid visa. We would never be allowed to leave Antigua without paying this syndicate. I walked away from that conversation in a bit of a daze. How could I, a guy who has lived a relatively clean life, so easily stumble across this and homeland Security cannot even get a whisper of it? Certainly they must know that these small inclusive governments are corrupt.

I tied to keep Jose's interest by saying that we had to bring Adianec's family out of Cuba as well. I told him that his was a nice option due to timing, but I was low on money - actually out of it - and we still had to save up for the others. He dropped it down to $6,000, but that was just for Tortola. I would still have to get her to St. Thomas on my own. It was difficult to negotiate with him because he lied about everything and his story constantly changed. Though I guess I would do the same if I were a soulless trafficker of human beings.

I told Adianec that I would need to leave in a few days. I reluctantly explained, "We're kind of, well, out of money right now, and I have to go home and generate some business. It'll just be for a little while."

I tried to act matter of fact about it when I told her, but the idea of leaving her here alone was destroying me. I had heard about another smuggler on the island, his name was Henry. We agreed to meet late that night in a part of the island that I was unfamiliar with. We drove out in a heavy rainstorm, turning down a dark street that had not been maintained. The potholes had turned to ponds, some with water as high as the door handles on our car. I parked at the designated spot and waited. Suddenly, out of nowhere, I heard a deep voice behind me. I turned, but didn't see anybody. The disembodied voice spoke again. It was so dark that night I couldn't see a thing, but I knew the voice was within a few feet. It was very disconcerting not being able to see the person I was speaking with. I didn't know if it was the situation, or him, or both, but the hair was standing up on the back of my neck. "Hey man, what's up with you?"

"Not much. I hear you may have an option for me."

"Options! Yeah options." I never heard the word "options" sound so dark and ominous. "Man, let's do it."

"Do what?"

"Find you one of them options." I asked him to tell me. Talk was not his game. "Talk talk talk, my man, ain't gonna solve your problem. Let's take action."

"Right, ahh, okay."

After a few minutes, I could make out a silhouette. It was difficult to understand what he meant because he was very good at speaking around a question without answering it.

I asked him what his plan was. When he asked me, "What's your problem, my man?" I wasn't sure what he was implying, did I have a problem with him, or what problem did I need him to remedy. I was wholly confused, but when you're desperate, you want to believe in anything. "We need to get to St.

Lucia. I'll get her to St Thomas from there. It's what, only eighty-five miles, with islands in between?"

"That's it."

Neither of us said anything for a long time. It was a long, uncomfortable silence. Finally, I asked. "So, can you help?"

"My man, that's what I'm telling ya." I asked him what do we do. He replied simply that we get her to St. Lucia. But I needed to know how, when, where, who, how much and how long it would take. "A lot of those questions can be answered by you, my man. You're the boss. I take my orders from you. You're in charge here."

I had a very uneasy feeling about this. I was pretty non-committal and tried to sound like I'd consider his offer. "I'm not sure...ok, alright, great, let's ahh, we'll get our thoughts together and give you a call."

I drove away slowly, not knowing if we had made a deal or not. What I wanted was for him to sail us to St. Martinique or Lucia and from there I could rent a boat to take her the last few legs.

I had nightmares about him the entire night, which I thought was strange. Not knowing how our negotiations went the night before, I called Henry again and scheduled another meeting that night, but in a populated area. We met that night, but again, he stood in the shadows and I never got a good look at him. This time I kept calling him on not giving me a direct answer. "Hey, Henry."

"Ready to do this thing?"

He wouldn't say anything directly. I never really knew what we were saying. "You tell me, what thing? Do you own a boat? What kind, how big?"

"What size you lookin' for?"

"Henry, what size and make of boat do you have?"

"You know my man, anything you want."

I was getting more and more upset and frustrated. This guy wouldn't tell me anything. "Okay, I'm- look, we need...okay let's- I'll tell you what, let's do it. I'll give you a call as soon as we have the money."

The next day at Francis's store I was telling his uncle about the meeting. He asked me if the man's name was Henry. I said, "No, but tell me about this Henry."

He leaned in and whispered, "He is very dangerous man. He will take people's money, get them just off shore, then slit their throats and dump their bodies overboard."

It was no wonder I had nightmares. This guy was pure evil. We seemed to meet a lot of his kind during our adventure. I didn't know what to do. I certainly didn't trust Jose either, but he seemed to have some integrity about his illegal activity. Dishonest, yes, but I didn't see him as a throat-slitting, dumping-bodies-overboard murderer.

I told Francis that I was putting Adianec in his care. He seemed to take great pride in that. He also had video internet so we could speak to and see each other while I was home. Francis said he would check on her everyday, even though our place was ten miles out of his way. The night before I was to leave her, yet again, she was very distant and I knew she was scared. She had left her family for me, and now I was abandoning her.

Francis took me to the airport early the next morning. Adianec held me tight. "Promise to get back soon."

She never asked for anything, so I knew she was really scared. I left my cell phone with her and would pick up another when I got home. I called her when I got home late that night. She had cooked dinner for herself and her new friend, a neighbor's German shepherd. I got a call at six the next morning. She was at Francis' store and asked me to hook up the laptop video monitor. We talked and watched each other as I woke up, then walked the computer around her new home so she could see it for the first time. I was pressed for time, so I carried her around with me as I got ready, showered and had breakfast. In a strange way, I felt she was finally home.

I had lunch with Barry and Lisa that afternoon. At that point, they were both so caught up in the drama and small successes they seemed to want her home as much as I did. I told Barry I needed a few more clients. I was broke and almost $40,000 in debt now. By the end of the week, I had three new remodels, one of which could start the next week. Herb was now available, but due to unpredictable weather, our Plan B was at least a month out, and that put Adianec in a bad situation. I also went to the bank and took out a personal loan. At least for now I still had my good credit.

Over the next two weeks, I put the jobs together and gave Luis a daily schedule for the time I'd be gone. The internet café in St. John also had cameras and it gave us more privacy, so that became Adianec's breakfast spot. Every morning at six, Adianec would call and I'd turn on the computer before I even opened my eyes. Her beautiful, far away face would be the first thing I'd see to start my day. "Okay, Amore, wake up."

"Hhmmm, mornin', girl."

"Turn on the computer."

"It's on…See Me?"

"Oh baby, you are beautiful. I love that face."

It's hard to describe how amazing that is to hear in the morning, especially when you look like I do in the morning. "That puffy face, you mean?"

"Lee, *por favor.*"

"Well, that's the real me, embrace it. You wanna see your new home, again?"

She was very excited and we went through the same routine every morning. I picked up the laptop and carried it around, showing her her new home, as if for the first time.

"Ahh! Is that my kitchen? Oh Lee, it's beautiful."

"And here's your bathroom."

"Amore, are you naked?" "Baby, there are people here. They can see you."

I showered as we spoke. To her complete embarrassment and joy.

I had been in contact with Jose often during that time, and we came to a tentative agreement. I also let him know, "Jose, this world does not hold a dark enough hiding place for you if anything goes south."

We had established a nice rapport. For someone who dealt in human cargo, he could be quite charming. Less than three weeks after I left her, I was able to return, with Jose's guarantee that she would be heading for Tortola within four days of receiving the cash from me.

Watching the emerald dot, that was Antigua, in the middle of the vast blue sea grow bigger by the minute, I cannot recall ever being so excited to see someone. I knew she and Francis would be waiting for me. As we flew over the island, I could make out all the secluded beaches and coves Adianec and I had visited. The all-consuming heat that greeted me that afternoon felt like a friend. It was familiar now, and I associated it with her. There I was on the tarmac with all the other tourists anticipating their carefree vacations, yet I was anxiously walking into another dangerous situation. I wondered if we would ever have a moment in some beautiful place to just numbingly enjoy it.

Adianec's smile was the most beautiful I had ever seen. There was nothing shy about it this time. She felt very small and vulnerable as I held her, something I had never noticed before. We drove back to the beach house to drop off my bags, and then Francis took us to pick up another car. We spent the entire rest of the day just lying on the beach, holding each other. We went snorkeling at dusk under a soft orange sky, in water that seemed to be the same temperature as the air.

The next morning we showered together in the ice cold shower, not the most pleasant experience before the sun heats things up. As we drove into St. John, Adianec told me, "No, don't park here. Park over there. That's the best place to park."

This was Adianec's town now. I was her guest. She seemed to know where everything was and knew all the girls that worked in the clothing stores. I couldn't have been more proud of her. We went to her internet café to plan the final leg of our journey after she got to Tortola. We found a boat rental place on the eastern edge of St. Thomas. The plan was that I would take off from there and navigate through the Virgin Islands to Tortola at the far end of the island chain. Then I would find her, pick her up, and deliver her to the United States. Steve said it should take a little more than three hours to get back to St. Thomas.

On the northern edge of St. John, there sits a centuries-old church and cemetery. The church was built in the same style as Catholic cathedrals I had seen on my travels throughout England. This particular one was in serious need of repair. My client, Jane, had a great-grandfather who had been governor of Antigua and she asked me to find his plaque in the sanctuary and take a picture. All the interior walls and floors were filled with plaques dedicated to those who had gone on and left behind broken hearts and lives. We came across a faded marble plaque over 150 years old. It was from a young man, dedicated to his nineteen-year-old bride who had died in an accident. He wrote of his unceasing pain and the hole her leaving had left in his heart. He went on to say her memory would never fade in his love and he apologized for bringing her there to that distant land so far from her family. It gave Adianec and me pause as I translated it for her. At the end it said he promised to raise their baby son in a loving environment, just as she would have done.

All my life, I had perfected the art of shielding myself from the potential of that kind of devastation by keeping a wall of humor and sarcasm between me and the people in my life. Reading that plaque, I felt I was that young man. I had a love now. I had allowed it to settle inside me. I knew that if I lost Adianec, I would be devastated. Though we had made an agreement to give it one year and see how it went, we both knew the entwining of our souls had already happened.

We drove over to see Paul and get in an afternoon dive and vomit. I took in the familiar drive so I could commit it to memory and enjoy it in a calmer future. It was all as I had left it, the beaten-down school and soccer field, the shacks on the side of the road that someone called home, the Friendship Bridge dedicated from the people of China to the people of Antigua. On both sides of the Friendship Bridge, swamps were filled with coconut and banana groves.

That night, we went to see Jose. I still had many unanswered questions that he was able to side-step on the phone. He asked me, "You bring my money?"

As much a statement as question. "Some. You have dates and times?"

"Lee, what you playing me for?"

"Don't fuck around, Jose. When is she flying out?"

"A few days, that's my word."

With smugglers, a "few" could mean anything. "Jose, what's a few days… two? Three?"

"Okay, this week for sure."

Again, nothing committal. I was about to lose it. "JOSE! Dammit, what flight, what day?!"

"I will tell you, when I certain. I don't lie to you. But listen. We're close, so we need to get the passport." I had no idea what he was talking about. "Lee, she can't get in with her Cuban passport."

"I thought you had this thing wired on that end."

"I need $1,200 for this final piece and then she is free."

"Jose, you're truly a piece of shit!"

Jose was still keeping the intricacies of the plan to himself. This guy was so crooked he couldn't see straight.

The deal was that in the next few days, Adianec would fly to Tortola. I would fly to St. Thomas the day before, grab a boat, and be waiting for her at the airport.

Adianec still had the contact number in Miami for the woman she had met at the Cuban holding house, so we called it that night. The woman had already made it to the U.S. but as we had assumed, there was a big catch. When they got off the plane in Tortola, they were essentially kidnapped and held for ransom. They were told that Jose only paid for the immigration bribe but they still owed money for transit to St. Thomas. Relatives were phoned in Miami and sent into a panic to raise as much as they can, before their family members can be shipped to St. Thomas. Now that we knew she would be kidnapped, we had to come up with our own plan to avoid that little inconvenience. With Adianec having an American boyfriend, that ransom could be tens of thousands. Coming up with the extra ransom fee was not an option, as I had no more money.

I was trying to behave as if things were normal, but Adianec was showing the strain. I had grown accustomed to this *Alice in Wonderland* world, where laws of humanity did not apply. No despicable behavior from smugglers, cheats, crooks or con men could shock me anymore. I attempted to keep Adianec busy with diving and exploring our natural paradise. After a few days, we got a panicked phone call. Jose had been arrested in St. Lucia. Our smuggler was now in jail and though it was where he belonged, he had left us in the lurch. I paid his bail, and came to the realization that I would have to leave her again. I would have to go to Barry, Herb and Bill and make my plea. Though there was no question that they wanted to go forward, I would have to convince them that it might have to be in unpredictable weather. When I told Adianec I would have to leave, she just looked at me with sad eyes of resignation, and nodded. We told Jose we were still on board, just in case he came through. If he did get her to Tortola, I would fly in the day before and meet her at the airport before she could be kidnapped. Then we would jump on the boat and head for U.S. soil.

I was overwhelmed with emotions as my plane taxied out. I wanted to jump off the plane while I still had the chance. I felt something devastating was going to happen to her and she would be gone. I was feeling guilt, anger, fear and several emotions I couldn't name. I needed something to go right. We needed a hand of compassion. As the plane took off, I looked down at the beautiful colors of the shoreline. We passed over the island/peninsula where Oprah has a home, and I thought, "Oprah, where are you?"

If there was a way to contact her, she could get Adianec home. I was really feeling desperate and I would have done anything at that moment to get her home safe. As the plane turned up the coast, our beach came into view. We were still low enough, probably ten thousand feet, to see the shape of our home and beach, but too high to make out anything else. Through the blur of tears that came out of nowhere, I thought I saw movement by the front door. I wondered if it could be her watching me fly away, again. I put my hand to the window to touch her and tell her, "I will love you forever."

I knew that to be a fact. I would love her forever. No one should ever have to feel the intense emptiness I felt at that moment. For the rest of the flight, I was angry that we had to do this alone. I knew when it was over, and it would be, the depth of our bond would be incomprehensible.

I stood outside by the front door and watched Lee's plane disappear for America. I was alone again and I missed him so much already. I went back inside and cried for hours. I couldn't help but think that he would never be able to get me to Los Angeles and I would one day have to return to Cuba. To lose him and my freedom, I would rather not go on living.

I didn't eat that day or night. I was so scared of being alone again in that house. Every sound made me hold my breath. I just lay there all day until it turned dark and waited for him to call.

I called as soon as I was in the cab heading to Santa Monica. How could I convince her that I never quit until I achieve my goal? This was much more than a goal; she was my life. When I got home, I went through my mail. I had been willfully ignoring my bills for the previous two months. Out of curiosity, I opened my cell phone bill to see how much all those roaming charges cost. I absolutely froze in panic when I saw the numbers. "Seven thousand dollars?!"

It was so astronomical, that as soon as I started to breathe again, I burst out laughing. I didn't care I would file bankruptcy when this was all over. My life had become a joke. I thought, "The world can be, and seems to be, against us...to hell with 'em all, she's my girl."

I called her two or three times that night…that'll teach AT&T. I called Barry and told him, "Pal, it's desperation time. We need to move now!"

He said he would check immediate availability on the boat and the guys. Bill and Herb were packed and ready. I would be responsible for weather forecasts.

During the next several days, Adianec and I spoke on the phone for hours. Whatever the bill was going to be, it was going to be. I had to make her feel safe. The weather was not cooperating and Adianec was worried she would have to deal with a hurricane alone. I was also taking every job that came my way, and hired extra guys. It was going to take a couple of years to dig out of the financial hole I had dug. Rather than panic about it, I was uncharacteristically calm. I didn't care. So what! It was only money.

Chapter thirty-eight

August 15, 2006

Nine days after I left Adianec, I got the call. She was flying out in the morning. I hung up the phone, immediately called the airlines, and then the boat rental place. I would be flying out at ten that night for New York City, and then catch a 6 a.m. flight to St. Thomas, U.S. Virgin Islands. It was the earliest I could get there. It would be one hour after she had landed, a fact that made me nervous. I was sure that Jose intended for her to arrive before me, giving the kidnappers the opportunity to control the situation…game on.

We had one thing on our side. We knew what they were going to do, and they didn't know we knew it. It was going to be tricky and dangerous, but we had come up with a plan.

I didn't call anybody to tell them that our final run was about to go down, or even that I was leaving. I needed to have total focus. There was no way I could catch any sleep on the plane. I was so agitated I could barely stay in my seat. When we were one hour outside of St. Thomas, I knew that she had landed on Tortola and was making her way through immigration. I could just imagine that immigration jackass smiling to himself, "I got my money." As soon as my plane landed, I turned on my cell phone. It rang immediately. It was her captors. I didn't let on that I knew they were not going to just hand her over.

They acted all chummy saying she was there with them but they wouldn't tell me where. Plan A was for her to not leave the airport with them, if she could do so without making a scene; they always had the option of sending her back to Cuba. But if that was impossible, she was absolutely not to let them take her to a private residence. She would demand they take her some place public, offering money if need be.

Going through immigration that morning I was terrified, but it all went smoothly. They didn't even look at my fake Spanish passport. I had on an arm bracelet that let them know I had paid. I was with two other Cuban men. When we came out, there was a man waiting for us. I told him I had to wait there but he told me that was not possible. I had to go with him or there would be a problem.

He took us to a "safe house," and said he needed money for the ride. The Cuban men said, "the girl will pay, she has an American boyfriend." and they took all of my money.

I refused to go into the house with them, but two large men in the house came out and said I owed them money. I said they would have to speak to my boyfriend, and that they had to take me to town to see him and find an ATM. When we got into town, we tried for ten minutes to call Lee. Finally, he answered. Lee and the man had difficulty understanding each other and he handed the phone to me. Afterward, the man was pressing me for information on Lee's boat and where he was landing it. The man was getting very nervous and told me I had to stay in that restaurant or I would be arrested.

It was difficult to understand them. They had very thick island accents. Plus, the connection was garbled. What I got from the conversation was, this guy saying, "You…Lee…"

"What? Hey, we have a bad connection say that again."

"I say-"

"I'm sorry, man. Put the girl on the phone."

Adianec sounded scared. I asked if they were big, and she said, "Yes."

"Are you in a public place?"

"Yes."

"Do they know our plan?"

"No."

"Are they mistreating you?" No answer.

"Okay, be strong, and I'll tell you when to move."

She said okay, and one of the guys got back on the phone. He wanted to know where I was going to be landing the boat. I told him I'd let him know when I knew. I joked with him a bit to set him at ease. His voice was still garbled, but I managed to catch, "When—?"

"When am I coming?"

"That's it." I told him I wished I knew and that I wasn't even sure how I'm getting there. "…make sure she's safe…"

"Yeah, sure," I assured him. "I'll take care of you, really appreciate your help."

"Need me…"

"Sorry, this phone is bad you keep fading in and out. How 'bout I buy you lunch when I get there, I need to speak to Adianec again."

I jumped into a cab and told the driver I'd give him twenty extra to drive insanely. He did, but it still took forty minutes. The kidnappers kept calling me, wanting an update. I was trying to placate them to stall for time before they announced their true intentions. When I arrived at the marina, Adianec had been with them for two hours. I knew they were nervous, which made me nervous.

I ran down to the dock to the boat rental place, but they only had one guy working and he was dealing with a group of Europeans that didn't speak English. Beyond floating, they had no idea what a boat did. My cover was a one day pleasure cruise, so I couldn't show too much anxiety. As I impatiently sat there, it occurred to me I was totally unprepared, again. No charts, no GPS, no radio and no memory of how to drive a twin engine boat. This had all gone down so quickly, I hadn't had time to prepare.

When the guy was finally available to help me twenty minutes later, I told him, "Yeah, I'm picking my girlfriend up on St. John and then we're heading to Tortola for lunch."

"Oh, I don't think you have time to make Tortola and be back here by five."

Plus, he didn't have any charts on how to get there. He just pointed in the general direction. All I could see was ocean and many islands in the distance. I asked which one was Tortola. He said it was too far to see.

While he prepared the boat, I ran up to the shopping area to find a marine store that had a chart. But no marine store, no chart. I did find a café that had dinner place mats with a cartoon drawing of the Virgin chain. It wasn't nautically accurate, but it gave me the general direction and shape of Tortola. I ran back down and quickly filled out the rental paper work. I asked the guy if he would start the engines while I called my office. This was the same trick I had used almost a year earlier. It worked again. I called Adianec's phone. She sounded angry. Demanding, *Amore mucho tiempo…why?*"

"How many are with you now?"

"One."

"Time to make your move, I'm jumping on the boat and I'll call back in ten minutes."

After an hour, the man told me to stay in my seat while he walked outside. Something told me he was going to get immigration to arrest me. Lee called and I was in a panic. I told him I could get away right then.

Stealing Castro's daughter

He told me, "Run and find a lady with a child, or a baby." I did, and she helped me find the hotel. Even in the lobby, though, I thought they would find me.

Our Plan B was for Adianec to excuse herself to use the bathroom. Since we weren't supposed to know she was being held, they wouldn't expect her to run. But that is exactly what she had to do. When I called back, she said she was with a woman and put her on the phone. I explained that Adianec was in trouble with some unsavory characters, and that she didn't know the area and we needed her help. The lady was very concerned and understanding. I asked her, "Ma'am, if you could please get Adianec to the nicest hotel on the water in Road Town. Please. This is an emergency. We will pay you for your trouble. Also, Adianec does not speak English very well, so you'll have to take her there rather than give directions."

She told me, "Don't worry. I will take her."

I told Adianec I would call back in a of couple hours when I pulled into Road Town.

As I pulled away from the dock, banging as I went, I looked around for a recognizable object high on the surrounding mountains so I could sight this area on the way back. I decided to use a grouping of communication towers on the bluff above the mouth of the bay. As I pulled out into the ocean, I looked at my cartoon map and figured the large island just to my center right a few miles away was St. John. This boat, though two feet longer, was much less stable than my Boston Whaler. The throttles were very loose and I had to keep constant pressure on them to keep my speed up, otherwise they would slip back to idle. It had been completely overcast since I landed, and just as I got up to speed, the dark grey clouds gave way. I couldn't see more than fifty feet in front of me and the driving rain was making my cartoon chart run. I studied it quickly and hard to memorize my route before it turned into pulp. All the islands were quickly becoming one giant drooping landmass. It looked like a Salvador Dali painting. The route seemed simple enough, I just needed to keep St. John on my right, even if I had to skirt around the other small islands. When I got to the far tip of St. John, I would know that by the fact that there would be no more islands on the horizon, just open sea. I would follow the tip straight out and in the distance I should see the mountains on Tortola.

Although I was focused on keeping my sloppy boat in line, I knew I was driving through my childhood fantasy. This was Robinson Crusoe territory. I was surrounded by tropical islands, with some only 200 yards away. Most were uninhabited due to their size, but all were lush and mountainous. St. John is a big island and very beautiful. Most of the coastline looked impossible to put ashore due to thick tropical vegetation and at times sheer cliffs jutting up hundreds of feet. It reminded me of the tropical paradises from the movies where people get shipwrecked. The storm had passed and I even got a glimpse of the sun as I rounded another small island. I sometimes had to stay very clear of St. John due to reefs close to shore. My back and neck were beginning to ache and tighten up due to the physical and emotional stress. This boat would not have made it ten minutes in the Gulf Stream.

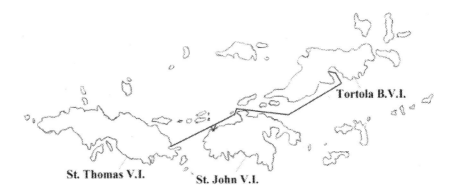

"St. Thomas route"

After a little over an hour, I saw the open rough sea with only one more island further ahead on the horizon. I was hoping it was Tortola, and it was actually not quite as far as I had originally thought. I slowed down to get my bearings and see if my "chart" still had any outlines. My phone rang. It was Adianec. She was stressed and nervous. I was concerned she would bring attention to herself and expose our plan. "I'm in the hotel, but they will kick me out. What do I do? Baby, I'm scared." Her voice was quivering.

She was thinking as if she was still in Cuba. She was convinced the men were going find her before I did. I could not calm her down and found myself yelling. I said, "Baby, I can see Tortola. I will find you, but I will not get there before I get there, okay? You have to be strong."

A little over thirty minutes later, after dealing with some rough water at the end, I pulled into Road Town. I wasn't quite sure at first that it was actually Road Town, but confirmed it a moment later as I shouted to a boat sailing out. The harbor is about a mile-wide and a half-mile deep. There seemed to be a waterway that continued a little further into the island. I could make out a marina deeper in. In front of me to the left was a very long dock and loading area. Along the extensive dock was a triple-deck high-speed ferry being loaded. The port and immigration buildings were at the land end of the dock. About 400 yards to the right of the loading dock was a rock jetty as long as the dock, creating a safe harbor. In fact, the entire shoreline between the dock and jetty was built up with huge boulders, except for a small twenty-five yard beach near the immigration office.

I slowly pulled near the jetty to figure out where Adianec might be. I called, but the wind was blowing so hard we had trouble hearing each other, and in our nervousness, neither of us could speak the other's language. "Amore, look out into the water. Do you see a boat with a blue top? She didn't know what blue was. I didn't take into account she didn't know what BLUE was. "BLUE! Blue like the sky!"

"Okay, no yelling. No, I don't see."

I took a breath. "Amore, we can't do this all day, they'll see me. First, look toward the ocean. I'm the only boat coming in."

"Lee, I sorry, *no comprende.*"

How could she not see me? I was right there. "Okay, do you see big rocks?"

I guess I wasn't much calmer, because now she was crying. "I don't know what is 'rock' baby."

Oh, boy. What's a rock? "Rocks, Amore, *Mondo* earth, hard earth."

Alright, I admit, that was a terrible explanation of what a rock is. "Amore, *no sabe.*"

If she couldn't find me, I had to find her. "Okay, don't walk away, I'm going to try to find you. Go near the water I'll call you back in a minute, my battery is low."

"What?"

"I'll call in five minutes."

She was growing more panicked by the second. "What? Lee, please, they will find me soon."

I had to hang up to save the battery, and sped toward a far shore that I presumed was where the hotel was. I called several minutes later. She picked up, far less calm than before. "Amore, I scared, you will not find me."

"Okay, let's slow down. Let's start again. Look again for a boat going crazy, *loco.*"

I was yelling above the wind for her to look out to the water. It would be easier for her to spot me. I was the only moving boat and there were dozens of buildings. I was spinning around, not knowing what boating laws I was breaking. I did know, however, that I was drawing attention to myself. I started to put the boat into tighter circles. Finally, "I see you! I see you!"

That was progress, step one. But where was she? "Good, Baby, good. Where are you? I'm going to move slowly. Tell me when I am heading toward you."

After a few minutes of going in circles like a drunken sailor, I got the answer to step two. "I see you! I can see you…your face!!"

"Okay, you are near the rocks!"

"Si, yes, I am near them, ahh oh…rocks?"

Three minutes later I saw her. "Baby, amore, coming to get you. Love you. We're almost there."

The only place to pick her up was the small beach near the immigration office and this would have to be quick. They would be looking for us. I pointed out the beach. We were now close enough to yell back and forth.

For some unknown reason, I guess because I didn't think anyone would ever believe this moment, I picked up the video camera and began to film her rescue. She was walking over to the beach like it was a Sunday stroll. I couldn't believe her casualness. She was smiling and taking her time.

The shore was built up with giant boulders, with no place to land, and no place for her to come to me. It had to be the beach near the immigration office. "Adianec, do you see the playa?" She didn't. "Run ahead, you'll see it."

Just then two immigration officers came out of their office to our left. The beach was exactly between them and her.

She was now laughing and walking slowly toward the beach. "I see it, amore."

I implored her to pick up her pace. "Run, baby, run," I was getting panicky. But she was still *walking* and smiling at me! She hadn't seen them. I suggested, again, that she speed up a bit. "Would you please fucking run… NOW!"

(Several weeks later, after we had viewed that video a few times, she informed me I was no longer allowed to use the word fuck in front of her, I haven't.)

After two hours of waiting for Lee, he finally called. I was so nervous. I knew he was close but I couldn't see him. When I finally saw him in the water, I felt even more desperate. I wanted to be in the boat immediately, but looking at the shore, there was no place for Lee to come in and get me. I wanted to jump in the water but I couldn't swim. Lee was yelling and pointing to a place up the shore. It took a few minutes to see it, and by that time we had got the attention of the men looking for me. Lee pulled me on the boat and we took off.

Chapter thirty-nine

Sprint for home

As I sped to the beach, the water got very shallow and I had to tilt the engines up to get in. I hit the beach pretty hard. It dawned on me that I was being an idiot trying to film this. I threw the camera down and pulled her on board. Immigration was yelling something but I was not going to stick around to find out what. I put the boat into reverse and nothing happened, we were stuck in the sand. I dropped the engines a bit more, told her to get to the back of the boat and I began to swing the boat back and forth in reverse. We freed ourselves quickly and I spun around and took off just as the ferry pulled away. As the ferry hit open water and sped up, we stayed within a hundred feet of her stern. I knew they would be coming after us, maybe with a gun boat, and I wanted protection. The crew kept waving us off, but I just shook my head.

I pointed straight ahead and yelled to her, above the sound of engines, crashing waves and wind, "That mountain on the horizon there, do you see it? That's the United States!"

She gave me a questioning look like she didn't believe me. "But what about the men?"

"If they come after us, I'm going to ram this boat right up their ass! We're not going back, we're going home, baby." We were too close to give up.

Twenty minutes later and with no immigration boat chasing us, I backed off a few hundred yards from the ferry. The water was pretty rough and was tossing Adianec around. One time we caught a wave wrong and almost flipped. She looked at me with huge eyes, as if wondering what the hell I was doing. I just shrugged.

Nothing seemed real anymore. I don't even know if I was scared. I was getting beat up by the rough boat ride but I didn't care. I wanted to fly as fast as we could.

We continued following the ferry until she turned to the right at the end of Tortola to follow the channel. I continued straight for St. John. I wanted Adianec to be within jumping distance of American soil if something happened. When we got close enough to shore where I could react if the Coast Guard spotted us, I started to relax. We were cruising fifty feet from shore at times. I said, "Amore, that right there, is dry U.S. soil. All you have to do is touch it and you're free."

She looked at me with a small, insecure smile. I knew she was overwhelmed and probably not as much of a fan of these adrenaline-filled situations as I. Although we weren't finished, she still had to put one foot on dry land. I knew we had succeeded. I wanted to celebrate. She was still traumatized by the whole deal so I had to save my festive attitude until she was ready.

As soon as we could see St. Thomas in the distance, I pulled into a calm, shallow, natural harbor on St. John. There was a sailboat anchored in water so clear that the boat looked like it was floating on air. We sat in that beautiful large cove with a white sand beach for a while, letting whatever heat we might have created calm down. I sat on the rail of the boat enjoying the surrounding beauty and let her be with her thoughts.

That last day seemed unreal and frightening until we got close to St. Thomas. There on the shore, waving in the breeze, was a giant American flag. I felt like I was in a dream. Until that moment I didn't believe we would make it. I had never seen the United States flag in person, only in pictures. Even as I think about it now, my heart starts beating so hard. I knew then that I was free. Lee told me that he had heard other people tell of similar reactions when they saw the American flag for the first time. I know from my own experience on that day, it will always have a special meaning for me.

After an hour, we pulled out of the serene cove and headed for the marina on St. Thomas. A mile or so from shore I looked up and saw a Coast Guard vessel heading straight for us. My heart sank in disbelief…we were so close. No sacrifice was too great now, I made up my mind to out run them and crash into shore, giving Adianec a chance to touch dry land. I would have to accept the consequences. I pushed hard on the throttles and the engines began to whine. The boat was slamming hard against the waves that were coming off the open ocean squeezing between the two islands. Adianec looked at me with curiosity until she noticed the Coast Guard boat, too. "Amore, this is it! When we hit land you have to run, don't worry about me, don't look back until you're way above the shoreline." She nodded. Just as I began to make a maneuver to slip by them, the cruiser turned away in the opposite direction toward the open ocean. I pulled the throttles back to neutral and slumped into the captain's chair not knowing if I should laugh or cry, or both. After a few minutes of processing a myriad of emotions, I set off again. As we pulled up to the fuel dock I told Adianec to get off the boat and keep walking until she hit dirt. "Do not stop for anybody. You have to put your foot on dry land." I got up on the dock and watched my girl walk to her new life. Just as she hit dry U.S. soil, my phone rang. It was my mother, whom I had not spoken to in weeks. She asked how Adianec was doing.

"Well, she has been a free woman now for twenty seconds. I can't imagine she could do much better."

My mother cried.

After I fueled up and turned in the boat, my last boat rental in this lifetime, I walked up the dock to look for my girlfriend. I should have known. She was standing across the street at a pizza parlor. We checked into our condo rental on the beach, with an incredible view of the area we had just raced through. I called Barry and got his voice mail. I left a cryptic message. "Barry Meepos…mission accomplished."

Ten minutes later he called back. "Where are you?"

"I'm in St. Thomas."

"Where is Adianec?"

"She is in St. Thomas."

He was quiet for a moment not quite comprehending what I was saying and then almost as if he was talking to himself. "You did it? I can't…you really…she's…so she's…wow you really…she is there with you?"

He spoke with her for a few minutes, welcoming her to the United States, and got back on the phone with me and stammered some more. I was a bit overwhelmed at his and my mother's reactions.

We showered and napped before Adianec's first American meal. We chose Italian. I had checked my email at the lobby on our way to dinner. Bill had sent a message saying how amazing it all was. "I'm so incredibly proud of both of you. The Mojitos are on me."

Adianec was, surprisingly, very quiet at dinner, and never once let go of my hand. She would remain that way for weeks. We woke early the next morning. I'm not really sure if we slept at all. We had a nice breakfast at a quaint harbor restaurant before she went to immigration. While we were eating, Jose called. He was furious. "What the fuck? How you fucking do that to me, I come through for you!"

I couldn't help but laugh. He was basically upset that we didn't let him screw us, again. Then he screamed at how selfish we were for leaving the other Cubans on Tortola. I told him, "Jose, first of all, aside from the fact that I did not agree to bring anybody else over, I didn't even know there were other Cubans with her. We never agreed to anything other than that you were supposed to get her safely through immigration. You failed. You see the difference between you and me? You, you cretin, are a smuggler. Me? I'm not a smuggler. I'm just a man in love…with a free woman."

He couldn't wrap his mind around that fact. After a few minutes of laughing at his idiocy, I hung up the phone. We were out of that dark and septic world. Our experience in it, thank God, was over.

After breakfast, I videotaped Adianec as she tentatively walked through the door of Homeland Security. I whispered on the video, "The next time I see you, you'll be a legal resident of the United States of America."

I took a cab back to the condo and tried to keep myself occupied. Processing Cubans apparently can take a couple of days. Several hours later, I was walking down the beach, exploring a wrecked sail boat that had washed ashore, when Barry called to get an update. As we were laughing about the past two years and the unbelievable adventures I had gone through, I got another call. I came back to Barry several minutes later and said, "That was Adianec. She's heading for the airport. Be home soon." She was processed and released in less than four hours.

I've spent my entire life fearing authority. I had always been treated with disdain in Cuba because I was Cuban. But the man in the Homeland Security office looked me in the eye, and treated me with so much kindness and respect. He said, "You no longer have to worry about Fidel. You are free. Welcome to the United States."

He told me I looked tired and I could rest as he processed the paper work. I knew then that everything I had heard was true, the United States was different. With the kindness that that government official should me I was finally sure my life was going to be as I had always dreamed.

I quickly packed and began to check out when I realized I didn't have a ticket for Adianec. I had my own return ticket, but not one for her. I would just have to change my flight. But I had no way of buying her ticket. I was out of money and my cards were full. I called Steve and left a message, "Hey, buddy, I, uh, need your help. Call me back."

Before I had finished checking out, Steve's assistant Shannon called, and asked for details. She called back again as I was in the cab heading for the airport. She had booked Adianec on the next flight out in three hours and had changed my ticket as well.

Adianec had a window seat all the way to Los Angeles and I was right beside her. We would have one stop: Miami.

When I pulled up to the airport, she was waiting for me with the documents that would allow her to enter the United States. Both Jay and Kevin called to congratulate her when we were in the terminal waiting for our flight. The flight home was quiet but emotional. Neither of us spoke a word. We flew over Miami as the sun was setting, casting an incredible orange glow over the city. As we passed the airport on our right, her forehead was pressed against the window and she had a soft serene smile on her face as she viewed her new country for the first time. We made a hard banking turn, putting the entire city and ocean into view. I could feel her excitement. The city she had always heard of as if it were from a fairy tale was now a reality. As the wheels of our plane touched down, I almost said to her, "Now it really is over."

But I realized it was not over. It was just beginning.

We arrived in Los Angeles about 1:00 a.m., and were awakened early the next morning by the constant ringing of my phone. Everybody in my world wanted to meet and welcome Adianec to America. As she showered, I made French toast and orange juice. After breakfast we went for a walk on the beach. We sat on the sand at the water's edge, the exact spot where I had sat late one night, long ago, wondering about a mysterious and beautiful Cuban woman I had just met.

The first three weeks in Los Angeles were a blur. I just could not believe I was actually in America. I do remember Lee taking me to his favorite sushi restaurant for my first lunch. He was busy talking on his phone and hadn't warned me about the green stuff (wasabi), I thought it was Japanese candy...it wasn't!

I met Barry and Lisa that afternoon. They made me feel like I was a member of their family, as did all of Lee's friends as I met them over the next several weeks. Everything was more than I expected; the shelves at Costco piled high to the ceiling, the produce aisle at Whole Foods with all the colors and abundance was so overwhelming I had to walk out. Lee took me to Aspen, Colorado that first winter and I saw and felt snow for the first time in my life. I couldn't stop laughing. I feel so blessed to have been welcomed to this country.

The greatest joy of my life has been to be by Adianec's side these past two and a half years as she discovers herself in a free world. Nearly everyday we wakeup grateful for her freedom and for the life we have created together.

EPILOGUE

On September 30, 2008, high above Paris on the Eiffel Tower, and far from the world she had left behind, I told Adianec I would always love and protect her. I then lowered to one knee and proposed. We married in Rome, Italy on August 9th, 2009. Our first child, a boy, is due May 19, 2010.

Authors note

We are often asked, respectfully, how much of our love story is true. We made a conscious decision from the very beginning not to embellish the story of her rescue. And why should we, the truth was already unimaginable. In fact, we have downplayed many aspects of our journey. This story is absolutely true in its content, and the events did take place in the way written, though some names have been changed. Also, I had to paraphrase some conversations, especially the ones during our arrest, due to their actual length (up to 2 hours). However, their substance is factual. So please enjoy our love story with the knowledge that it is true.

I have many personal opinions and realizations borne out of our two-year struggle that I would like to share here. Though we are extremely grateful for Adianec's freedom, we feel a deep sadness due to the fact that there are still eleven million Cubans living under the oppressive rule of a dictator, and isolation due to our embargo.

The more I've studied Communism the less sense it makes. The most surprising thing I realized during this time is that the leaders of all communist countries, it seems, are actually pure capitalists (in their personal lives). Fidel is considered by *Forbes* magazine to be one of the richest leaders in the world. If the goal of Communism is to serve the masses, why do all communist societies have to, literally, fence their population in, and murder anyone who tries to leave? And why do the leaders live such decadent life styles while their people suffer so greatly? Not just Cuba, but North Korea, and to a large degree China and Vietnam, until they somewhat embraced capitalism. It was the same with the old Soviet Union and East Germany. If you're going to embrace

Communism as a leader, whose standard is equality, then live as the peasants do, not as a king.

I began to form my own opinion of our embargo. I completely understand why Cuban Americans would want to destroy Fidel Castro's regime, and have their country restored to freedom. He stole their homes, their property and their businesses, and then forced them to leave their homeland with only one suitcase and no valuables. Then they had to suffer the humiliation of starting their lives over in a new country with a foreign language. And they proved to be the lucky ones as Fidel, Che and his "comrades" murdered their family members and friends. Many of the people that were executed had actually helped bring Castro to power. But then they made a fatal error when they questioned his sudden turn to Communism.

Not that I'm an expert by any means, but what I don't think some Cuban-Americans understand or at least acknowledge is how devastating this embargo has been for the eleven million people left behind. Not to mention the three hundred million Americans who are being denied our rights: freedom of movement. It adversely affects people I know directly and care for. More than just on a personal level, the embargo is universally considered, by most experts outside of the Cuban community, to be a half-century-old failure. Fidel needs the embargo if for no other reason than to have a scapegoat for any of his and Communism's failings. There are many experts that say Castro would have been unseated long ago if not for the embargo. In fact, he has seemed to radicalize his policy whenever it looked like the U.S. was going to soften its stance. For decades the entire world, the UN and all our allies, has condemned our embargo. I've seen its devastating effects on food, medicine and basic needs. Without question, Fidel Castro is completely responsible for raping Cuba's infrastructure and progression, and doing all he could to kill the spirit of the Cuban people. But, I feel guilty over our embargo; I think we will see it some day as one of our biggest humanitarian blunders.

Acknowledgements

This story would not have its fairytale happy ending had it not been for an army of friends, and strangers that became friends. Barry Meepos, Jay Roberts Jr and Kevin McCorkle. Love you guys, you are above the standard. Steve Meepos, thanks for refueling my tank in Antigua, and giving us the final push. Lisa, thank you for treating Adianec as a sister and helping her discover L.A. Luis Carbajal for holding down the fort as I hop the globe. My mother (Jean Colby), for waiting patiently. Bill Bryan, Phil Colius and Herb Lurie for logistics and a sense of hope. Nicole Lawrence, for your expertise. Dr Tom Stelmach, thank you for the supplies that went to Cuba. Jenny Roberts, your buyers intuition was a life saver. Captain Paul Roos for taking a risk with a couple escapees on the run and your continued friendship. Junior "Jesus" Knowles, thanks for the tow. Leslie Steinmetz and Danny Klein for your "rolodex." Dr John Williams, Fred Johnston, Nicky and Dr Gold, hard to believe you were ever "just clients." Lisa Campbell McCorkle, your passion for this story has kept me in the game. Gabe and Steph Lakatosh, what would we do without you two? Dr Michael "The Title Maker" Gold. Dana Meepos and Shannon Holt thank you for showing me the difference between a gerund and a dangling participle. Robert Natureman, for sweeping the broom through my writings and putting the shovel in my hands making me dig deeper. Amira Rida, and Nina Golden, for helping me edit and making me change my changes. Ben Corbett, it would have been a tougher climb without all the advice. Julie Blivas and the Brentwood Book Babes, Michael Mercier, Joann Meepos, Tammy Sue Roberts, Joe and Christine Neuman, Mike Jacobs, Erika Malcolm, Rich Miller, Bobby Fahn, Kirk Jones, Bobby and Patty Meepos, Maureen Kedes, Dawn Ann Ritter, Jan R. Remmers, Peter Loewy, Jeff Kershner, Randy Kershner, Michael Silver, Mark Robbins, Andy Fox, Dave and Nancy Fordon. My attorney $cott $chwimer, thanking you in advance. Sri Sri Ravi Shankar and Mitra Rahbar for your love, guidance and for keeping the path lit.